RAYNAUD'S DISEASE (LOCAL SYNCOPE, LOCAL ASPHYXIA, SYMMETRICAL GANGRENE): ITS HISTORY, CAUSES, SYMPTOMS, MORBID RELATIONS, PATHOLOGY, & TREATMENT

Published @ 2017 Trieste Publishing Pty Ltd

ISBN 9780649686759

Raynaud's Disease (Local Syncope, Local Asphyxia, Symmetrical Gangrene): Its History, Causes, Symptoms, Morbid Relations, Pathology, & Treatment by Thomas Kirkpatrick Monro

Edited by Trieste Publishing Pty Ltd.
Cover @ 2017

www.triestepublishing.com

THOMAS KIRKPATRICK MONRO

RAYNAUD'S DISEASE (LOCAL SYNCOPE, LOCAL ASPHYXIA, SYMMETRICAL GANGRENE): ITS HISTORY, CAUSES, SYMPTOMS, MORBID RELATIONS, PATHOLOGY, & TREATMENT

Trieste

RAYNAUD'S DISEASE

(LOCAL SYNCOPE, LOCAL ASPHYXIA,
SYMMETRICAL GANGRENE)

ITS HISTORY, CAUSES, SYMPTOMS, MORBID RELATIONS, PATHOLOGY, & TREATMENT

BY

THOMAS KIRKPATRICK MONRO, M.A., M.D.

PHYSICIAN TO THE GLASGOW ROYAL INFIRMARY;
EXAMINER IN THE UNIVERSITY OF GLASGOW

GLASGOW
JAMES MACLEHOSE & SONS
Publishers to the University
1899

GLASGOW: PRINTED AT THE UNIVERSITY PRESS
BY ROBERT MACLEHOSE AND CO.

To

THE MEMORY

OF

MAURICE RAYNAUD

PREFACE.

THERE has long been need of a new account of Raynaud's disease, which should not only give due recognition to the work of its brilliant discoverer, but also incorporate the advances in our knowledge of the affection which are based on the large number of cases that have been published since Raynaud's time. With the exception of a few articles in British and Australian journals there has, until quite recently,[1] been practically no attempt to give, in English, a systematic and at the same time sufficiently comprehensive description of this disease; nor am I aware of the existence of any such treatise in a foreign language, a translation of which might have met the needs of the case.

The special interest which I have taken in Raynaud's disease for a considerable number of years past, on theoretical grounds, has been fostered by the number and character of the cases that have come under my own observation; and thus, encouraged by the knowledge that something of the kind was required, I began, more than two years ago, to prepare this essay.

[1] Dr. Barlow's article in Professor Clifford Allbutt's new *System of Medicine* meets, in considerable measure, the need referred to, but the present essay was approaching completion when I first heard of its appearance.

The work is based on all published cases, the records of which have been accessible to me, and on various cases with which I have myself met. The Bibliography, apart from the theses, is limited to writings which have been examined in connexion with the essay, and though it cannot profess to be complete, it will probably be found to be lacking in little that is of genuine importance on the subject of Raynaud's disease, in English, French, or German.

The numbers given in foot-notes refer to the corresponding entries in the Bibliography. Various other writings, which have been utilised in the preparation of this essay but which have only an indirect bearing on the subject, are referred to by their titles in foot-notes, and are not included in the Bibliography.

In the case of Raynaud's *Thesis* and *New Researches*, the references, unless the contrary is stated, are to Dr. Barlow's translations.

The frontispiece, showing the title-page of Raynaud's *Thesis*, with his signature on it, is reduced by photography from the original copy in the library of the Faculty of Physicians and Surgeons of Glasgow.

My thanks are due to Dr. Walter L. Watt of Winnipeg for valuable assistance in proof-reading.

10 CLAIRMONT GARDENS, GLASGOW,
October, 1899.

CONTENTS.

xii   *CONTENTS.*

BIOGRAPHICAL NOTE.

MAURICE RAYNAUD, the son of a distinguished university man, and nephew of the French surgeon, Vernois, was born in 1834, and studied in Paris. He became interne in 1857, doctor of medicine and doctor of letters in 1862, physician to the hospitals in 1865, agrégé[1] in 1866, officer of the Legion of Honour in 1871, and member of the Academy of Medicine in 1879. He lectured at the Lariboisière and Charité hospitals, and had as part of his duty to supplement the teaching of Piorry in the chair of clinical medicine at the Hôtel-Dieu, and of Monneret in the chair of pathological medicine. He had also charge of a course of mental and nervous diseases.

Raynaud was to have read (in French) the address in medicine at the International Medical Congress in London in 1881, and had chosen for his subject "Scepticism in Medicine." His unfinished paper was read to the Congress after his death by his friend, M. Féréol. He had long been conscious of the gradual onset of organic heart disease, but he continued to work without ceasing. On Wednesday, the 29th June, 1881, he went to his country house in apparently

---

[1] One who has, by *concours*, or public competition, obtained the position of assistant to a professor.

good health, and after dining with his family, was playing with his children, when he was seized with violent pain in the region of the heart, and in three hours he was dead. He was scarcely forty-seven years old.

The one ungratified ambition of his life was a chair in the Faculty of Medicine, and his disappointment perhaps hastened his premature end. Notwithstanding what M. Peter said on the occasion of the obsequies, it is probable that Raynaud never would have been elected to a professorship. He was a devout Catholic, and did not conceal his religious convictions. This taint of clericalism was enough to prevent the Faculty from nominating him to a chair for which he was admirably qualified, that of the History of Medicine. The profession as a whole fully recognized the great injustice of this failure to appreciate, and duly reward, the truest merit. The seat at the Academy was a partial compensation.

Raynaud, at one time, had some thoughts of entering political life, but after a reverse which he sustained at the Paris municipal elections, some months before his death, he seemed to reserve himself entirely for his numerous patients, his private studies, and his clinical teaching.

His principal writings were his inaugural thesis, *Sur l'asphyxie locale et la gangrène symétrique des extrémités*; his theses for the doctorate of letters, *De Asclepiade Bithyno medico ac philosopho*, and *Les médecins au temps de Molière*; and his agrégation theses, *Sur les hyperhémies non phlegmasiques*, and *De la révulsion.*

He wrote also numerous articles in Jaccoud's *Dictionnaire de Médecine*, and amongst his frequent communications to learned societies may be mentioned one made to the Academy, *Sur l'infection et l'immunité vaccinales*, with a memoir, *Sur le traitement du rhumatisme cérébral par les bains froids.* Shortly before his death he had made, in conjunction with Mm. Pasteur and Lannelongue, a research of some importance, *Sur la salive d'un enfant mort de la rage.*

We are apt to think of Raynaud, principally or exclusively, as the man who first recognized the existence of the disease which has long been associated with his name ; but the value of his work in a different direction has been testified to by Roux, who, at the Congress of Hygiene and Demography held at Budapest in 1894, said that "the question of preventive and therapeutic serums was born with the experiments of Maurice Raynaud on the blood of heifers inoculated for cow-pox ; and with those of Richet and Hericourt, on the serum of dogs and rabbits vaccinated against septicaemia (1888)."

Raynaud's character was spotless, and his great abilities and high intellectual attainments gave him the title to be regarded, as M. Peter remarked, in the fourfold character of physician, savant, philosopher, and man of letters.

Gaz. hebd. de Méd. et de Chir., 1881, pp. 424, 439 ; *Bull. de l'Acad. de Méd.*, 1881, 2ᵉ série, T. x., pp. 865-867 ; *Biographisches Lexikon d. hervorragenden Aerzte*, 1886, Band iv. ; *Brit. Med. Jour.*, 1881, ii., 53, 92, 268 ; *Lancet*, 1881, ii., 72 ; Lennox Browne, *Diphtheria and its associates*, 1895, 233, 234.

ANATOMICAL AND PHYSIOLOGICAL
CONSIDERATIONS.

THE capillary wall, it will be remembered, consists of a single layer of flat nucleated epithelial (endothelial) cells united by cement substance, and continuous with the epithelial lining of the arteries and veins.

The wall of an artery is generally described as consisting of three layers. In the very finest arteries the inner coat, or intima, is made up of the endothelial cells, and a transparent fenestrated elastic membrane which supports them. The middle coat, or media, is represented by bundles of plain muscular fibres, arranged transversely or spirally around the intima, and embedded in, or situated between, elastic tissue lamellæ. The outer coat, or adventitia, is a comparatively thin fibrous tissue membrane.

In arteries of larger size the inner coat is thicker, and possesses, in addition to the endothelium, an inner fibrous layer, and a layer of fenestrated elastic membranes; whilst the middle coat is made up of numerous layers of plain muscular tissue, together with a good deal of elastic tissue.

The smaller the artery the more purely muscular is its middle coat, so that the smaller the artery the more capable is it of active changes in calibre.

The smallest veins are not unlike the smallest arteries, but are of rather wider calibre, and possess less muscular tissue in their walls.

The larger veins vary considerably in structure, but can generally be recognized as possessing three coats which are comparable, in some degrees, to those of the arteries. The walls of veins, however, are, on the whole, much thinner, much less elastic, and much less muscular than those of arteries of corresponding size. While the media is the principal coat in arteries, the adventitia is generally the thickest in veins. Some veins have no muscular fibres at all, whilst others have one, two, or even three layers of muscular tissue.

Nutrient vessels (vasa vasorum), both arterial and venous, and lymphatic spaces and vessels are found in the outer and middle coats of arteries and veins of large or medium size.

Nerves, too, are distributed to arteries, and also, though much less freely, to veins. They penetrate the outer coat to reach the muscular tissue of the media, and are derived from the sympathetic system. Their fine non-medullated fibres are found to accompany the smallest arteries and veins, and sometimes to form plexuses around them. Small groups of ganglion cells are occasionally present on these minute nerves.

The muscular tissue, which is so important a constituent of the walls of the finer arteries, is controlled by two kinds of vasomotor nerves, viz. vasoconstrictor and vasodilator. These reach the vessels by way of the peripheral nerves, and a given nerve trunk may contain vasomotor fibres of either kind, or of both kinds. Both classes of vasomotor fibres take origin in the central nervous system, but they reach their destinations by very different routes. In the case of mammals, all vasoconstrictor fibres, so far as is known, leave the cerebro-spinal axis in the middle (dorsal and upper lumbar) region of the spinal cord. They pass, by way of the anterior root, to the mixed trunk, and leave the anterior primary division of the latter by the visceral branch (white ramus communicans) in order to join the sympathetic chain, in the ganglia of which (vertebral or lateral ganglia) they lose their medullary sheaths. They thence reach the abdominal viscera by way of the splanchnic nerves, the limbs by way of the grey rami communicantes and brachial and sciatic plexuses, and the head and neck by way of the cervical sympathetic. These vasoconstrictor fibres, as they pass out in the bundles of the anterior spinal roots, are extremely fine, having little more than one-tenth the diameter of the accompanying motor fibres for the skeletal muscles.

The course of the vasodilator fibres, which are also of very fine size, has not been so clearly ascertained, but it is supposed that they pass out from the medulla, and from all parts of the spinal cord, by anterior roots, follow a tolerably direct course to their destination (instead of passing through the sympathetic system), and retain their medullary sheaths till they reach collateral ganglia or terminal ganglia, or, in other words, till they get near their termination in the tissue to whose blood-vessels they are distributed.

Different tissues have different kinds of vasomotor supply. For example, the vasomotor fibres of the skin are mainly constrictor—perhaps because control of the body temperature by control of the surface radiation is one of the most important functions of the skin. On the other hand, the vasomotor fibres which are present in the nerves of muscles are mainly dilator. The alimentary canal and its appendages resemble the skin in being furnished principally with dilator fibres.

All the evidence goes to show that vasoconstrictor fibres are, under ordinary circumstances, constantly conveying impulses of moderate strength, which keep up in the arteries that moderate degree of contraction which is spoken of as "tone." This activity may be either augmented or diminished, so that either narrowing or widening of the vessels may be induced by agencies operating upon the vasoconstrictors. On the other hand, there is no evidence of continuous activity on the part of vasodilator nerves, so that any agency acting upon them can only lead to dilatation of the vessels.

Moreover, the influence of the dilators is principally local, and their activity is usually part of a reflex process; whereas the constrictors may act either locally or over extensive areas.

The existence of vasomotor and vasodilator nerves of arteries has been recognized for many years, but the occurrence of vasomotor nerves in the portal vein was only proved in 1890, and in the superficial veins of the extremities in 1893.[1]

Vasomotor centres. Vasoconstrictor nerve fibres may be described as arising from three orders of cells : (1) Cells in the medulla oblongata, from which fibres pass partly to the nuclei of certain cranial nerves, and partly down the lateral columns of the cord, to end, in either case, in close relationship to vasomotor cells of the second order. (2) Cells situated at various levels in the cerebro-spinal axis, and giving off fibres which pass out in cranial and spinal nerve-roots to sympathetic ganglia. Cells of the second order are normally subordinate to those of the first, but

[1] Howell, *American Text-Book of Physiology,* 1896, p. 485.

are apparently capable of acquiring powers which compensate for destruction of the medullary centre. Thus, if the spinal cord be divided, the vessels innervated through the cord below the level of the lesion are paralyzed, but if the animal survive for a considerable time, arterial tone is regained. (3) Cells in sympathetic ganglia (proximal or distal) from which bundles of non-medullated fibres pass to the vessels. Certain experiments suggest that even these sympathetic cells may act as subordinate centres.[1] An additional point of interest is that arteries, whose vasomotor nerves have been divided, appear to be sometimes able to regain their tone through the inherent contractile power of their muscular tissue.[2]

It is not possible at present to point to any similar series of vasodilator centres. None are yet known to exist in the bulb. The centre of origin of any given vasodilator nerve is believed to be situated in the cerebro-spinal axis, very close to that of the ordinary (skeletal) motor nerve which the dilator nerve accompanies.[3]

Vasomotor phenomena (constrictor and dilator) have been observed on stimulation of various parts of the brain (crura cerebri, corpora quadrigemina, and especially the motor area of the cortex); but it is not certain that these are not reflex.

The medullary vasomotor centre has been found by experiment in the rabbit to be bilateral, each half being situated in the lateral portion of the bulb rather nearer the anterior than the posterior surface. Its length is (in the rabbit) 4 mm., the upper limit being 1 or 2 mm. below the corpora quadrigemina, and the lower limit 4 or 5 mm.

[1] Howell, *American Text-Book of Physiology*, 1896, pp. 488-491.
[2] Foster, *Text-Book of Physiology*, 5th ed., 1888, Pt. i., pp. 328, 329.
[3] Foster, *op. cit.*, p. 331.

above the point of the calamus scriptorius.[1] Each half of this centre corresponds in position to the lateral nucleus of the medulla (Lockhart Clarke's antero-lateral nucleus), which is situated not far from the surface of the lateral area, behind the inferior olive, in front of the ascending root of the fifth nerve, and rather nearer the anterior than the posterior aspect. The lateral nucleus appears to represent a portion of the lateral horn of the spinal cord cut off from the rest of the grey matter by the crossing of the pyramidal tract.

Gaskell[2] distinguishes two kinds of cells, a larger and a smaller variety, in connection with the intermedio-lateral tract, or lateral horn, in the thoracic region. The larger cells are represented higher up by the group which gives origin to the phrenic nerve and the external part of the spinal accessory, and still higher by the nucleus ambiguus (accessory vagal nucleus), the nucleus of the seventh nerve, and the motor nucleus of the fifth nerve. The smaller cells found in the lateral horn of the cord are regarded by Gaskell as the source of the katabolic, or motor nerves, of the vascular and glandular systems.[3] As the antero-lateral nucleus is not known to give rise to any out-going fibres in the region of the bulb, and as experimental results place the vasomotor centre in this region, and also suggest that fibres pass down from it in the lateral columns of the cervical cord to be distributed in the thoracic outflow of vasomotor nerves, Gaskell concludes : " I am inclined to

[1] Foster, *Text-Book of Physiology*, 5th ed., 1888, Pt. i., p. 326.
[2] *Journal of Physiology*, 1889, x., 153 *sqq.*
[3] Mott's investigations lead him to favour the view that the intermedio-lateral tract gives origin to the splanchnic efferent fibres of the anterior roots (including the vasomotor fibres). ("The Bi-polar cells of the spinal cord and their connections," *Brain*, 1890, Pt. iv., 433 *sqq.*)

look on this antero-lateral nucleus as serially homologous with the smaller cells of the intermedio-lateral tract in the thoracic region, and to consider this chain of nerve nuclei as giving origin to the motor or katabolic nerves of the vascular system." [1]

The theory of the vasomotor function of the lateral nucleus is far from being established. The strongest argument in its favour is the correspondence of the nucleus in situation with the seat of the vasomotor centre as demonstrated by experiment. But this correspondence is not exact, for the lateral nucleus can be seen in sections of the closed part of the medulla, and of the lower part of the open medulla in man, whereas the lower limit of the vasomotor centre in the rabbit is at some distance above the upper end of the closed medulla. The idea of a serial homology between the lateral nucleus and the smaller cells of the intermedio-lateral tract is not necessarily weakened by the fact that the lateral nucleus lies at some distance anteriorly and. laterally to the nucleus ambiguus (which represents the larger cells of the intermedio-lateral tract), but is seriously weakened by the fact that many of the cells of the lateral nucleus are of relatively larger size. [2]

[1] *Journal of Physiology*, 1889, x., 161.
[2] Quain's *Anatomy*, 10th ed., 1895, p. 52.

STATISTICS.

RAYNAUD'S disease, particularly in its severer aspects, is by no means a common ailment. Even if it did at times cause death, its frequency would not entitle it to, and it does not obtain, any separate mention in the Reports of the Registrars-General for Scotland and England. In the seven years, 1881 to 1887 inclusive, out of more than thirty-six thousand cases treated in the wards of the Glasgow Royal Infirmary, not one is entered as Raynaud's disease. In the decade commencing 1888 (the year in which Raynaud's works were published in English), there were 8 cases of the disease among 54,793 patients; or 4 males among 35,679, and 4 females among 19,114. If we consider the medical wards only, so as to exclude accident cases, we have 7 cases among 21,328; or 4 males among 13,086, and 3 females among 8242. As might be expected, the cases were not equally distributed among the years; the first was in 1891, the next two were in 1893, then four in 1895, and one in 1896. It will be seen, therefore, that about one case in three thousand admissions to the medical wards represents the frequency of Raynaud's disease. It is probable that this is really an under-estimate, since the affection is frequently associated with some other ailment, which may be more important from the point of view of survival, and so more likely to appear in the returns.

There were 1918 admissions to the Hospital for Sick Children in its first five years (1883-1887), and among these there was one case of "symmetrical gangrene" in 1887. In the next decade (1888-1897), 5961 cases were treated in the wards, and these included a case of "gangrene of fingers" (1890), and a case of "Raynaud's disease" (1897). During the same decade, 54,148 cases were seen at the Dispensary of the Hospital, and these did not include a single case of Raynaud's disease, unless three cases classified simply as "gangrene" (one in 1890, and two in 1897) may be supposed to have been examples of the disease in question. It will be seen therefore that hospital cases among children gravitate to the indoor department, and that the proportion of cases to the total admissions to the wards is almost the same as on the medical side of a general hospital, namely, one in three thousand. Even if we assume that all the cases of "gangrene" were examples of Raynaud's malady, the proportion of cases at the Dispensary would only be one in eighteen thousand.

To illustrate the frequency from the point of view of dermatology, we may take the statistics published in the *Transactions of the American Dermatological Association* for 1895.[1] The returns are for the year 1894, and include 2 cases of Raynaud's disease out of a total of 24,321 cases, or scarcely one in twelve thousand.

[1] 1896, xix.

TERMINOLOGY.

MANKIND has long been aware that under the influence of cold the fingers may undergo a change of colour, becoming sometimes white, sometimes blue. What Raynaud accomplished was to show that the circulatory disturbances which are manifested to the eye by such pallor or lividity may supervene with undue readiness, and may actually be so severe or so prolonged as to destroy the life of the tissues.

A finger which is the seat of pallor of this kind is commonly spoken of as "dead" (digitus mortuus, doigt mort, todter Finger). The condition is familiar to many who wash with cold water on a winter morning, and can scarcely be regarded as morbid, or as meriting by itself the designation, Raynaud's disease. Raynaud called it *local syncope*, since it is due to a local deprivation of blood, and is thus comparable to syncope or fainting, which depends upon a more general deprivation. Later writers have proposed other names, such as "local anaemia" (Hardy), or "regional ischaemia" (Weiss).[1]

The blueness of a part that has been exposed to cold is the ocular manifestation of a condition which Raynaud called *local asphyxia*. He borrowed the expression from

[1] *Wiener Klinik*, 1882, viii., 373.

Boyer, from whose treatise on surgical diseases he transferred to the title-page of his original thesis the pregnant
remark : " La gangrène est à l'asphyxie locale ce que la
mort est à l'asphyxie générale." Weiss has proposed the
expression "regional cyanosis" in place of "local asphyxia,"[1]
and Barlow has suggested "local cyanosis" as more appropriate than "local asphyxia," since the capillaries contain
imperfectly oxygenated blood.[2] Raynaud points out that
Boiseau, in 1832, named the same condition "uterine
cyanosis" on account of its association with suppression of
the menses.[3]

Sir George Johnson disapproved of Raynaud's termin-
ology, and said that what Raynaud called "local syncope"
ought to be termed "local asphyxia" (arrested circulation
due to arterial contraction, asphyxia meaning pulselessness) ;
and that what Raynaud called "local asphyxia" ought to be
termed "local apnœa" (presence of unoxygenized blood in
the implicated tissues).[4] On etymological grounds, Johnson
was perhaps correct, but an attempt to carry out both the
changes he proposed would simply lead to confusion. On
the other hand, "local cyanosis," as proposed by Barlow,
would be an improvement as regards accuracy, and could
lead to no mistake.

Many years ago a French writer[5] called attention to the
tendency to regard syncope and asphyxia as synonymous
terms, and this is still apt to cause some obscurity in French
writings on the subject. Thus, Moursou refers to local

[1] *Loc. cit.*

[2] *Illustrated Med. News*, 1889, iii., 176.

[3] Raynaud, *Thesis*, 1862, 102 note.

[4] Johnson, *An Essay on Asphyxia* (*apnœa*), London, 1889, pp. 7, 52;
British Med. Jour., 1894, i., 900.

[5] Beau, *Arch. gén. de Méd.*, 1864, i., 5.

syncope as local asphyxia of the first degree, and he speaks of local asphyxia when the detailed description points really to local syncope.[1]   And Raynaud himself, in his article in the *Nouveau Dictionnaire*, describes local asphyxia as taking two principal forms—local syncope and local asphyxia proper.[2]

The climax of Raynaud's disease is *symmetrical gangrene*; symmetry was to its discoverer one of its characteristic features.   Moreover, it is so much an affection of early life that he felt tempted to call it "juvenile gangrene."

In a part which has been for some time subject to attacks of local cyanosis, chronic changes may occur in the skin. One of these consists in the development of *tachetées* (an old French term), which are reddish blue or purple patches, not removable by pressure, sometimes very persistent, and apparently due in great measure to the presence in the deeper layers of the skin of the pigment of extravasated blood.   Such a change has been called "tachetic."   Weiss applies the designation "regional rubor" to isolated spots which become red like fuchsin, or like a raspberry, with elevation of temperature and injection of vessels.[3]

Another series of terms that must be mentioned here consists of compounds derived from the Greek word ἄκρεα, extremities.   On the analogy of the older word, "acrodynia" (the name of a disease which appeared as an epidemic in France in 1828, and among whose symptoms were pains in the hands and feet), Dana proposed the designation "acroneuroses" for an extensive group of neuroses of the extremities, of which Raynaud's disease is but one example.[4] At a much earlier date, Laveran had proposed the name

---

[1] *Arch. de Méd. navale*, 1880, xxxiii., 342-345.
[2] Similarly Ritti and Rognetta (Nos. 153 and 155).
[3] *Loc. cit.*, 373.   [4] *Medical Record*, N.Y., 1885, ii., 57.

"acrocyanosis" (acrocyanie) for local asphyxia of the extremities.[1] And at a later date, Mr. Jonathan Hutchinson suggested "acroasphyxia" as a good term for asphyxia of the extremities (Raynaud's "local asphyxia"); "acrosphacelus" for gangrene of the extremities; "acroscleriasis" for the sclerotic changes in the tissues of the extremities, which are sometimes found in association with, and sometimes apart from, Raynaud's disease; and "acroteric," as an adjective, to be used to describe conditions in which the extremities (hands, feet, face, etc.) are the parts most affected.[2]

Such a disturbance of the cardio-vascular equilibrium as is met with in Raynaud's disease on the one hand, and Graves's disease on the other, has been called "vasomotor ataxia."[3]

The disease was first called after the name of its discoverer by Laveran. How long ago this was I have not been able to ascertain, but Calmette alludes to it in 1877. Mr. Hutchinson admits that he had a good deal to do with introducing it to this country, and it will be useful to bear in mind his hint that we may sometimes conveniently speak of "Raynaud's phenomena" when the circumstances of the case do not altogether justify the expression "Raynaud's disease."

That "Raynaud's disease" is the best name for us to use will appear on a consideration of the objections that can be put forward against other designations. In his original thesis, Raynaud styled it "local asphyxia and symmetrical gangrene

---

[1] Calmette, *Rec. de mém. de méd., de chir. et de pharm. milit.*, 1877, xxxiii., 25.

[2] *Arch. of Surg.*, 1892, iii., 95; *Med. Week*, 1893, i., 85; *Arch. of Surg.*, 1895, vi., 351.

[3] Solis-Cohen, *Amer. Jour. Med. Sc.*, 1894, cvii., 130.

of the extremities," but as he pointed out in his *New Researches*, it is undesirable to use two names for what are but different degrees of one disease. He further pointed out that "symmetrical gangrene" will not satisfy requirements, since gangrene is often absent, and that "local asphyxia" is objectionable if it leads to the inference that the disease is purely local. He therefore styled the disease "local asphyxia of the extremities," with the proviso that this is but a name.

B

HISTORY.

LACHMUND (1676) has preserved for us a narrative of a curious case met with by Bernhard Schrader when the latter, as a student of surgery, was travelling, in 1629, with his brother John and a companion named Alexander Lax. The three put up at an inn in a place called Geest, and they then found that the daughter of their host, a girl of twenty-three, suffered every month from considerable pain in her fingers and toes and in the tips of her ears and nose. There was also oedematous swelling of the hands, feet, and face, whereupon there followed, shortly before and after full moon, mortification of the parts, so that the ends of these, having become white and dry, dropped off in little pieces, without feeling, pain, moisture, or bad odour. That which survived of the affected parts retained its natural form and appearance. And when Schrader made further enquiries, the father showed him a box in which were stowed away a hundred or more pieces of dead tissue that had fallen off in the course of three years.[1]

Hertius, of Nassau (1685), tells of a woman of that town,

[1] *Bibliography*, No. 100. It is Case xx. in Raynaud's *Thesis*. Those who are curious may read in the original Latin how the narrative was rescued from oblivion.

aged twenty-six, who, after being long tormented with heat and pain in her hands and feet, tried to ease her suffering by plunging them into very cold water. The consequence was that gangrene supervened, and she lost portions of all her toes and of many of her fingers.[1]

Raynaud places in his group of doubtful cases two which were published in 1808, by Bocquet and by Molin. The histories are scarcely sufficient to enable us to determine their exact nature.[2]

Rognetta (1834)[3] tells of a patient in Dupuytren's clinique whose hands and feet were in a condition of dry gangrene. The fingers were white and cold as ice, and the last phalanges were mummified. The toes were nearly as bad, and the ears, nose, and lips showed great want of vitality. The patient was a man of forty, and had been ill from time to time for four years, though not completely

---

[1] Raynaud, *Thesis*, Case xxi. The reference given by Raynaud, and by Dana, is to *Miscellanea curiosa sive ephemeridum medico-physicarum Germanicarum Academiae naturae curiosorum.* Annus tertius, Anni MDCLXXXIV. Nuremberg, 1685. There is some mistake here, for a careful search through the volume has not enabled me to find any such case recorded by Hertius. I have, however, found two very similar cases reported in the same volume by J. L. Hannemann (*Obs.* lvii., pp. 145, 146). In one instance a young man, suffering from burning fever, plunged his hands into cold water, and kept them there during the daytime. When he drew them out they were black and almost dead. The other case was also that of a young man with high fever, who immersed his hands in icy cold water. When they were taken out they were livid black and devoid of sensation; a thing, adds the narrator, which can the more easily happen, since the loss of whole limbs has been observed in some cases, either spontaneously or under the influence of malignant fever.

[2] Cases xxiii. and xxiv. Case xxv., the last in the *Thesis*, was originally published in 1703, and is of still more dubious character.

[3] No. 155. This Case is xi. in Raynaud's series.

disabled as regards his hands till four months previously. In other respects he enjoyed good health. Exposure in the course of his employment as a farm-servant to the great heat of summer was precisely the thing that made his ailment worse. Dupuytren employed the same treatment as he regularly used for senile gangrene, viz. bleedings, poultices, and reduced diet, and after a week of these measures the parts were restored to a healthy condition as if by magic.

It is noteworthy that Rognetta speaks of the "glacial torpor," or "asphyxia of the digits."

Raynaud quotes from Godin (1836), Topinard (1855), and Bernard Henry (1856), three cases in which lesions of the circulatory apparatus disclosed after death appeared to account in part for the symptoms observed during life.[1]

Portal (1836) records the case of a man who, after camping out in the fields at night for some weeks, began to suffer from pain and numbness in the fingers and toes. He ultimately lost the terminal phalanges of all the digits of both hands and feet, his health being completely restored after their removal.[2]

Raynaud quotes from Marchand (1837)[3] the case of a woman who, after several attacks of malarial fever, became very susceptible to the influence of cold, so that if she went out in cool weather her extremities became pale and sometimes blue, or even deep purple.

A case which, though possessing very little relationship to the ordinary forms of Raynaud's disease, is sufficiently curious to deserve mention here, was published by Samuel Solly in 1839 and 1840. The patient was a boy of three, whose feet became purplish black, in August, 1838. In the

---

[1] *Thesis,* Cases xviii., xix., and xvii.
[2] No. 141. Case xvi. of Raynaud's series.   [3] *Thesis,* Case vi.

following month some sloughing took place on the legs, and
gangrene involved the left foot so severely that by the end
of the year it had dropped off. By the end of January
the right forearm was gone, partly amputated by nature;
amputation was proceeding in the middle of the left upper
arm; the left foot and some phalanges from the right foot
were also gone. The gangrene extended for a time in the
left leg, and involved the tip of the nose, but by the middle
of February it ceased to progress, and for a time the patient-
got on very well. In July, however, the gangrene started
anew in all the limbs, and death took place in September,
1839. The post-mortem examination threw practically no
light on the nature of the case.[1]

Mr. Hutchinson[2] quotes a case published by Huguier in
1842. A boy of seven and a half years was admitted, two
months after a severe cold, with all the left finger-tips black,
and the right finger-tips somewhat dark. The middle toe of
the left foot was gone, and the others were black. The tips
of the right toes were black. The arteries were normal.
After a time (how long is not stated) the boy left the Charité
well, but having lost all his toes, all the left fingers, the
whole right hand, and the skin of the tip of the nose and
that over the cheek-bones, chin, and edges of the ears.

Henry Dayman reported, in 1846, a case that occurred at
Bere Regis in Dorsetshire, in the practice of Mr. Nott. A
boy, aged ten, was seen in the beginning of November,
1842, with slight febrile symptoms and a few petechiae on
the legs. Four days later the spots were gone, but the tip
of the nose, the pinna of each ear, the calves of the legs,
the lips, cheeks, and hands were of a dark colour as if from

[1] No. 171. Raynaud includes this in his group of doubtful cases;
Case xxii.
[2] No. 81.

effused blood. After some days the discoloured parts were found to be cold and devoid of sensation. In course of time the tip of the nose, ears, and lips dried up and dropped off, and a line of separation appeared on the right forearm and left hand. Death took place fourteen months after the onset of the disease. There was no autopsy.

The case was seen by many medical men, who made numerous conjectures—inflammation of the arteries, heart disease, ergotism, morbid conditions of the blood, etc., but no one of these theories was sufficient to account for the facts.[1]

Case viii. in the *Thesis*, rather a severe case of Raynaud's malady, was communicated to Raynaud by Landry. It had appeared, in an abridged form and under a wrong designation, in 1851.

Raynaud quotes from Gintrac (1853)[2] the case of a woman who, at the climacteric, suffered from local syncope and ultimately gangrene of portions of her fingers.

He quotes another case from Duval (1858),[3] that of a girl whose hands became the seat of severe pains and of local asphyxia, which seemed to be advancing to gangrene. Ultimately the loss of tissue, though extensive, proved to be quite superficial, but the patient died a few weeks later from acute phthisis.

This brings us up to the date of publication of Raynaud's *Thesis*; but it may be advantageous to continue this chronological list of cases to the time of Raynaud's *New Researches*; first, because his discovery remained practically unknown in other lands until about that period; and, second, because the new cases he gives in his last contribution to the subject are all drawn from his own experience.

A carefully observed case was published by A. S. Myrtle

[1] No. 36.   [2] *Thesis*, Case xiv.   [3] *Thesis*, Case vii.

in 1863.[1] A colonel who had been in the army for many years, and had previously enjoyed good health and lived well, began to suffer, early in August, 1862, from attacks of coldness and numbness in the fingers and tingling in the ears. The fingers were pale, except the ungual phalanx of the right little finger, which was blue. The ears were cold and mottled. In the course of a week the end of the little finger became black and shrivelled, and dead, while the ears rather improved. Severe pain in the feet then set in, and the ends of the toes became bluish. In the latter part of August there was desquamation in the affected parts of the fingers and ears. Eventually there was complete recovery except of the gangrenous part of the finger, which was amputated in the January following. There was no disease of the heart or arteries, and the symptoms were attributed to (1) deficient *vis a tergo*, and (2) "lowering of the vitality from deficiency of nerve force."

John R. Begg, of Dundee, reported in 1870[2] the case of a woman, aged twenty-one, who was seized, six weeks after a tedious labour, with itching followed by pain in both hands, while two fingers of the left hand became blue. Soon the left foot became blue, and then the right hand, right foot, and lobules of the ears. The blueness began at the tips of the digits and ascended. The patient had been troubled with coldness of the extremities for many years, even in the hottest days of summer. The blueness passed on to gangrene, and the patient lost the extremities of her four limbs, the tip of her nose, and part of each ear. Both legs were amputated forty days after the commencement of the gangrene, and both hands twenty days later. Patient regained her good health and spirits. Contrary to Begg's expectation, the tibial arteries in the mortified and amputated lower ex-

[1] No. 125.   [2] No. 17.

tremities were found to be pervious, and after considering and rejecting various other theories, he concluded that "the cause of the disease was organic changes in the capillaries."

In 1871, Sir James Paget recorded a case of local syncope,[1] and in the same year Mr. Hutchinson[2] published a case which is of historical interest. The patient was a woman who, after being out on a cold day, found that her nose and left ear were black and very cold. Parts of the asphyxiated organs became gangrenous. This woman, on being asked, said that her urine had often been dark. Another symptom was complete immobility of both pupils to light and accommodation. There was no history of malaria, and the attacks were not periodic. Mr. Hutchinson remarked on this patient's predisposition to gangrene, *i.e.* on unduly little exposure to cold. Though the urine was never found to contain blood-colouring matter when she was under observation, he considered the morbid state to be allied to "intermittent haematinuria"; and he suggested that the iridoplegia might be connected with the vasomotor disease.

In 1873, J. Moursou published an important paper in which he described a case of local asphyxia occurring immediately after an attack of intermittent fever. This communication will be referred to later on.

A well-marked case of local asphyxia and symmetrical gangrene of the extremities was recorded by Faure in 1874.[3] This need not be reproduced here; but it is interesting to note Faure's remark, that none of Raynaud's predisposing causes were present, this being the earliest recognition of Raynaud's work, so far as I know, by another writer in France. Reference, however, to *Raynaud's local asphyxia*

[1] No. 135.   [2] No. 74.   [3] No. 46.

had been made still earlier in Germany by Estlander in 1871; and also by an abstracter in Schmidt's *Jahrbücher* for 1872, in connection with some of the earlier cases which were published in Scandinavian journals. Two were recorded by Schuboe in 1869. One patient was a woman in whom patches of cyanosis appeared on various parts of the body, but the disease did not proceed further than the formation of blisters. The other was a chlorotic girl who suffered actual gangrene of the ends of the digits. In 1870, Bjering reported the case of a boy, in his second year, who had cyanosis and gangrene of some of his fingers and toes; and in the same year, Brünniche put on record two cases which occurred in boys, one in connection with "Typhus," and the other without any apparent cause. A well-marked, though not severe case, was reported by Riva of Bologna in 1871. In 1872, Holm (Norway) reported a case in which symmetrical cyanosis of several fingers and toes followed erysipelas, and led to slight gangrenous losses of tissue. Bull (Norway) reported a case in 1873; and in 1877, Nielsen recorded a very characteristic case which was met with in an elderly debilitated woman who had just recovered from pneumonia.[1]

Raynaud's own contributions to the literature of the disease which now bears his name are three in number: (1) his *Thesis*, published in 1862; (2) his article on "Gangrene" in the *Nouveau Dictionnaire de Médecine et de Chirurgie Pratiques*, published in 1872; and (3) his *New Researches*, published in the *Archives Générales de Médecine* in 1874. It will be well here to indicate shortly the contents of these writings.

The *Thesis*, in which Raynaud first communicated his

---

[1] Nielsen, however, remarks with regard to his own case, that ergotism, though improbable, could not be absolutely excluded.

discovery to the world of letters, consists of three chapters, the first of which is largely devoted to general considerations on spontaneous gangrene. Earlier observers had pointed out the association of gangrene with the late stages of severe fevers, with diabetes and with senility; but Raynaud now proposes to show that there exists a variety of dry gangrene which has not hitherto obtained due recognition—a variety characterized by its involving the extremities of the limbs and sometimes the nose and ears, by its symmetrical distribution, and by the absence of disease of the blood-vessels, and he hopes to prove that its cause is a vicious innervation of the " capillary vessels." He duly recognizes the merit of Zambaco, who in his thesis on "Spontaneous gangrene produced by nervous perturbation " demonstrated that "there are gangrenes without alteration of vessels," though that writer went too far when he claimed that the nervous element predominates in all gangrenes. He attempts to prove that the fundamental fact of gangrene is the diminution or absence of oxygen necessary for the life of a tissue, and then proceeds to define his use of the expressions "local syncope" and "local asphyxia."

Raynaud's attention was first called to the subject of spontaneous symmetrical gangrene by a case which he saw in the early part of 1861.[1] By looking around him carefully, and by searching through medical literature, he was able to put together twenty-five cases, five of which were original. The second chapter of his *Thesis* is occupied with an account of these cases. Some of them are instances of local syncope only, others of both syncope and asphyxia; some go on to gangrene of various degrees of severity; some are found by post-mortem inspection to be associated

[1] He says 1860 at p. 21, but the history of the case makes it clear that 1861 was the year (p. 76). See pp. 45, 88 of original.

with cardiac disease; and some, he frankly admits, are of doubtful value.

The third chapter contains an elaborate study of the disease from various points of view, the pathology in particular being discussed at great length. Raynaud here propounds his theory of a spasm of arterioles and venules in the affected parts, and he suggests, in a cautious way, that electricity may prove to be of value in treatment.

In his article in the Dictionary, Raynaud reasserts as the two characteristic facts of the disease the absence of demonstrable changes in the vessels and the symmetry of the lesions, and he mentions that he has seen a case associated with a sclerosed condition of the skin. In the *Thesis* he had said that the pulse in the arteries of the affected limbs never ceases to be perceptible, though it may be altered. He now admits that the large arteries may share in the spasm, so that the radial pulse may be temporarily effaced.[1] Considerable portions of the third chapter of the *Thesis* are reproduced in this article.

The *New Researches* include six new cases of the disease, two of them being specially important because narrowing of the arteries of the fundus oculi could actually be seen with the ophthalmoscope, and several of them because of the great benefit received from electrical treatment. In one of the six patients, the gangrene was not strictly symmetrical, and this raises grave doubts in Raynaud's mind as to its right to be classed with the others. In this paper he develops more fully his theory of the disease, suggesting that the vascular contraction is reflex, that the starting-point of this reflex action is sometimes an irritation of the generative organs of the female, but more commonly a cutaneous temperature-impression, and that the occurrence of the

[1] *Thesis*, pp. 107, 113; *Nouv. Dict.*, xv., 651.

disease can only be accounted for by supposing that the vasomotor centres of the spinal cord are abnormally excitable.

As Raynaud penned his account of his new researches he was able to reflect with satisfaction that his earlier work had been accepted by the medical profession as a genuine contribution to the advancement of nosological science. It is enough at present to mention the names of the writers on this subject who followed Raynaud in the seventies. They include Hamilton (1874), Fischer (1875), Calmette (1876 and 1877), Mills, M'Bride, Englisch, and Nedopil (1878), Hutchinson, Wilks, Warren, and Vulpian (1879). The attention of physicians in this country was first definitely drawn to the subject by Dr. Southey in 1880, and by Mr. Hutchinson about the same time. Among others who wrote upon it in the same year were T. Smith, Moursou, Debove, and Richard. Sainton wrote in 1881; Hutchinson, Makins, Leloir and Merklen, Verdalle, Saint-Philippe, Ritti, Hastreiter, and Weiss in 1882; Barlow, Southey, Fabre, Petit and Verneuil, and Roques in 1883.[1] Curiously enough, though Dr. Barlow published several cases under the title of "Raynaud's Disease" in 1883, the malady obtained no mention in the second edition of *The Nomenclature of Diseases*, published by the Royal College of Physicians in 1885.[2] There is no doubt, however, that interest in this strange disease was greatly quickened by the publication, in 1888, of Dr. Barlow's English translation of Raynaud's *Thesis* and *New Researches*.

[1] For references, see *Bibliography*.

[2] It has duly found its place in the third edition (1896).

ETIOLOGY.

Mr. Hutchinson [1] has given us the following list of the local effects of exposure to cold:

Pallor (emptiness of arterial and venous capillaries);

Brick-red congestion (fulness of arterial and venous capillaries);

Plaice spots—lighter spots occasionally scattered over the brick-red skin (unexplained);

Cyanosis (weakness of venules, usually associated with contraction of arteries);

Sclerosis (induration of skin with pale marbling);

Sphacelus (sloughing from arterial constriction);

Onychitis and arthritis;

Chilblain and other forms of inflammation.

Certain of these conditions constitute the essential phenomena of Raynaud's disease.

Some light is thrown upon this subject by a consideration of what takes place in ordinary frost-bite. The freedom with which the ether spray can be used for the production of local anaesthesia shows that the skin can be actually frozen without serious consequences, if this condition be not kept up for more than a minute or

[1] No. 86, p. 86.

so. But if the skin is exposed to a very low temperature for a prolonged period harm will result. There is first contraction of all the unstriped muscle of the part, so that the arterioles are narrowed until, it may be, their lumen is obliterated. Consequently, the arterial blood supply is cut off, and the part becomes shrunken and pale, or "dead." Since no warm blood reaches it, it now freezes readily if the exposure be continued, and if this persist still longer, necrosis of the part will take place, and thereafter, even if warmth be applied, the circulation cannot be restored; the affected part remains pale and cold. If, however, warmth be applied in time, even after freezing, the vessels will dilate. The blood may then re-enter the part with a rush so violent as to be hurtful. Exudation may take place through the walls of the vessels whose nutrition has meanwhile suffered, and may cause not only swelling, pain, etc., but even sufficient pressure upon the vessels to arrest the circulation again. This arrest is probably aided by increased adhesiveness of the blood-corpuscles within the vessels. In this way a part that has escaped death from exposure to cold may die from the effects of the reaction after the cold has been withdrawn.

If there be no necrosis, inflammation, often with vesication, ensues. This varies in degree according to circumstances, and in slight cases may be manifested merely by redness, swelling, and burning pain, or severe itching. The phenomena of these slight cases are exactly the same as those of chilblain. The one point of difference is that the degree of cold which is required to produce the common chilblain is by no means severe; the exposure is slight, but the person is unduly susceptible. Even in chilblain, however, the inflammation may be associated with vesication and necrosis of a portion of the true skin.

In chilblain, then, the morbid process is inflammatory, and while it occurs apart from any very severe exposure in those who possess a special susceptibility, it corresponds strictly in its nature to the reaction that follows upon exposure which while severe is yet not serious enough to cause death directly. On the other hand, Raynaud's disease, while likewise occurring apart from any necessarily severe exposure in those who are susceptible, is the type of what occurs in ordinary individuals in consequence of exposure so severe that death of the part occurs before any reaction can take place. If necrosis of tissue occurs in the former case, it is due to the inflammation of tissues whose vitality has been impaired by cold or otherwise. When necrosis occurs in the second case, it is due to vascular spasm and consequent deprivation of a proper blood supply, acting upon tissues whose vitality may at the same time be reduced by cold or otherwise. This does not mean that all cases of Raynaud's disease are associated with gangrene; a large proportion, indeed, are not. But even where the vascular spasm passes off before any of the tissues die, there is but little tendency to inflammatory reaction. It is true that after attacks of this kind a reaction frequently does occur in the form of excessive vascularity with redness and discomfort or even pain, but even then inflammation is commonly but slight. The obtrusive features of the condition are the vascular spasm and its direct results; whereas in chilblain the characteristic features are of a definitely inflammatory nature.

These two types of lesion, chilblain and Raynaud's disease, depend upon different susceptibilities which may be, but frequently are not, combined in one individual. There

is a history of liability to chilblain in less than 12 per cent.
of the cases of Raynaud's disease, though this doubtless
understates the proportion, since the absence of chilblain
is definitely reported with regard to less than 6 per cent.
of the cases. The probability is that a good many of those
who are not reported to have suffered from chilblain did
suffer in this way in childhood, but got over the tendency
as they grew up. Of 17 cases reported by Mr. Hutchinson,
2 never had chilblains, though one of these had always
been liable to cold hands and feet; 2 had been liable to
both chilblains and local syncope almost all their lives;
6 had suffered from chilblains slightly or severely in early
life; and with regard to 7, chilblains are not mentioned.
The experience of other observers, though less extensive,
gives the same results. Short has reported the exceptional
case of a woman who had suffered from cyanosis of the
hands for four years. Her toes had formerly been affected
with chilblains, but had ceased to trouble her since the
fingers became blue.

The essential lesion, then, in chilblain is inflammation;
in Raynaud's disease, vascular spasm. Chilblain is mainly
a disease of childhood; the youthfulness of the tissues may
account in part for their susceptibility to cold. Raynaud's
disease, while not infrequent in childhood, is in the main
an affection of early adult life, when the nervous system
is reaching or has just reached its full maturity. Both
these conditions resemble frost-bite and the local results
of cold in general in affecting most readily the peripheral
parts of the body, and especially those which possess a
large extent of cooling surface in proportion to their size,
viz. the fingers, toes, nose, ears, etc. Mr. Hutchinson
remarks on the liability of young pigs that are born in
cold or chilly weather to lose their tails by frost-bite,

probably on account of their deficiency in a protection of hair or fat.

Since chilblain and Raynaud's disease are both expressions of an undue susceptibility to cold—the former on the part of the tissues, and the latter on the part of the vasomotor system—it naturally follows that cold is one of the most potent agents in inducing them ; but in those who are very susceptible, chilblain may be caused by a breeze in summer, and Raynaud's disease may occur not only after a trifling exposure, but even, there is good reason to believe, as a pure neurosis.

Since the phenomena of Raynaud's disease manifest themselves as a rule first and principally in the " extremities," it follows that anything that diminishes the activity of the circulation in the periphery will tend to make these phenomena more marked if they are present ; or call forth an attack—it may be even the first attack—in those who are predisposed to it ; or give rise to appearances very similar to Raynaud's phenomena even in those who are but little predisposed. In these ways numerous difficulties of diagnosis arise, and there is often room for much difference of opinion as to whether a given case which presents " Raynaud's phenomena " can be justly styled a case of " Raynaud's disease." Thus an excessive accumulation of uric acid in the blood appears to be capable of causing arterial contraction and local cyanosis, and Raynaud's disease may develop in characteristic form in the course of chronic Bright's disease. Similarly congenital abnormality or structural disease of the arteries may be a contributing cause.

Weakness of the heart's action, howsoever induced, cardiac valvular disease and pericarditis may have a share in causing the peripheral disturbance of the circulation. The

c

disorder may appear to consist simply in an undue excitability of the vasomotor system, or this may be part of a more
widespread neurosis, as when it is seen in the subjects of
hysteria, epilepsy, or insanity. It may result from a concussion which involves the vasomotor centres of the bulb
and cord, and it is sometimes met with in cases of
organic disease of the central or of the peripheral nervous
system.

The following statistical tables, except where otherwise
stated, are founded on 180[1] of the most characteristic cases
reported by others, or met with by myself, and selected for
the purpose from the much larger number on which this
essay is based.

Nationality. There is some reason to believe that
Raynaud's disease is not so common in German-speaking
countries as in Britain and France. Of course to make sure
of this, it is desirable to consider only those cases that have
been published since the disease became well known in all
the countries compared.

In 1878, Nedopil, of Vienna, spoke of it as rarer in his
country than in France. Weiss (Austria), writing in 1882,
refers to symmetrical gangrene as "an extremely rare
neurosis." Schulz, in 1884, calls the disease a "quite extra-
ordinarily rare one."[2] Hochenegg (Austria) speaks, in 1885,
of the poverty of German literature with regard to this
subject, and collects 16 German as against 35 French cases.
Scheiber (Austria) collected 26 cases in 1892, as a supplement to the 93 collected by Morgan, and published in the
Lancet in 1889. Of these 26 cases, 12 were recorded in
British, 3 in American, 1 in Australian, 3 in French, and 7 in

---

[1] The totals do not always amount to 180, because some of the reports
are defective in certain details.

[2] *Deut. Arch. f. Klin. Med.*, 1884, xxxv., 183.

German literature. Of the 180 characteristic cases collected by myself, 145 were recorded in English, French, or German *periodical* literature in the years 1881-1897, thus :

British, - - - - - - - - 90	
American, - - - - - - - - 24	
Australian, - - - - - - - - 5	119
French, - - - - - - - -	21
German, - - - - - - - - 4	
Austrian, - - - - - - - - 1	5
	145

So that 62 per cent. appear in British periodicals, and 81 per cent. in journals in the English language. The French cases are less than one-fourth of the British, and the German and Austrian together less than one-fourth of the French. It is probable that these figures exaggerate the differences in the liability of the different nations, because they do not take cognizance of the cases studied in French and German dissertations, nor of several collections published by French writers with the special purpose of showing the relationship between Raynaud's disease and malarial fever. If we eliminate these sources of fallacy by considering the number of *authors* whose names appear in the *Bibliography* of Raynaud's disease (including 15 French and 6 German writers of theses), we get the following :

British, - - - - - - - - 84	
American, - - - - - - - - 24	
Australian, - - - - - - - - 3	111
French, - - - - - - - -	52
German, - - - - - - - - 16	
Austrian, - - - - - - - - 9	25
	188

British authors therefore constitute 44 per cent. of the whole, and 59 per cent. of all write in English. Authors who use French are less than half as numerous as those who use English, and German authors are less than half as numerous as French.[1]

Sex. Of the cases I have collected 62.6 per cent. were females, and 37.4 per cent. males. Raynaud found that 80 per cent. of his cases were females,[2] and if we eliminate from his 25 cases those that are doubtful or insufficiently described, we find that 8 out of 9, or 88 per cent. of the genuine cases, were females. Yet of the 6 cases in his *New Researches*, 4 were males, and only 2 females. The cases admitted to the wards of the Glasgow Royal Infirmary during a recent decade were equally divided between the sexes, and the same proportion exists among the cases in my own note-books. The reason for this great discrepancy is probably to be found in the severity of the early reported cases, which attracted the notice of Raynaud and those from whom he quoted in a way that milder cases would not. It would appear that this neurosis resembles hysteria in its tendency to assume its worst forms in the adult female, and the special liability of women in France to the very severe forms of hysteria may be analogous to their special liability to Raynaud's disease. Thus, while the percentage of cases in English-speaking countries is 61.5 females to 38.5 males, and in German-speaking countries 57 females to 43 males, in France it is 68.4 females to 31.6 males.

[1] It must be admitted that a certain amount of fallacy must creep in here through the inaccessibility of provincial French and German periodicals. So far as the different languages are concerned this will be partly neutralized by the same condition applying to American contributions.

[2] *Thesis*, p. 115.

Age. The average age of the collected cases was 30.9 years for both sexes, or 32.2 years for males, and 30.4 years for females. This, however, means the age at which the patient came under observation. In a third of the cases (20 males and 41 females out of 180), it is definitely reported that the patient was subject to the disease for more than a year before he or she reached the age given. This period of preceding liability varied from 1 to 38 years for both sexes, or 1 to 12 in males, and 1 to 38 in females. It averaged 6 years for both sexes, or 4.5 years for males, and 6.7 for females. If the 6 years be distributed among the 180 cases, it will be seen that the average age at the onset of the disease should be 28.9 years for both sexes. Similarly, if the 4.5 years be distributed among all the males, it will be found that 1.3 years should be deducted from 32.2, so that the average age at the actual onset is 30.9. And if the 6.7 years be distributed among all the females, 2.5 years must be deducted from 30.4, leaving 27.9 years as the average age at the commencement in females.

In addition to the cases just dealt with, where Raynaud's phenomena were of more than one year's standing, there were 7 cases out of the 180 in which there had been liability for more than a year to attacks of dead fingers (local syncope). These were 3 males and 4 females, with ages varying from 18 to 50. Their liability to dead fingers extended back in 3 cases for a number of years, in another case (aet. 50) almost to childhood, and in the others over practically the whole of life.

Table I. (page 38) shows that a considerable number of cases occur in the first ten years of life, and that after a falling off in the next five years the cases become numerous again between 15 and 30. This has doubtless some relation to the evolution of the nervous system, especially in females, and to occupation, especially in males. After another falling off, there is again an increase as the degenerative period of life sets in, the explanation probably being that anatomical changes in various organs, but especially in the cardio-vascular system, operate as contributory causes. Raynaud noted the increased liability about the age of 40.[1]

TABLE I.

SHOWING INCIDENCE OF RAYNAUD'S DISEASE IN THE TWO SEXES, IN DIFFERENT RACES, AND AT DIFFERENT AGES.

Age in Years when seen.	Britain, Australia, and United States.		France.		Germany and Austria.		Totals.
	Males.	Females.	Males.	Females.	Males.	Females.	
– 5	3	6	1	1	1	...	12
– 10	3	7	1	1	...	...	12
– 15	3	3	...	...	...	...	6
– 20	4	12	1	4	...	1	22
– 25	3	8	1	4	...	...	16
– 30	9	10	...	2	...	...	21
– 35	5	2	...	2	1	2	12
– 40	5	5	2	2	...	...	14
– 45	5	9	1	2	...	1	18
– 50	2	6	2	5	1	...	16
– 60	3	6	1	2	...	...	12
– 70	3	4	1	...	...	...	8
Over 70	...	1	1	...	...	...	2
Totals,	48	79	12	25	3	4	171

[1] *Thesis*, p. 116.

The table also shows that the preponderance of the female sex holds good at almost all ages. A preponderance of males, however, is found among the English-speaking cases between the ages of 30 and 35. Two of these males became ill in consequence of exposure, and in another the disease was apparently induced by the same cause acting on a malarious subject.

The oldest male of the collected cases was aged 74, and had suffered, especially in winter, for six years. This man was of sober habits, and had previously enjoyed good health. His arteries were supple. His fingers and toes, one after another, became the seat of mortification, and there was cyanosis of the nose and ears (Saint-Philippe).

The oldest female on the list was a widow aged 77, whose case is reported by F. P. Henry. She had been liable to symmetrical local disturbances of the circulation for twelve winters, and the first attack, which involved the ears, came on under the influence of exposure to a cold wind. After ten years the cheeks became similarly cyanosed in winter. Some months before admission the upper limbs became affected, and about the same time bullae developed on the feet. Portions of both ears became gangrenous.

It must be admitted that it is difficult to regard Raynaud's phenomena when they occur in advanced life as manifestations of a neurosis, and nothing more. Yet why should this be? Senile insanity may be associated with mental exaltation, and it is not unreasonable to suppose that the vasomotor centre may suffer from the same perversion of function as the cerebral cortex. It is to be noted that so experienced an observer as Mr. Hutchinson describes cases of Raynaud's disease in women aged 64 and 62; the latter he calls a typical example.

The youngest patients in the list were a boy of 19 months, who had been ill for 5 months, and a girl of 15 months who had had an earlier attack when she was 9 months old (Deck; H. Mendel). But the disease sometimes occurs at a still earlier period of life. Thus a patient of W. W. Johnston's, a girl of 5 years, was reported to have had a similar attack when aged 3 months. Defrance records a case occurring at 9 months, and quotes from Friedel a case which occurred in an infant of 6 months.

Heredity. In nearly 8 per cent. of cases (8 males and 6 females in 180) there is a history of Raynaud's phenomena in some antecedent or collateral member of the family. Thus two patients were brothers; another two were brother and sister. A patient of either sex might have father, mother, brother, or sister affected with some form of the same complaint. One young man who had suffered much from ague developed local cyanosis with loss of epidermis; his father and two other members of his father's family had suffered habitually from coldness and numbness of the hands (C. Beale). Colman and Taylor report the case of a young girl whose first symptom was deadness of the distal part of the right middle finger, coming on in summer and without obvious cause. In later attacks other fingers of the right hand became involved after the middle one; and on one occasion the left fingers were also involved. The attacks generally came on in the morning while patient was washing, but the temperature of the water had no influence on their occurrence or duration. This girl's maternal grandfather suffered for some years when he was an elderly man from exactly similar symptoms, limited to the right fingers, and induced as readily by hot as by cold water; and this man's brother, when over 70, was subject for some years to similar attacks, which, however, involved both hands, and occurred in cold weather only. Among the collected cases are three instances in which a child of a female patient showed a tendency to suffer from Raynaud's phenomena; one of these is Case xv. in the *Thesis*.

Occupation. This is of importance chiefly in so far as it entails exposure to cold. It is possible, however, especially in the case of females, that a sedentary occupation may contribute as a cause by fostering a neurotic constitutional tendency. The following are the occupations, where these are recorded, of the male patients among the collected cases: farm-worker (3), traveller, peddler, car-driver, omnibus-conductor, carter, ballaster, footman, groom (2), colonel, hussar, mason (2), labourer (2), quarryman, builder, drill-instructor, schoolboy, teacher, waiter (2), house-painter, journeyman printer, locksmith (2), bookbinder, door-keeper, potman, lawyer (2), and merchant. It will be seen that the occupations in the earlier part of the series involve constant exposure to the elements, and as to the remainder, the teacher was a poor lad who taught languages to beginners during the day, and studied at night in a cold room; the door-keeper was much exposed, and had been a policeman for many years; the potman became ill after exposure to cold, and one of the lawyers suffered in consequence of driving several miles in an open sleigh on a winter's night. But in a number of cases the occupation had no obvious connection with the disease. Another patient whose case has been published was a sailor.

The occupations reported as having been followed by the female patients are these: domestic servant (8), house-wife (3), charwoman, worker in the fields, washerwoman, seamstress (4), machinist, weaver (2), mill-worker (2), laundress, florist, French polisher, polisher of plate, confectionery worker, and school-girl. Some of these occupations do not involve exposure, but rather the reverse. With regard to two of the seamstresses, there was no obvious cause for the illness; in a third the disease seems to have been brought on by mental strain and hard work, and in the fourth by anaemia and debility induced by prolonged lactation. The machinist was a girl of 21, who had suffered from the disease only during the seven years in which she had followed this occupation; the relationship is not further explained. There seems to have been no special exposure in the case of the weavers and mill-workers. The confectionery-worker became ill after prolonged fatigue and exposure when melting snow was on the ground. The florist had to put her hands in cold water. The case of the French-polisher was peculiar; her father was liable to local syncope in cold weather, but she first became subject to it in the extreme heat of summer. The polisher of plate probably owed her illness to severe mental strain and hard work, but her occupation involved fatigue of the fingers. No cause is reported for the laundress's illness.

Cold. One of the most important of all etiological influences is exposure to cold; not uncommonly it is the immediate cause of the first onset of the disease. This was reported to be the case with 22 patients out of the 180, namely, 13 males and 9 females. In many reports the cause of the first attack is not stated, so that 22 is probably much less than the correct number. There can be little doubt that the preponderance of males is due to the influence in them of exposure from occupation. On the other hand, the records show that in 21 instances the first attack was not due to cold, and here the proportion of the sexes is reversed (7 males, 13 females, 1 not stated). Far more frequently cold induces a fresh attack, or aggravates an existing one; this applies to at least 29 males and 39 females of the 180. In other 5 cases, cold had no influence in exciting fresh attacks. In none of these 5 is cold reported to have caused the first attack, and of 2 of them the contrary is reported. In another case (not due to cold) the symptoms varied in the course of the day, and were at one time relieved and at another time aggravated by cold water (Raynaud, *Thesis*, Case viii.). In another instance (also not due to cold) the patient preferred to sit in cold air (Renshaw).

The exposure which induces the first onset of a certain proportion of cases of Raynaud's disease may be a trivial matter, and is frequently nothing more than the patient and thousands of others like him have long been liable to in connection with their occupations. For instance, a car-driver began to suffer after working late one winter's night (Thomas). Exposure to cold, or to cold and damp, or to a cold wind; working out of doors in severe frost, or on a snowy night, or moving into a damp house may be followed by the first manifestations of Raynaud's disease. But a quite ordinary degree of cold may produce the same phenomena in a predisposed subject. Thus a factory girl was affected when going to work on a morning in early autumn (Mills). In more than one instance, a malarious subject has taken ill on the voyage home (Barlow, Fairland). An epileptic was admitted to an asylum with acute mania, and for a whole week in winter refused to stay in bed, and stood during the night with bare feet; Raynaud's disease ensued (Bland). Another patient was a woman who, after getting heated by working in the fields in August, bathed her hands and feet in very cold water (Faure). In another instance, the cause was standing in cold water under a shower-bath every morning for a week (Paget).

Fatigue, especially from walking, appears to make the influence of exposure more potent, and in one of Affleck's cases, a long walk seems to have been the exciting cause; in his other case, prolonged fatigue co-operated with exposure. In a case reported by Dixon, a girl of 19 had temporary numbness in the left foot after walking three miles in fine weather at the ·beginning of winter. A fortnight later she started to walk four miles in rainy but not very cold weather, when suddenly both feet became cold and devoid of sensation, so that she was compelled to discontinue her walk, though not before her left foot and several toes of her right foot had become purple. Noyes describes a case where the fatigue of a heavy day's washing seemed to be the cause. The patient had a constricted feeling in the feet that evening, and later on tingling and burning, which continued during the succeeding night and day; on the second morning, several toes and portions of both ears were black.

When Raynaud's disease results from exposure, the symptoms set in almost at once in a considerable proportion of cases. The patient may begin to suffer while still exposed, or may not be conscious of serious harm until later. Thus an adult may be seized with burning pain in the affected region on getting into shelter in a warm room. Or a child that has been out on a cold day may be found on coming home to have cold and livid feet. Sometimes, however, the onset is delayed, and it may even appear to be brought about in an indirect fashion. The lawyer who suffered after driving in an open sleigh found his foot slightly frost-bitten when he got home, but managed to restore the circulation by vigorous rubbing; the symptoms set in a few days later (Garland). Faure's patient, the woman who, when heated, bathed her hands and feet in cold water, suffered for a time from some gastric disturbance with fever, and was confined to bed for ten days. Raynaud's disease did not manifest itself till 31 days after the cold water had been used. A patient of Affleck's was much fatigued by walking in melting snow. Pain began in both feet two days later, and was experienced during several hours daily for a week. Twelve days after the exposure, swelling and blueness were present in addition to the pain. A case mentioned by Hochenegg may be cited as a type of a certain class. A young soldier who had hitherto enjoyed perfect health underwent extreme fatigue in a march home from Bosnia, with little rest, and that only on damp ground. When he arrived at his station his hands and feet became livid, cold, and insensible. Most of this passed off under appropriate treatment, but the terminal phalanges of several toes in each foot were lost through gangrene. The heart, vessels, and kidneys were normal, and other causes of local asphyxia and gangrene could be excluded.

Season. Some indication of the season of onset is given in 73 of the 180 cases, and here again the influence of cold is apparent; thus: January 2 cases, February 5, March 2, April 4, spring 3, May 3, June 3, July 1, summer 3, warm day 1, August 5, September 5, October 9, autumn 2, November 5, December 6, winter 14. Cases that begin in hot weather may nevertheless be due to cold, as in the case of the woman who, when overheated, bathed her hands and feet in very cold water; or they may be due to an emotional cause. But there may be no explanation for such cases. Some of them may be peculiar in other respects. For instance, the affection may remain uninfluenced by weather, or if attacks are induced by washing, these may occur with equal readiness whatever the temperature of the water employed.

Emotion. Mental strain and violent emotion are occasional causes of Raynaud's disease, chiefly in women. The cares of life have pressed heavily upon a poor widow (Barlow); a young woman, worn out by nursing her dying mother, has her emotions deeply stirred by watching the corpse (*Thesis*, Case v.); a mother is overwhelmed with grief at the death of her only child (Hutchinson); a woman is terrified by an attempt at indecent assault (Dehio). These are actual cases. The circulatory phenomena may appear at once after a fright, or may be delayed for a couple of days.

Malarial Fever. The relationship which is now known to exist between Raynaud's disease and paludism was scarcely appreciated by Raynaud himself. This was perhaps because his cases were comparatively few, and because a considerable proportion of them were not characteristic. Nevertheless several of the cases he records were malarious subjects. Thus Case vi. in the *Thesis* was a woman who had several attacks of tertian fever in March, and became liable to local syncope and local cyanosis towards the middle of April; and Case viii. was a woman who became affected with Raynaud's symptoms some months after recovery from a tertian intermittent fever of three months' duration. Among the cases which Raynaud himself terms doubtful, there were two (xxiii. and xxv.) in which the patients suffered from an undefined fever. Case i. in the *New Researches* was a man who had had intermittent fever many years before; while Case v. was a young woman who began to suffer almost immediately after a series of febrile attacks which had gone on for a fortnight. In connection with this last case, Raynaud asks what share intermittent fever had in the development of local asphyxia. He finds the question a difficult one to answer, but says that the fact of the association ought to be borne in mind in treatment. In the *Thesis* he had definitely alluded to a preceding intermittent as of no special importance.[1]

Some very important papers have been published by French writers on the relations that subsist between paludism on the one hand, and local asphyxia and symmetrical gangrene on the other; and in particular by Moursou (1873 and 1880), Calmette (1876 and 1877), and Petit and Verneuil (1883). The mere fact of the coincidence of the two conditions had of course been recognized long before any of these observers published his experiences, for Case vi. in Raynaud's *Thesis* had been recorded by Marchand in 1837, and Case viii. had been published as an example of acrodynia in 1851. Rey, in 1869, reported the case of a corporal of marines who, after suffering from intermittent fever in Senegal and later on in France, became subject to syncope, cyanosis, and losses of epidermis in the extremities; and Marroin published, in 1870, the case of a soldier who had intermittent fever at Jerusalem, and became subject, a couple of years later, to local syncope and cyanosis. Rey accepted Raynaud's theory without attributing any influence to the intermittent fever, while Marroin raised and rejected the theory of a connection between the two disorders. Moursou first clearly laid down the doctrine of this relationship when he published, in 1873, a case in which local asphyxia of the extremities followed an attack of intermittent fever, and he not only recalled Rey's case in support of his view, but also suggested a theory to explain the relationship.

The writings of Rey, Marroin, and Moursou cannot have been known to Raynaud when he published his *New*

[1] P. 116.

Researches in 1874, since he does not allude to them. It is all the more curious that he dismissed the subject so briefly, since two out of his six new cases were paludic subjects. Even in connection with his older collection of cases, he had become familiar with the fact of intermittence of the vascular disturbances in the extremities, and he had also known sulphate of quinine to destroy the intermittence. The fact remains, however, that Raynaud, who in 1872 wrote[1] that he knew of no instance of "gangrène propre à la cachexie paludéenne," still failed in 1874 to recognize the intimate relationship between malaria and the disease which was soon to bear his name.

In 1874 Charpentier communicated to the Society of Medicine the case of a' man who had local asphyxia of the upper extremities from 12 to 4 p.m. every day during the first four months of a certain year. In the following year, during the same period, and at the same hours, he had gastric pains (without other digestive disturbance) which yielded only—like the attacks of local cyanosis— to sulphate of quinine. Five months later the attacks of local asphyxia returned, but these again ceased under the influence of quinine. Durosiez, who was asked to report upon this case, expressed the opinion that the local asphyxia was but one of the manifestations of intermittent fever. Foulquier (who recorded this case) and Bréhier both issued their theses in this year, and appear to have been largely inspired by Durosiez's report.

Calmettè's attention was drawn to the subject during his residence in Algiers, where he saw many cases among natives and Europeans. He showed that local asphyxia of the extremities may follow, accompany, or precede an attack of

[1]No. 147, p. 679.

intermittent fever. In the ' cases quoted, it followed the fever. One or two examples may be selected from Calmette's experience. An Algerian woman was admitted for palustral cachexia with anasarca, enlarged spleen, and marked pigmentation of the skin. Cyanosis of the four extremities had occurred at intervals during some months past. Drops of water projected on the skin would bring on an attack of symmetrical cyanosis. There was transient amblyopia during the attacks, with constriction of the arteries of the papilla. The patient had repeated attacks of fever in its three stages, and as soon as the hot stage set in, the extremities became the seat of local syncope and asphyxia—there being a perfect alternation between the febrile cold of the whole organism and the arterial spasm. In another instance, a European colonist, after numerous attacks of fever, became subject to cyanosis of the extremities, which sometimes coincided with feverish periods, and was associated with ocular troubles. A soldier who had long been in Africa, and had suffered badly from intermittents in 1868 and 1869, was admitted in 1875 for a recurrence of the fever. By this time he had been subject to local asphyxia for more than a year, but now the attacks came almost every day, invading the three middle digits of each hand and all the toes. The application of water promptly brought on this condition, and exposure to fresh air induced it less readily. Otherwise an attack would occur spontaneously quarter of an hour before the feverishness began, and would persist till after the commencement of the cold stage. In another case (a European colonist, who was the subject of malarial cachexia), it seemed to Calmette that the attack of arterial spasm in the extremities, occurring as it did daily between 2 and 2.30 p.m., replaced the ordinary febrile attack. A female of Spanish descent

D

had several attacks of fever, and afterwards, without obvious cause, suffered seriously in her limbs. Both thumbs remained almost intact, but of the remaining digits in each hand the middle finger alone retained a rudiment of the third phalanx, the others having only the first. The great toes still had two phalanges each, but all the others were reduced to one phalanx apiece.

As an instance of the actual concurrence of Raynaud's phenomena and malarial attacks, Calmette mentions the case of a soldier who, having been for some years in Africa, came under observation with a large spleen and commencing palustral cachexia. He was taking attacks of fever at least once a month, and local asphyxia frequently coincided with the cold stage. It did not occur apart from the feverish attacks. The normal algidity of the first stage was exaggerated till there was actual cyanosis of the four extremities.

To exemplify the occurrence of intermittent fever after an attack of symmetrical gangrene, Calmette quotes from Pitron and Regnault (1836) the case of an officer who, after staying for four months at a post in the Pyrenees, found that his lower limbs frequently became frozen. Numbness, itching, and sensations of cold and heat followed. Dry gangrene ensued, and the left leg, which was the more extensively affected, had to be amputated. The patient had an attack of intermittent fever during convalescence, but recovered completely.

Vaillard recorded, in 1877, the occurrence of local asphyxia in a man who had had attacks of tertian fever. Moursou published his important contribution in 1880. He had gained his experience principally in Cochin-China, and he was now able to collect 22 cases showing the influence of paludism in the genesis of Raynaud's disease

(Moursou, 9 cases; Raynaud, 4; Rey, Marroin, and Vaillard, each, 1; Calmette, 6). He pointed out that malaria was not always a cause, and considered that quinine would then be useless, whereas in malarial cases it would succeed admirably. He asserted that local asphyxia frequently occurs after intermittent fever, and especially after its more obstinate types (quartan and tertian), and occasionally in connection with pernicious fever, while it also follows paludic diarrhoea. Cold and heat, he said, have a similar occasional influence on the onset of attacks of local asphyxia and of intermittent fever.

Petit and Verneuil (1883) recognized these two categories : (1) local asphyxia contemporaneous with the attack of fever, the circulatory disturbance slightly preceding the shivering, or coinciding with the shivering, or with the sweating ; (2) local asphyxia chronologically independent, the ischaemia following, replacing or alternating with the fever, but itself apyretic. In the latter group the fever might precede the local asphyxia by years, so that the connection could easily be overlooked. Petit and Verneuil further pointed out that, in view of the extreme frequency of intermittent fevers, local asphyxia was rare. The malarial poison of itself was not a sufficient cause ; other factors must enter into the etiology, and one of these was undoubtedly exposure to cold. The season of the year in which local asphyxia began was mentioned in 16 cases out of 23 collected by these writers ; 12 of the 16 began in winter, 2 in spring, and the other 2 in autumn.

Of the 180 collected cases, 15 at least (8 males and 7 females), or 8.3 per cent., had malarious antecedents, whilst with regard to 28 (10 males and 18 females), or 15.6 per cent., there was good reason to believe that the patient was free from any such infection. In the large proportion of 76 per cent. (137 cases), the report does not give the necessary information. To put these figures in another way: Of the sufficiently reported cases, 8 males out of 18 (44.4 per cent.), and 7 females out of 25 (28 per cent.), or 15 patients out of 43 (34.9 per cent.) were paludic subjects. It is quite possible that this over-represents the frequency of a malarious history, but on the other hand it should be stated that the papers of Moursou and Calmette[1] have not been utilized in drawing up the list of 180 cases. If we added the cases collected by these writers to those that are not published with the special purpose of showing the connection between malaria and Raynaud's disease, we should get a considerably increased proportion of malarious cases. The statistics will doubtless be very different in malarious and non-malarious countries.

The interval between the malarial attack and the onset of Raynaud's disease varies considerably. A third of the 15 cases began within the year, either during the later of a series of febrile attacks, or immediately after the fever, or several weeks or months after a tertian fever. If Raynaud's disease does not appear within a few months after the malarial attack, it is not very likely to do so for a good many years. The intervals in some of the 15 cases were 11, 14, 34, 35, and 47 years. More than once the fever is noted as having been severe. The patient may have enjoyed a long period of good health. For instance, the first case in Raynaud's *New Researches* was a man of 59, vigorous and healthy looking, of temperate habits, and favourably situated as regards food and lodging, whose only illness had been an attack of intermittent fever 35 years before.

[1] The cases collected by Petit and Verneuil are almost all quoted from other writers, principally Moursou and Calmette.

One of the 15 cases was a woman, aged 42, who came under the observation of Englisch in January, 1877, with gangrene of the toes. Her illness began in 1875, and it is reported that she had intermittent fever for 8 weeks in 1876.

Intermittent fever may play its part in the etiology of non-typical cases of Raynaud's malady. Thus Hutchinson tells of a dressmaker who had intermittent fever at 12, and numerous severe attacks of quinsy. The last and worst of these left her very weak, and about a year later, when aged 22, she became liable to painful lividity of the nose (*nasus mortuus*), the hands and feet being always normal. The first attack was due to exposure, but afterwards the nose would become very cold on a very hot day.

Sexual Disorders. To what extent disorders of the sexual organs can influence the development of Raynaud's disease is very uncertain. There is no doubt that Raynaud himself attributed considerable importance to diseases of the female generative system. In connection with Case v. in his *Thesis* he remarks upon the striking coincidence between the affection of the extremities and the suppression of the catamenial flux, and he calls attention to the close similarity between this case and the one he cites next. Later on he says, "the only well-marked exciting cause has, in several instances in women, appeared to be suppression of the menses; and on the other hand we have seen considerable improvement, or even complete cure, coincide with the re-establishment of that function."[1] In the *New Researches* he discusses the sensory origin of the reflex vascular contraction, and whilst admitting that it probably varies much in different cases, and that it is most commonly an impression produced by temperature upon the cutaneous

[1] *Thesis*, p. 131 (original).

nerves, he says it has appeared to him "in several cases
that it ought to be sought in the genital apparatus of
the female."[1] The experience of most later observers,
however, has scarcely borne out what Raynaud was perfectly justified in concluding from his own experience. It
is quite true that some disorder of menstruation is present
in a certain proportion of cases, but the two seem to be
more frequently related as common effects of some more
general condition than as cause and effect. Menstruation
may be absent throughout the course of Raynaud's disease
and return on improvement or recovery; or the flow may
return without affecting the circulatory trouble (*Thesis*, Case
ii.); or the irregularity may commence after Raynaud's
disease has set in; or the function may be regular before,
during, and after the illness. Deficiency or absence of the
flow is no doubt often due to chlorosis. In Case v. of the
Thesis, Raynaud's disease and amenorrhoea set in gradually
together in consequence of emotion and nervous exhaustion.
Case vi. was somewhat similar, but tertian fever seems to
have been the cause. In Case ix. both conditions came on
suddenly in consequence of a fright. The disease may
begin at or after the menopause, which may have been
preceded by excessive menstruation. In one case a second
attack (several years after the first) was brought on by a
miscarriage (James). A lady slipped in going downstairs,
and fell on her back. Next day the menses which she
expected did not appear, but as she felt well she went
to a ball in the evening. On the following day she began
to suffer from symptoms of concussion of the spinal cord
involving the vasomotor elements. The menses appeared
five days after the accident, but recovery was not complete
for nearly three months (Marfan). Raynaud tells of a lady

[1] P. 181.

who had been subject from childhood to attacks of local syncope, and who learned to regard the complete disappearance of this liability as the first indication of a commencing pregnancy; menstruation had no influence upon the symptom (*Thesis,* Case i.). Pregnancy may be an indirect cause of Raynaud's disease by giving rise to nephritis, which sometimes becomes complicated with the vasomotor disorder.

TABLE II.

SHOWING RELATION BETWEEN RAYNAUD'S DISEASE AND THE FEMALE GENERATIVE SYSTEM.

Raynaud's Disease in females of all ages, - - - 111 cases.
,, ,, above 14 years of age, - 93 ,,
No report as to uterine functions, which were therefore
    presumably not seriously disordered - - in 60 cases.
Menstruation normal or regular, - - in 7 cases.
  ,, regular but painful, - - 1 ,,
  ,, absent or scanty or irregular, 15 ,,
  ,, excessive, - - - - 3 ,,
  ,, began at 20 years of age, - 1 ,,
Menopause, - - - - - - 2 ,,
Uterine engorgement after labour, - - 1 ,,
Pregnancy, - - - - - - 1 ,,
Recent tedious labour, but complete .
  recovery, - - - - - - 1 ,,
Attacks of faintness and palpitation since
  confinement 4 years previously, - 1 ,, 33 cases. 93 cases.

It may be said, then, that disorders of the generative organs are not frequently the cause of Raynaud's disease. There is no reason to believe that the loss of blood in normal menstruation is ever the cause, and it is very doubtful whether in the few cases in which haemoptysis, haematemesis, or epistaxis has occurred, the haemorrhage has had any causal relationship; indeed, haemorrhages of this kind have been repeatedly found to supervene in persons who were already the subjects of vasomotor symptoms.

Sexual and alcoholic excesses are not often mentioned as causes of Raynaud's disease, and appear to be at most only contributory agents. In the recorded cases there has almost invariably been some other possible cause, such as undue exposure, fatigue, malaria, or neurotic tendency.

Less Common Causes. It has been already mentioned that Raynaud's disease may occur in connection with diseases of the nervous and vascular systems, and that certain morbid blood-states may cause it. It has been observed also in a case of lead poisoning (Sainton). It may follow specific fevers, such as measles, or measles and whooping-cough together, typhus, enteric, influenza, diphtheria, and perhaps pneumonia and erysipelas. It occurs at times in the subjects of syphilis—the acquired disease occasionally, but much oftener the inherited disease. Among other possible causes are phthisis and struma, acute and chronic bronchitis, rheumatism, quinsy, dyspepsia, enteritis, chlorosis, anaemia, and rickets. To these Mr. Hutchinson would add inherited gout. The disease has been met with in association with diabetes insipidus, and it has an intimate relationship with paroxysmal haemoglobinuria. It has been induced by a dog-bite in a subject of inherited syphilis (Pasteur). It has resulted from giving up the habitual use of morphia and chloral (v. Hoesslin). Gangrene of the lower extremities has been attributed to contusion of the solar plexus (Curtis)[1]; and in a case of Collier's, peritonitis, especially marked in the region of the solar plexus, was regarded as the cause of the local syncope, asphyxia and gangrene which were observed.

[1] Sajous' *Annual of the Universal Medical Sciences*, 1890, ii. c. 48.

LOCAL SYNCOPE.

OF the 176 cases tabulated on page 58, there were 3 in which local syncope was alone observed, 20 (4 males and 16 females, together 11.4 per cent.) in which it was associated (not necessarily at the same time) with local cyanosis, and other 66 (19 males and 47 females, together 37.5 per cent.) in which necrotic or sclerotic processes were added to the local syncope—almost always, but not invariably, after a stage of local cyanosis. On the other hand, there were 28 cases (9 males and 19 females, together 15.9 per cent.) in which local cyanosis alone was observed, and other 56 cases (28 males and 28 females, together 31.8 per cent.) in which necrotic or sclerotic changes followed upon local cyanosis without any stage of local syncope being noted. All the 13 cases (7.4 per cent. of the whole) in which scleroderma occurred were females. It is interesting to note the equality of the sexes among the severer cases in which local syncope was not observed. This is doubtless to be explained in part by differences of occupation leading to different degrees of attention to slight symptoms. Dead fingers speedily interfere with various female pursuits such as sewing, and if they set in when the individual is sitting in a warm room cannot escape notice ; whereas if they are

TABLE III.

SHOWING THE INCIDENCE OF DIFFERENT PHENOMENA OF RAYNAUD'S DISEASE IN THE TWO SEXES AT DIFFERENT AGES.

Age.	Sex.	Class I.	Class II.	Class III.	Class IV.	Class V.	Class VI.	Totals.	
− 5	Male	—	I	—	I	3	—	5	
	Female	—	I	—	—	6	—	7	12
− 10	Male	—	—	—	I	3	—	4	
	Female	—	5	I	—	2	—	8	12
− 15	Male	—	—	—	I	2	—	3	
	Female	I	—	—	—	2	—	3	6
− 20	Male	I	2	—	I	1	—	5	
	Female	—	3	4	2	7	2	18	23
− 25	Male	—	3	—	—	1	—	4	
	Female	—	—	5	3	3	I	12	16
− 30	Male	I	—	—	3	5	—	9	
	Female	—	3	I	I	6	I	12	21
− 35	Male	—	I	I	—	4	—	6	
	Female	—	I	I	I	4	—	7	13
− 40	Male	—	—	2	I	4	—	7	
	Female	—	I	I	I	2	2	7	14
− 45	Male	—	—	—	I	6	—	7	
	Female	—	2	2	—	6	2	12	19
− 50	Male	—	I	—	I	4	—	6	
	Female	—	2	I	I	6	I	11	17
− 60	Male	—	I	I	I	1	—	4	
	Female	—	I	—	I	3	3	8	12
− 70	Male	—	—	—	I	3	—	4	
	Female	—	—	—	I	3	I	5	9
Over 70	Male	—	—	—	—	1	—	1	
	Female	—	—	—	—	1	—	1	2
Totals,	Male	2	9	4	12	38	—	65	
	Female	1	19	16	11	51	13	111	176
	Both Sexes	3	28	20	23	89	13	176	

Class I. Local Syncope.[1]   Class II. Local Asphyxia.   Class III. Syncope and Asphyxia.   Class IV. Including slight losses of tissue, trivial ulceration, etc.   Class V. Severer grades of tissue loss.   Class VI. Scleroderma associated with the other changes.

[1] It need scarcely be explained that mere liability to dead fingers is not considered in this Essay as equivalent to Raynaud's disease.

not associated with pain, they may hamper the work of an outdoor labourer but slightly, and may be attributed to climatic influences alone, so that they may be forgotten immediately after the condition has passed off. Whether this can be regarded as accounting in full for the extraordinary contrast in sex-proportions between this group and the others is by no means certain.

In the cases of 2 males and 1 female included in the table, syncope and gangrene alone were recorded, though this does not necessarily imply that no local cyanosis was observed. Similarly with regard to 3 males, gangrene alone was mentioned. All the cases in which scleroderma ensued, with one exception, included a stage of local syncope; all except one had a period of local asphyxia; and 7 were associated with tissue necrosis.

Local Syncope,[1] the first of the three characteristic stages in a typical case of Raynaud's disease, cannot of itself be regarded as a disease so long as it amounts to nothing more than the familiar "dead fingers." The condition is in the first instance, as a rule, protective in its nature, the purpose being to cut off the access of blood to those parts that most readily lose heat by radiation, in circumstances where cooling might take place to a degree dangerous to the whole organism. That dead fingers, however, cannot be looked upon as normal is evidenced by the impairment of function, and especially of the tactile sensation necessary for the execution of delicate movements, that so constantly

---

[1] The late Sir (then Dr.) B. W. Richardson, who was apparently unacquainted at the time with Raynaud's work, proposed, in 1885, to give this same designation "local syncope" to the same condition of "suspended life in local surfaces." Mr. Henry Hudson, whose pupil he had formerly been, suffered from attacks in the second and third fingers of his left hand.

accompanies them.   Local syncope is the result not of a normal physiological process, but of the exaggeration of a normal process.   The stimulus that gives rise to this exaggerated result may be the same as would give rise to a strictly normal result in a normal individual, or it may be impossible to recognize the action of any specific stimulus. But in a large proportion of cases of Raynaud's disease, the living tissues by whose activity this normal process is carried out have been rendered abnormally sensitive to the influence of ordinary stimuli, and have acquired the habit of giving a greatly exaggerated response to such stimuli.

The most characteristic feature of local syncope is the corpse-like pallor of the affected part, but the phenomena are usually both subjective and objective, though they vary greatly in different cases.   The pallor has been described as waxy, tallowy, dull, or leaden; it is apt to be associated with a recognizable degree of lividity which can be seen in the nail.   Rarely it is snow-white.   Occasionally, however, the tint is yellow, and this may even be so striking as to suggest jaundice to the patient.   Though the change in colour sometimes attracts attention, it is commonly some disorder of sensation that first gives notice of the abnormal condition. This is often a numbness or blunting of the sense of touch which interferes with any delicate operation in which the patient is engaged at the moment; or it may be a pricking pain, or severe pain, or a feeling of stiffness.   There may, however, be no pain at any period of the attack.   Exceptionally a livid pallor has been observed to set in over the whole surface of the body, and then gradually localize itself in the hands.   In cases where both syncope and cyanosis occur locally, syncope is the earlier phenomenon in the great majority of cases, but in occasional instances the reverse order is seen. The two phenomena may be present at the same moment in different parts of the extremities; they may even be seen at the same moment in one hand. As compared with the digits, it is seldom indeed that the nose, chin, cheeks, and ears suffer from local syncope. The tip of the tongue is but rarely affected.

When the condition of local syncope is established, the local temperature becomes reduced, so that the part is cold to the touch. Tactile sensation is diminished or lost, but other forms of sensation are not necessarily affected in the same degree. The part may be painful when touched, or devoid of the sense of pain. The sense of heat and cold may be lost along with the sense of pain in one case, whilst in another the temperature sense is preserved, and touch and pain are completely lost. The temperature sense, or the sense of pain, may be impaired more than that of touch. The patient's suffering may simply amount to discomfort, or it may be aching, or tingling, or severe pain, and the parts may feel stiff as well as numb.

The power of movement is sometimes said to be diminished in the affected digits. So long as the syncope is limited to the fingers, paresis obviously cannot depend upon the long flexors or extensors, and it is very doubtful if it can be attributed in any degree to the lumbricales or other small muscles of the hand. Doubtless Raynaud's suggestion[1] that the impairment of movement is due to defect of afferent impulses rather than to muscular weakness is correct. In exceptional cases the skin of the affected part is covered with perspiration.

The distribution of the lesion varies indefinitely in different cases. It may attack one or several of the fingers, or all of

[1] No. 147, p. 638.

them. It may be unilateral or bilateral, and sometimes the symmetry is so exact that the same two digits are involved in each hand; this may be not only in the earlier attacks, but until the disease has progressed to the length of gangrene. The digit may have its tip only affected, or the syncope may extend centrally so as to involve one or more or all of the phalanges. The condition may be confined to the digits, or may involve the whole foot or hand. Although all kinds of deviation from the rule are met with, the general tendency is for the upper extremities to suffer sooner, more frequently, and more severely than the lower. The thumb escapes more frequently than any of the fingers, but there does not appear to be any great difference in susceptibility among the four fingers, or between the two sides of the body.

Local syncope may involve one finger only in the earlier attacks, and spread to others in later ones; or it may confine itself for many years to a single digit of one hand. I have at present under observation (January, 1899) a man who has been subject for over a year to attacks which are always confined to the left ring finger. An attack may suddenly involve all ten fingers simultaneously; or one finger of each hand first, and then another may be involved, until perhaps both hands are in a state of syncope. The one hand may become affected as the other is recovering. A peculiarity in the mode of onset may, like a peculiarity in the extent of the affection, be persistent in a given case.

Cases of Raynaud's disease which manifest a stage of local syncope are due to the same conditions (heredity, exposure, emotion, malaria, Bright's disease, specific fevers, phthisis, etc.) as have been described in connection with the general question of etiology. While occasionally met with at the extremes of life (as early as the second year, or in advanced age), local syncope is chiefly seen in the period of active sexual life. Another way of stating the same fact is to say that cases of Raynaud's disease in childhood seldom manifest a stage. of local syncope. Sometimes, however, the patient, commonly a woman, has been liable as long as she can remember to attacks of local syncope, and the more immediate cause of her illness (exposure, malaria, etc.) has intensified rather than originated the tendency to Raynaud's disease. A case has been recorded by Taylor where the susceptibility began during pregnancy, possibly, however, owing to exposure; and Raynaud tells of a lady who found that her liability to local syncope always ceased at an early period of each pregnancy. In Marfan's case (quoted in the section on Etiology), local syncope followed an accident which probably involved concussion of the vasomotor centres.

A fresh attack of local syncope may be excited in one who is liable to it in various ways, but especially by exposure and by emotion. Anything that happens to worry a susceptible subject may cause an attack forthwith. Fatigue also may induce it. The special time for its occurrence is in the morning after washing; but washing with cold water in the warm part of the day, or handling a cold article may induce it. Occasionally it is induced by washing in the morning, whatever the temperature of the water may be. In some cases an attack may come on at any hour without obvious reason. It may occur pretty regularly at a certain hour in the morning and evening, or it may follow a regular daily intermittent type.[1] It may be relieved by the taking of food, or may set in during the early stage of digestion. Dancing may bring it on—apparently through the agency of

[1] As in Cases iii. and iv. in the *Thesis.*

the accompanying excitement, since in the same patient a smart walk may be beneficial.

The pallor of the fingers may be associated with flushing of the face, which may be the occasion of great mental distress to the patient, especially when such changes occur at meal times, and are conspicuous to others.

The duration of an attack varies greatly, even in the same person; it may be minutes, or hours, or days. In the simplest cases the attack fades away into a completely normal condition. Even though it has persisted for half to three quarters of an hour, there may be no pain or undue warmth when restoration sets in. But very often a more or less marked reaction ensues for a time, accompanied by a sensation of tingling, burning, or even pain, and followed by a restoration to the normal. Or the pallor may give place to cyanosis, the second stage of Raynaud's disease, and if there was severe pain in the first stage this may now lessen.

The frequency of the attacks likewise varies greatly. It may be once, several times, or ten, twenty, or thirty times a day. It may be once a week at first, and ultimately come to be once a day in the same case. Persons again in whom cold is specially influential in bringing on an attack may suffer comparatively seldom, or not at all, in the summer time ; or after suffering in winter only, for some years, their liability may extend to the summer also. Similarly a person who suffers only occasionally during many years may come to suffer every winter.

Friction applied to the part which is the seat of local syncope may rapidly restore the circulation, but sometimes it has little influence. Swinging the arms and the local application of warmth or of electricity may also be beneficial. It might be anticipated that the condition, especially if brought on by slight exposure, would rapidly disappear in a warm atmosphere, but this is not always the case; the deadness may continue for three quarters of an hour or an hour after the individual has gone into a warm room.

It seems clear that exercises (walking, riding on horse-back, etc.) which increase the activity of the general circulation are one means of warding off attacks of local syncope, though it will be remembered that walking has, in one or two instances, appeared to be the exciting cause of Raynaud's disease. On the other hand, there is reason to suspect that such exercises as piano-playing, sewing, etc., which involve only a limited number of comparatively small muscles, and involve the activity of susceptible parts, may actually promote an attack. It may be that the rigid flexion of the digits in striking the notes, and the pressure of one digit against another in holding the needle may have the mechanical effect of diminishing the local blood-supply sufficiently to stimulate the unduly sensitive nervous mechanism of the vascular system in the same way as an impression of cold would do.

To judge of the effects of such exercises as dancing, the associated mental excitement must be borne in mind as well as the mere muscular activity. Thus in one neurotic young woman, a few minutes' dancing would cause the fingers, and to a less extent, the toes, to die (Hutchinson); and Mills has reported the case of a young woman with phthisis and Raynaud's disease in whom, on one occasion after dancing, the tip of the tongue became bluish white and numb, and talking was at the same time rendered somewhat difficult.

Although as a rule the arteries that are accessible to palpation (radial, etc.) are not involved to any extent in an attack of local syncope, it occasionally happens that their pulsations may be greatly reduced if not actually abolished. There is every reason to believe that this is due to the

E

abnormal contraction which is generally limited to the smaller vessels extending up to the larger arteries. Thus, in Case iii. of Raynaud's *Thesis*, the one radial pulse became very feeble and the other almost imperceptible, and the one proof that there was no clot obstructing the calibre of the vessel consisted in the regularly recurring appearance and disappearance of the pulsations. More frequently, however, any alteration in the pulsation of the larger arteries is such as may be attributed to the increased resistance in the periphery, or to the constitutional effects of the cause (emotion, cold, etc.) that excited the attack.

An interesting and important observation on the state of the blood in local syncope has been published by Colman and Taylor. A girl, aged 10, was the subject of Raynaud's disease which did not go beyond the stage of syncope. There was no blood or blood-colouring matter or albumen in the urine. Blood was removed for examination on several occasions from an ischaemic finger. This was done by putting a ligature loosely round the finger before the attack was expected, and drawing it tight when ischaemia was established. The insensitive finger was incised and was not squeezed. The blood was transferred to the slide by contact, and quickly covered with a thin glass. It was then found that the liquor sanguinis was coloured; many red corpuscles were shrivelled and irregular; some were nearly normal in shape but devoid of colour. The white corpuscles were normal in appearance. There was no increase of haematoblasts. There were no blood-plates. In short, there was a condition of haemoglobinaemia, though there was no haemoglobinuria. It must not, however, be assumed that the blood is usually or even frequently in such a state in an attack of local syncope.

If local syncope attack a part frequently and severely, it

tends in the long run to produce a thin, conical form and parchment-like appearance. Very often, however, no such change is produced ; and Raynaud mentions the case of a young lady whose fingers, though they had long been liable to become dead, were yet extremely gross and soft.[1] More-over, even when the shape of a part has become altered by the long duration of the impaired blood-supply, some improvement may take place if the circulation is thoroughly restored. Thus Rognetta (1834) tells of a countryman whose hands and feet had been affected from time to time for four years with the variety of gangrene which some called "white." The fingers were white, conical, and cold as ice ; the two last segments atrophied and mummified, and the last segments completely insensible. In the earlier years of the disease this "glacial torpor or asphyxia of the digits" lasted only a few days, but on the present occasion it had continued for four months. Dupuytren treated this man by bleedings from the arm, poultices, and moderate diet, and after eight days the hands and feet were restored as if by magic to a healthy state, the fingers even appearing to lose to some extent the conical shape which they had manifested before treatment began.

The relative frequency with which the thumb escapes probably depends partly on the fact that it is shorter and thicker than the fingers, and thus possesses a relatively smaller cooling surface, and partly on the anatomical arrangement of its blood supply. In one of Affleck's cases, the right hand suffered more severely than the three other extremities, and as no brachial, radial or ulnar pulse could be felt on this side even after the girl had been dismissed from hospital, and as, although the patient was right handed, the right arm was somewhat smaller than the left, it was con-

[1] *Thesis*, Case ii.

cluded that there was some congenital abnormality of the
arteries, which gave a comparatively inefficient supply to the
most affected limb.   Mr. Hutchinson[1] in endeavouring to
account for the complete escape of the thumb, little and ring
fingers (not only at the stage of syncope, but even when the
stage of gangrene was reached) in a case where the index
and middle fingers of each hand were involved, says that it
cannot be explained by the nerve supply, and suggests the
(normal) arterial arrangement as a partial explanation.   The
ulnar artery is continued into the superficial palmar arch
which gives off digital branches to the three inner fingers
and the ulnar side of the forefinger; while the radial artery
supplies digital branches to the thumb and radial border of
the index finger.   So far as the digits then are concerned,
the index finger gets the last of the supply brought by the
radial artery, and the index and middle fingers get the last
of the supply brought by the ulnar; so that Mr. Hutchinson's
theory is so far borne out.   But this in no way accounts for
the striking relative immunity of the thumb; I think this is
best explained by the proportionally smaller radiating surface.   Moreover it is quite possible that the nerve supply did
have something to do with Mr. Hutchinson's case.   It is
obvious that the daily occurrence for a year of *digitus
mortuus* in two fingers of each hand was not a morbid
state limited to the affected fingers; the central nervous
system was necessarily implicated.   Now morphologists
have clearly established with regard to the cutaneous
nerves of a limb that its distal part is supplied from
the middle nerve-roots that enter into the limb-plexus,
while the fibres of the upper nerve-roots are distributed to
the preaxial side, and those of the lower roots to the
postaxial side of the limb.   If the vasomotor nerves conform

[1] No. 82, pp. 311-314.

as the cutaneous nerves do to this morphological law of distribution, then the middle digits will get their vasomotor supply from or through the middle region of the cervical enlargement, and not from a part which, like that at the first dorsal level, is concerned also in the supply of the chest-wall. And thus, just as the upper extremity is the most typical seat of local syncope, so the central or most typical portion of its periphery, both as regards anatomical configuration and innervation, is the part that is most susceptible to local syncope.

Local syncope, then, is the manifestation of a special susceptibility which, appearing for the first time in childhood, or in advanced years, or, as is much more frequently the case, in early adult life, often persists for many years or for the whole of life. It may become less troublesome with the lapse of time, but this may be chiefly owing to the sufferer having learned by experience to avoid the conditions that are likely to induce an attack. And in a certain proportion of cases, local syncope becomes replaced by, or associated with, one or more of the other phenomena of Raynaud's malady.

LOCAL ASPHYXIA.

THE mere aspect of a part is not so characteristic of local asphyxia as of local syncope, because the morbid conditions that induce a cyanotic colour of skin are much more varied than those that cause deadness. The actual tint differs widely in different cases. It may be bluish white, and the skin may then seem unduly transparent. Or it may be simply dusky; or it may be definitely blue, slate-coloured, dark blue, or quite black. Sometimes, however, it is violet, or bluish red, or red with almost no admixture of blue. A violet colour may become replaced by black as the attack continues. Such a part is rendered pale by pressure, and the sluggishness with which the blood flows through it is shown by the great tardiness with which the pale portion becomes livid again after removal of the pressure. Elevation of the part may promote a gradual disappearance of the cyanosis if it is not severe.

Instead of the more uniform discoloration just described, or associated perhaps with it in a more proximal part of the same limb, there may be a livid marbling of the skin, or a mottling of red and blue.

Local syncope is often observed at some stage in the same case as local asphyxia, but almost as frequently it is not. When both occur, syncope is almost always the earlier phenomenon, but in exceptional cases the reverse order obtains; a cyanotic part has been seen to get as white as snow, but in a few minutes the whiteness would disappear and the blueness return.

The conditions that render an individual liable to attacks of local cyanosis are of the same varied description as those that cause a liability to local syncope, and have been discussed at length in the section on etiology.

Local asphyxia may, like local syncope, be the result of an accident. Thus Skipton has reported the case of a carter, aged 57, who enjoyed good health till a mass of lime fell upon him from a height, knocking him down and rendering him insensible for a time. From that date till his admission, four weeks later, the following symptoms were present: diminished surface temperature, inability to move the toes or to flex the fingers of the right hand, anaesthesia of the limbs, from the fingers to above the wrists, and from the toes nearly up to the knees. The following additional symptoms occurred only at intervals, generally twice a day: extreme lividity of the ears, lividity of the nose and of the dorsa of the hands, and lividity of a small area over the left shoulder. Numbness and extreme cold were experienced in the affected parts during the paroxysm, and heat, tingling and severe pain as it passed off. The lower limbs did not get blue, but rather pale and cold. There was some mental depression, and at times giddiness, but otherwise good general health.

Whilst local syncope is seldom seen anywhere except in the limbs, local cyanosis attacks the ears and face with great frequency. The principal parts that are liable are the extremities of the limbs, the ears, and the nose; less commonly the lips,[1] cheeks, chin, tongue, and any part of a limb or of the trunk. Raynaud speaks of a painful neurosis of the breasts, accompanied by very pronounced lividity, which would almost merit the name of local asphyxia of the mammae.[2] Patches that occur on the trunk or on the proximal segment of a limb are sometimes different in character from those that are seen on peripheral parts, and will be discussed later.

There is endless variety in the distribution of the affection and in the manner in which one part becomes involved after another. The hands may be the first to suffer, or the ears, or the nose. Thus the order of invasion may be : hands, then cheeks, ears and legs ; or ears, then fingers in following year, and toes several years later ; or nose, then hands and feet, then ears ; or hands, then toes, nose and ears ; or ears, then nose, then fingers ; or ears for ten winters, then ears and cheeks for two more winters, then limbs also ; and so on. In a given case, the order in which the parts are invaded may vary in the different attacks. The hands alone may be affected, or the nose alone, or the ears alone. The combinations include : hands and feet, or fingers and toes ; fingers and nose ; fingers and ears ; four limbs and ears, with or without cheeks and chin ; nose and one or both ears, with upper or lower limbs, or the four limbs, etc. The lower limbs tend to be affected less frequently and less severely than the upper, but, on the other hand, the toes may suffer seriously while the

---

[1] Raynaud (*Thesis*, p. 101) said he had never observed in local asphyxia the blue colour of the lips which is constant in cyanosis (*morbus caeruleus*). The occurrence, however, has been repeatedly noted, and at least one case in which it was sometimes seen has come under my own observation.

[2] *Thesis*, p. 168, note.

fingers practically escape, and in paroxysmal cases, the feet may be attacked much oftener than the hands. Different localities may be affected in different attacks. The thumb is, if anything, less susceptible than the fingers. It is rarely that the tongue is involved. Powell has reported the case of a man of forty-eight, who, when convalescent from sore throat (diagnosed as diphtheria), found one morning that his nose was blue and swollen. In a day or two his ears and the four fingers of his right hand were similarly affected, and a few days later the left little and ring fingers were in the same state. The tongue became livid, swollen, and painful. The thumbs and the fingers not already mentioned were cold and dusky red at their tips. Partial gangrene of several fingers and of one ear took place, with slighter losses of tissue in two toes and in the tongue near its tip.

While scarcely a case is met with in which local syncope is not absolutely "acroteric," involving principally or only the most peripheral parts, this is by no means so characteristic a feature of local cyanosis. Even though it be present on the digits, it may be more conspicuous on the hands, but the fingers and palms may remain free for some time after the dorsa of the hands and forearms, and even portions of the trunk have been invaded. Moreover, it may involve a large portion of a limb, from the extremity upwards. It may not be confined to the digits or to portions of them, but may affect the hands and feet, or forearms and legs. In cases where the discoloured area is of a very dark blue, the boundary line between this and the normal skin may be pretty sharp.

The distribution is generally roughly symmetrical, but one side of the body may be invaded some time before the other. The side that is first affected does not necessarily suffer most in the long run. The disease, however, may continue for years to be a unilateral affection. On the other hand, a case may commence and persist for some time symmetrically, and then begin to manifest a unilateral distribution. As a good illustration of a case where the phenomena were almost confined to one side, one recorded by Pasteur may be mentioned. A boy, aged nine years, who had never been liable to cold or blue hands or feet, but who was probably the subject of inherited syphilis, was bitten by a puppy on the back of the left hand. Once or twice in the first two days his mother noticed that this hand was slightly blue. Five days after the bite, the wound began to suppurate, and the whole hand became icy cold, dark blue, and very painful. A poultice seemed to make it quite well again. Two days later he was admitted to hospital with his hand oedematous, painful, and bluish black. The lower half of the forearm was also discoloured and the radial pulse was less full than on the unaffected right side. There was very slight lividity of both ears. The urine was (and remained) normal. This attack passed off two hours after admission. Six days afterwards, an attack, which lasted only ten minutes, took place in the morning; and later on in the same day, a mild one was induced by keeping the hand in cold water for some minutes. Meanwhile the wound healed rapidly, and the boy was dismissed cured three weeks after the accident. Three days later, there was a well marked attack of local asphyxia involving the whole hand for about an hour, and nine days after this, the left foot became cold and the great toe blue, after a warm bath. The boy subsequently remained free from attacks up till the time of reporting.

To illustrate how limited the extent of the lesion may be, and yet how great the suffering it may entail, I quote from Hutchinson the case of a dressmaker, aged 25, unmarried, who had intermittent fever at 12, "low fever" at 23, and about ten severe quinsies, the last and worst at 21. Menstruation was always behind time but rather profuse. The last quinsy left her very weak, and she became liable to cold nose about a year afterwards, the first attack taking place after she had been out on a very cold day. Her hands and feet remained quite healthy. Her nose was always worse in winter, but was liable to "die" even on a very hot day in summer. It would not remain in a normal state for two hours unless she kept absolutely still. Movement was the principal agent that caused the attacks, the nose getting "bluey-red" and cold to the very root, and very painful. Friction would not remove the attack, nor would a hot room prevent it. Even going to bed in a warm room did not ensure speedy relief.[1]

The immediate agent in causing an attack in this case was obviously not any emotion connected with movement, but the cooling influence exerted by air in motion upon the susceptible part. Thus the patient did not dare to go to the seaside.

As was pointed out in considering local syncope, cyanosis and syncope may be present simultaneously. For instance, the distal portions of the fingers may be white, while the remaining portions of the hands are livid, and this may continue for hours together ; or the fingers and toes may be white and the hands livid. In the case of a patient of mine who had paroxysmal cyanosis of both hands and one foot, it was reported that the backs of the ears were almost constantly yellow.

Local asphxyia may occur at any age. Several cases have been recorded as beginning so late as the seventh decade of life, and the disease is by no means rare in

[1] No 79, p. 228.

infancy, cases having occurred at 3, 6, and 9 months, and in the second year. In one of my cases, a child who had extensive congenital discoloration of the skin, the more characteristic phenomena of Raynaud's disease set in before she was twenty months old ; and in another patient of my own, the disease began at the age of four months. In infants, as a rule, no stage of syncope is observed, and a large proportion of them suffer some loss of tissue, either trifling or more serious.

The latter of the two patients I have just referred to was brought to me at the Dispensary of the Royal Infirmary, on 6th May, 1898, on account of vomiting and purging. She was then exactly six months old. When she came back a week later, it was found that the hands and feet were livid red and swollen—a condition that had existed for two days. The mother stated that she had noticed these parts get dark in colour, at times only, during the past two months, and she thought they must be painful because the child cried and pulled away her hands and feet when they were touched. The heart and lungs were healthy, and there was nothing important in the family history.

The swelling of the extremities passed off three days after it set in, and when patient was seen on the 20th May, the feet and hands were warm and free from swelling, lividity, or pain ; the reddish hue they still manifested was scarcely abnormal. The urine was free from albumen. The last note (January, 1899) states that there has been no return of the disorder of the hands and feet. The mother describes the colour which they formerly had as "pure blue," and she now adds that the face was swollen at the same time as the extremities, though not altered in colour. The child (who has been brought up on the bottle, as the mother had not enough of milk) is not very robust, and has still from time to time a tendency to diarrhoea, but for some months past she has remained free from vomiting, and the parents agree that she is not losing ground.

The following is a summary of the other case, which illustrates several unusual but important aspects of the disease.[1] The patient was first seen by me in May, 1893, when she was twenty months old. Local cyanosis had commenced in the feet about three weeks previously, and by the time of the visit, the second left toe was quite black, and a small ulcer had formed on the right great toe. The child was the subject of congenital hydrocephalus. There was a very striking discoloration of the skin over a large part of the body which was said to have been present from birth, and to have been indeed more general at birth than now. This was in the form of a bluish red mottling which was seen in patches in almost all regions of the body—face, trunk and limbs. Exposure to cold and crying always intensified this, while warmth diminished it. Most of it disappeared on pressure, and the individual vessels could not, as a rule, be recognized. In the face, the mottling was especially marked over the prominences, and it was also present on the ears. There was some on the upper part of the chest in front and on the back of the neck, and there was a patch lower down on the back. More or less of it could be seen over the whole extent of the arms. The palms of the hands and most of the fingers were very red with some whitish mottling. The discoloration was well marked on the left buttock and in slighter degree over both lower limbs down to the feet. There was a good deal of redness about the feet.

During the next six months, the child's condition

[1] A detailed account of the earlier stages of this case was published in 1894 ; No. 117, pp. 267-279.

improved somewhat, and the blackness of the toe was·
replaced by blueness. In the course of the winter, however, she suffered much from the cold and was constantly
crying; a dark blue, almost black, spot was frequently
present on the middle of each cheek ; the feet swelled up and
became more discoloured under the influence of cold, and
the toe did not look so well.   Moreover, since the date of
her first visit, patient had been found to have a hernia of
the mucous membrane of the trachea through a gap in its
anterior wall.   There was nothing to call for remark in the
family or early personal history, or in the state of the viscera
other than the brain.   Patient was subject to colds and
conjunctivitis, and was a noisy breather—for which her
narrow, highly arched palate was perhaps in part responsible.   The usual causes of Raynaud's disease could be
excluded.   Things got worse again in February, 1894, and
blisters appeared on the first right and third left toes.   The
gums became swollen about the same time, and the discoloration of the face and limbs was worse than I had yet seen
it.   In the course of examination, however, the child fell
asleep, and her colour then improved in an extraordinary
manner.

Some time later, improvement set in again, and the
piece of tissue that was actually lost from the second left
toe was surprisingly small.   The nail was also shed, and
replaced by a new one.   By the summer of 1895, there
was no local asphyxia in the usual sense of the expression,
but the discoloration was still present on the face, ears,
buttock and extremities, and still varied with the temperature of the atmosphere.   In February, 1896, she had an
attack of erysipelas of the right arm.   She recovered from
this and had good health till September, 1897, when she
had an attack characterized by sickness, haematemesis and

convulsions, and ending fatally after thirty-three hours. She was six years old when she died.

Apart from the hydrocephalus (which is noteworthy from the point of view of etiology) and the tracheocele, two features connected with the discoloration of the skin deserve attention : first, its widespread, almost universal distribution ; and second, its presence at birth, and persistence throughout the whole of life. But before commenting on these, it will be well to allude to a few other recorded cases which in one detail or another present some resemblance to my own.

Féré tells of a waiter who at the age of 40 began to suffer from epileptic attacks. Somewhere about the same time he became liable to local asphyxia of the hands, feet and nose. After he entered the Bicêtre, at the age of 48, it was found that his ears also would get violet, and it was noted that the whole surface of his body, both trunk and limbs, was marbled over with violet patches of a tint slightly less deep than that seen on the nose and digits. This colour was momentarily effaced by pressure, and became less marked in the great heat of summer. The heart and lungs were normal. Ultimately a small slough developed on one toe, but, although for a time the appearances in the feet were very threatening, the patient was improving when he left the institution.

Féré and Batigne report the case of a lad of 19, an epileptic subject, who had been liable all his life to attacks of local syncope, which affected his fingers both summer and winter, and his feet in winter only. On different parts of his body there were patches of a tint which varied between rose and violet. These identical patches had been present from infancy. The largest was on the lower part of the right thigh, and there was another on the left thigh, whilst others were situated on the trunk, and a small one was present on the left upper limb. They were effaced by pressure, and when the patient was warm in bed could scarcely be detected. The writers describe these congenital and permanent vascular spots as cutaneous angiomas (*naevus vascularis planus*), the histological condition being a dilatation of the vessels in the papillae of the skin. Cutaneous sensibility, though much diminished in other parts of the body, in this case was found to be normal in the angiomatous patches.

In one of Southey's cases, the whole cutaneous surface became readily mottled on exposure, and after a time this livid mottling was replaced by elevated, itchy patches, which were hot and painful at night, and were perhaps of an urticarious nature. Southey, remarking on this case (in 1883), suggested that what Raynaud called local asphyxia was the same thing as had been previously known in certain parts of France as "tachetée," and that his case was an instance of it. If, however, we are to continue to use the expression tachetée,[1] it is best to follow Barlow in his interpretation of it. One of the latter observer's patients had blue or purple patches on the buttocks, thighs and feet. These would persist for weeks or even months, and were at times the seat of coldness, tingling and aching. Barlow recognizes these cutaneous lesions— reddish-blue to begin with, and becoming rust-coloured, not disappearing on pressure, and long persisting—as a result of blood stasis, and due mainly to the deposition of blood pigment in the deeper layers of the skin. It

---

[1] As *tachetée* is originally the feminine form of an adjective, it probably represents a contraction of *maladie tachetée*, whose synonym is *morbus maculosus*. The full French expression seems to have been applied to other conditions besides purpura.

is to them that he applies the designation tachetée, and he distinguishes this from both erythema and ecchymosis.

It is clear from a comparison of these cases that the more widespread and permanent of the cutaneous lesions are not all of one nature. In the case of Féré and Batigne, they were present from infancy, and in my own from birth. They were in both instances effaceable by pressure, intensified by cold, and made less conspicuous by warmth, and were thus obviously connected with the presence of circulating blood in the vessels, so that we cannot be far wrong in regarding these permanent marks as naevoid in character.

The cases of Southey and Féré may have partaken to some extent of the same nature, but were perhaps simply instances of an unusually wide distribution of the lesion which is more commonly confined to the limbs, ears, and face. Southey's, however, presented the peculiarity that after a time local asphyxia gave place to urticaria—another cutaneous lesion in which the vasomotor system is involved.

Barlow again is doubtless right in recognizing the occurrence of patches which originate in the actual deposition of blood-colouring matter. This view is the more easy of acceptance since actual haemorrhage may occur in connection with this disease. Thus Calwell tells of a girl who, in the course of an attack of Raynaud's disease, had extravasations which underwent the usual changes on the left thigh and right forearm, and a considerable number of sufferers from this ailment have had epistaxis at one time or another.

In many cases local cyanosis is associated with local swelling, and as Raynaud pointed out,[1] this may precede the asphyxia. The swelling is oedematous and pits on

[1] No. 148, p. 172.

F

pressure, unless in parts such as the palms and soles where
the tissues are very dense, in which case the parts are
rendered hard. One part may be cyanotic and swollen,
and at the same time another part may be cyanotic only.
Or cyanosis and swelling of one part may be associated
with swelling only in another. The swelling may be
considerable, and has been described in at least one
instance as enormous. The liability to swell is not confined to the limbs, but may extend to the ears, the face,
and even the tongue. Occasionally the oedema may
commence several days, or even a fortnight (O'Conor),
before the cyanosis; and to judge from a case recorded
by Bland, we may even have to admit the paradoxical
position that an attack of local asphyxia may be constituted
by oedema alone without any local cyanosis. Bland's
patient suffered from an attack of slight swelling of the feet
without discoloration. After a fortnight there was a
renewed attack in which the swelling was associated with
more characteristic phenomena,—not only cyanosis, impaired
sensation and pain locally, but also ocular and urinary
symptoms.

Mr. Hutchinson describes the case of a woman, aged 24,
who suffered frequently from local syncope and local
asphyxia, and in whom little elevations of a deep purple
tint formed on the sides of the fingers. These thickenings
varied in size from a pin-head to large shot, and were not
removable by pressure. They were regarded as " thrombotic warts." [1]

The local temperature, of course, becomes much reduced
as the cyanotic state continues. It may be 35° or 40° F.
(19° or 22° C.) below that of the axilla. As showing how
closely the retardation of the circulation may allow the

[1] No. 80.

temperature of the affected part to approximate to that of the surrounding atmosphere, allusion may be made to Marchand's case[1] in which, while the external temperature was 54·5 F. (12·5° C.) the temperature of the palm of the hand was only 56·75 F. (13·75° C.), while between the fingers, which were even more affected than the rest of the hand, the thermometer only rose to 55·6° F. (13·1° C.).

In a considerable number of cases the cyanosed part sweats freely. When the livid part is pricked, dark blood may escape, but if the cyanosis has become so pronounced as not to be removable by pressure, and gangrene is about to begin, it may be that no blood will flow from a prick. The blood from an asphyxiated region may be normal, or may show only some diminution of haemoglobin. Haig has found great diminution of red corpuscles after an attack. In blood drawn during the attack of cyanosis, disintegrating red cells and an increased number of white cells were observed. In this case some of the attacks of local asphyxia were followed by haemoglobinuria.[2] It must not be supposed, however, that changes like those just described are usual in connection with local cyanosis. The superficial veins are occasionally distended in the affected part, or in a more proximal part of the limb. In rare cases spasm of the veins has been actually seen. Thus in Weiss's patient it was repeatedly noticed that single veins of the dorsum of the foot gradually narrowed their lumen to complete disappearance, while the dorsa of the toes became cyanotic in a corresponding degree. And Barlow, in a supplementary report in 1889 on a case he had first published in 1883, says: " The only fresh clinical feature to add is that I have in some of the

[1] Quoted by Raynaud, *Thesis*, p. 42.　　[2] No. 58, p. 143.

paroxysms observed a moniliform appearance in some of the dorsal veins of the hands. A series of small dark nodosities were seen along the line of the veins with narrow, almost colourless, tracts between them. Presently the dark nodosities were observed to alter their situation along the line of the veins, and likewise the colourless tracts. It was obvious that there was a wave of contraction of the walls of these veins causing narrowing of the lumen in certain parts, and temporary varicosity in others."

The subjective phenomena of local asphyxia are numerous, and often constitute a serious feature of the disease. They may be entirely awanting, as in the case described by Raynaud,[1] where the patient in the earlier period of his illness attributed the dark colour which came into his little finger every morning to the black dye of his trousers' pocket. A cyanosed part, though not painful spontaneously, may be painful when firmly seized. Coldness, numbness, tingling, aching, itching, pricking, burning, stinging as of nettles, discomfort, and pain of various kinds and of all degrees of intensity up to frightful agony, and radiating, it may be, widely, are among the sensations experienced. Even if the pain be continuous, it may undergo severe exacerbations from time to time, and when these occur at night, they may greatly interfere with sleep, and thus lead to exhaustion. Curiously enough the pain is sometimes relieved by cold, and aggravated by warmth.

Without entering into the subject of pathology at present, it is to be noted that the pain of local asphyxia and syncope probably depends upon more than one factor, since it attains its maximum at different stages of the disease in different cases. Thus in the case quoted by Raynaud from Landry,[2] pain was most acute when asphyxia supervened,

[1] No. 148, Case i. [2] *Thesis*, Case viii.

and diminished with the onset of syncope. On the other hand, the pain associated with syncope may lessen, and ultimately pass away, when asphyxia replaces syncope. Conversely, in a severe case which was under my charge for a time, it was reported that when the paroxysms of pain came on, the bluish tint became paler. Or the pain may be worst during the transition from asphyxia (following syncope) to the normal state. Or again, the whole series of changes, from normal through syncope, blueness and redness, back to normal, may be gone through with nothing worse than discomfort.

Sensation may not be appreciably diminished ; or there may be impairment of tactile and painful sensation, or preservation of pain with cutaneous anaesthesia. The sense of temperature may be preserved while tactile sensation is diminished or lost. In one case the painful part may be sensitive to the slightest touch, while in another, the sense of touch may be blunted in a part that is the seat of excruciating pain. Anaesthesia, as well as pain, may extend higher up a limb than the asphyxiated area. Patches of anaesthesia, and sometimes of hyper-aesthesia, were present at times above the ankles in a case where the feet often became black (Lunn).

Electrical sensibility may also be lost, as in the following case which was communicated by Riva of Bologna in 1871, and is worth quoting in abstract, because it was published before Raynaud's article in the Dictionary, and before the *New Researches.* A coffee-house keeper began at the age of 63 to suffer in winter from local asphyxia of the ears and nose with some loss of epidermis. Next winter the same thing appeared in the fingers, and in the third winter it extended over both hands. He came to the clinique when the affection was beginning to show itself in the fourth winter. As he lay in bed at this time, both hands were warm and whitish red, with scattered red spots which became pale on pressure, and without pain. The dynamometer registered 260. The temperature between the thumb and the index finger was 96·4° F. (35·8° C.), and in the axilla 98·2° F. (36·8° C.). The ears and nose were bluish. If he got out of bed and left his hands bare, these began in the course of a few minutes to get red and cold, especially at the finger tips. The redness and coldness increased, and after fifty minutes the hands were swollen, and blue as if coloured by indigo. The patient was then unable to close his fist, and he could not open it completely. To attempt either of these movements caused severe pain, which was also induced by pressure. Blood flowed freely on pricking. The temperature between finger and thumb was now 69·1° F. (20·6° C.), in the palm of the hand 74·1° F. (23·4° C.), and in the axilla as before. The dynamometer now indicated only 75. The toes were affected in the same way as the fingers. After the patient returned to bed, his hands and feet took an hour, and his ears and nose still longer to recover from their lividity. When the induction current was applied to the affected skin in the hands, it caused neither pain nor muscular contraction, though both were marked when it was applied to the forearm. Yet the slightest touch on the affected parts caused great pain. The patient was treated by the induced current daily, and at the fourth sitting, slight muscular contractions were observed in the cyanotic region. At the nineteenth sitting, faradic contractility was almost completely restored, and after thirty-nine sittings, the patient was permanently cured. He came under observation again in the course of the winter on account of transient albuminuria at a time when the temperature remained for weeks below freezing point, but his hands remained free from any abnormal condition.

Riva's case shows how severely voluntary muscular power and muscular response to electrical stimulation may be impaired in local asphyxia. It need scarcely be added that a comparatively slight degree of asphyxia may, by impairing cutaneous sensibility, interfere greatly with the ability to perform delicate movements. Movements may also be interfered with mechanically by the swelling of the parts, and again the great pain induced in some cases by voluntary movements of the affected parts may prevent the patient from making any effort.

In those who are liable to attacks of local asphyxia, its appearance is often determined by any exposure to cold. Such persons naturally tend to suffer most in winter, but in some instances weather has no influence. A person may be specially liable to local cyanosis on getting up, or it may tend to recur with some regularity at some other part of each day, or there may be no regular periodicity. There may be no obvious cause. In one of my cases, it was distinctly stated by the patient's mother that washing the child's hands with cold water did not cause them to get blue. Lividity might come on when she was running about the house and persist for hours. Emotion may induce an attack, but seems not to be so influential an exciting agent as in the case of local syncope. Some facts noted in individual cases are worthy of record as throwing light on the pathology of the disease. For instance, one of Hutchinson's patients had local syncope of the fingers all day after washing with cold water. He never used cold water again for washing, and when he used warm water the parts became quite blue.[1] A patient of Solis-Cohen had

[1] No. 86, p. 98.

dusky blue hands which upon immersion in ice-cold water soon became red. If one hand only was immersed, that one became red and the other acquired a deeper blue colour. In another case reported by the same writer, the patient was liable to attacks of cyanosis of the hands, both in consequence of and apart from temperature conditions. When the hands were put into water at 110° F. (43.3° C.), they became slightly red in a few minutes. If immersed in water at 40° F. (4.4° C.), they became distinctly red in a shorter time. If one hand was placed in cold water, it became red, while the other which was not immersed became blue. In connection with the first case it will be remembered that heat is often employed as a haemostatic as well as cold, and the two others show that the effect of temperature impressions upon the vascular arrangements of a part is by no means a purely local one. In one of Calmette's cases, an attack was readily induced in the susceptible parts by pouring cold water over any part of the body. Conversely, Raynaud found that electrisation of one hand brought about the disappearance of cyanosis from both hands,[1] and Israelsohn found that in his case of marked local asphyxia of the four extremities, the cyanosis disappeared from all the limbs when treatment (friction with spirit of camphor) was applied to the upper limbs only.

Sometimes when an attack is impending, the development of a blue or black colour may be accelerated, if not actually occasioned by the application of warm water. Raynaud tells us how alarmed he was by what happened on one occasion to the patient whose case was the starting point of his *Thesis* (Case xv.). Portions of the fingers were as black as if they had been stained with ink, and in the hope of

[1] No. 148, p. 178.

stimulating their vitality, Raynaud persuaded the patient to plunge her hands into mustard and water, with the result that in a few moments the limbs became quite black as high as the forearms.

The modes of onset are so various that it is scarcely possible to describe any one as typical. Discoloration or pain or some other abnormal sensation or swelling may be the first phenomenon, and the one may precede the other by a long or a short period. Pain and blueness may commence and increase together. The onset even of a deep blue colour is sometimes almost sudden. Swelling also may set in suddenly. The discoloration may spread, as we can readily understand, from the tips of the fingers upwards, but it may begin in the palm and extend downwards. An attack may pass off quickly, but the more characteristic process is that described by Raynaud, who remarks on the way in which less livid spots appear in the midst of the livid area, increase in size and run together whilst the periphery also gets invaded by a rosy colour until the cyanotic tint is entirely replaced by a ruddy or normal one. He says a dark red spot is the last thing to disappear. The early part of this process may be associated with formication, tingling, or stinging ; and for a short time after the blueness passes off, the parts may feel to the observer's hand hotter than normal.

The duration of the attack varies from a few minutes up to hours or even days. Several attacks may occur in one day ; or there may be only one a day, or one in several days or weeks; or the intervals may be much longer. Some cases of local asphyxia are in a high degree *paroxysmal*, whilst others which persist with but little change for prolonged periods can justly be described as *chronic*. The persistence of the latter group of cases may be such that the nails are allowed to grow very long on account of the pain caused by cutting them.

Syncope and cyanosis may exist simultaneously in one person. Sometimes instead of the whiteness of ordinary syncope, a yellow colour is associated with cyanosis, as in a patient of my own, who along with paroxysmal cyanosis of the hands manifested a yellow colour on the backs of the ears. In Tannahill's case, the attacks of local asphyxia were preceded by pallor of the eyelids and a yellowish hue of the eyeballs and lips. Occasionally the earliest phenomenon may be motor, as for instance flexion of the fingers, which in Dehio's case followed on a fright and was succeeded after two days by pains, blueness, and swelling.

Raynaud asserted in his *Thesis*, and reiterated the statement in the Dictionary, that "the pulse never ceases to be perceptible in the arteries of the affected limbs," though he admitted that "it may present remarkable alterations." "As to frequency: there may be at the time of the attack a little rapidity of the pulse, which never exceeds 100 a minute, and which is not accompanied by febrile heat of the skin. As to intensity: although ordinarily the pulse is full, it may become small, thin and compressible; but this is the exception." He also recognized that irregularities of rhythm might be observed in one case at the commencement of the disease, and in another case, not during the continuance of the disease, but long before and long afterwards. "In the great majority of cases, the pulse continued regular throughout."[1]

The irregularity is not very important, and is doubtless accounted for in some cases by the neurotic disposition of the patient. And in cases where the patient is suffering

[1] *Thesis*, p. 107.

severe pain, especially if he is exhausted by want of sleep, it is not surprising to find that some acceleration of the pulse takes place. The fulness and tension are much more important points in local asphyxia, and there can be no doubt that they are frequently altered from the normal, even if we make all reasonable allowance for errors of observation depending upon swelling of the parts overlying the vessel, congenital abnormality in its size and course, and so forth. As a rule, the pulse in the radial and other similar arteries is practically or strictly normal. But sometimes the radial (a better one to judge by than the tibial) is small, and sometimes almost imperceptible, though it may be normal in the intervals between the paroxysms. In a unilateral and paroxysmal case recorded by M'Call Anderson, the pulse was frequently absent, from the wrist to above the elbow, though at other times it was perceptible.

The pulse tension may be increased in connection with chronic Bright's disease and allied conditions with which Raynaud's phenomena may be associated. And similarly it will be understood that the constitutional state, the condition of the heart, and various other circumstances may in individual cases account for an intermittent, irregular or feeble pulse.

The bodily temperature may be subnormal, normal, or elevated during the attack, and it may be higher after than during the attack. In considering the temperature, it is necessary to make due allowance for the influence of concurrent affections, such as phthisis, Bright's disease, etc. On the whole, it would appear that in the absence of complicating conditions, the characteristic temperature of the blood in local asphyxia is normal or subnormal.

The general health of the patient is not as a rule

interfered with by local asphyxia itself, unless through the insomnia, anorexia and exhaustion caused by the pains. There may, however, be headache, sickness, epigastric pain, cardialgia or shivering at the onset, and languor or drowsiness in the course of an attack. Amenorrhoea has been noted in association with an attack prolonged over months. Other associated conditions will be considered later.

Of the more lasting effects of prolonged local asphyxia, tachetée has already been considered. The exudation which causes the swelling may persist for some time in the sheaths of the tendons, and is probably capable of giving rise to bands and contraction; these may, however, ultimately pass away. Unlike local syncope, it very rarely leads to scleroderma. I have seen a case of local asphyxia without syncope or gangrene, in which the fingers had a markedly tapering aspect, so that a mistake might have been made by a careless observer; the explanation appeared clearly to be that the soft tissues clothing the proximal phalanges were more swollen than those of the distal segments. Cases that go through the evolution from local syncope to well marked scleroderma almost always manifest the phenomena of local asphyxia at some stage.

Mr. Hutchinson is perhaps nearly right when he says that the liability to local asphyxia (without syncope) "is a constant one, and having once been developed, usually persists through life."[1] But it is doubtful if it is so constant or so persistent as the liability to local syncope, and whether or not, the intervals between the attacks may, in the early stages at least, be very prolonged. Certainly the liability may continue for many years (one of Hutchinson's patients was a woman who had suffered from the par-

[1] No. 83.

oxysmal variety of local asphyxia for ten years before her death from bronchitis at the age of 25), and those authors are somewhat hasty who describe their cases as permanently cured, if they mean that the liability to an attack is quite gone. Nevertheless cases are on record that make it clear that the tendency may long remain latent. Thus, W. W. Johnston tells of a girl who came under observation at the age of five years. The long series of frequent paroxysms of local asphyxia came to an end suddenly and permanently after two months. She had had a similar series of paroxysms which began when she was three months old and continued for three months. Though asphyxia was the principle feature in this case, local syncope also occurred ; the hands would suddenly get red, and soon afterwards the fingers would become white, then livid, then almost black. An attack of Raynaud's disease may be constituted simply by one attack of local asphyxia prolonged over months without interruption.

SYMMETRICAL GANGRENE.

WHILE local syncope is met with in 50 per cent., and local asphyxia in 94 per cent., necrosis of tissue, either slight or serious, occurs in 68 per cent. of cases of Raynaud's disease. Gangrene is almost always preceded by local asphyxia, and is often preceded by local syncope also. In less than 2 per cent. of cases, gangrene alone is mentioned in the reports, but a perusal of these makes it appear almost certain that there was a stage of asphyxia. In the same proportion of cases, syncope and gangrene alone are mentioned ; in the majority of these, asphyxia also was probable. With regard to the remainder, and in one instance where syncope, gangrene and scleroderma are recorded, the reports leave us in doubt.

The causes, numerous and varied as they are, that give rise to the symmetrical gangrene of Raynaud are practically identical with those that induce local syncope or local asphyxia, and need not be further referred to here. The age-relationships of symmetrical gangrene are similar to those of local asphyxia rather than to those of local syncope.

The parts most frequently involved are the extremities of

the limbs and the ears, either singly or in various combinations, and either bilaterally or unilaterally. In about 43
per cent. of cases with gangrene, this lesion involves one or
both of the upper limbs; in 24 per cent., the lower limbs;
and in other 22 per cent., both upper and lower extremities.
The thumbs are less liable to suffer than the fingers.
Portions of one or both ears are involved, either alone or
along with the limbs or other parts, in 22 per cent. of the
cases. The tip of the nose is occasionally lost in this way.
It is curious that Raynaud did not know of cases where the
ears became gangrenous. He says in 1862 and again in
1872, " the nose and the external ears are sometimes more
or less attacked; but I am not aware that in these situations
complete mortification has been observed."[1] " The lobule
and the alae nasi present, it is true, a black colour, livid
marblings extend to the cheek, but this coloration disappears on pressure, to reappear subsequently. The parts
become reanimated little by little, without even passing
through the period of desquamation."[2] "On one occasion I
have seen scars of quite minute size form on the point of the
nose."[3] In Dayman's extraordinary case, the tip of the nose,
ears, and lips were among the parts lost by dry gangrene.
In one of Raynaud's cases, a slough formed over the tip of
the coccyx.[4] In rare instances, tissue from the cheeks,
lips, chin, and less distal parts of the limbs, and even the
trunk may die. It has been asserted that other parts may
suffer, such as the nates, sacral region and labia majora
(Weiss), but it is doubtful if any such case yet recorded can

[1] *Thesis*, p. 105; No. 147, p. 642.   [2] *Thesis*, p. 105.
[3] No. 147, p. 642. Raynaud also quotes Solly's case in which the
scar due to a former slough on the nose became dark in colour as if
gangrene were about to begin anew in that situation (*Thesis*, Case xxii.).
[4] *Thesis*, Case xii.

be considered a genuine instance of Raynaud's disease. Some of those reported may be noma, scurvy, arteritis, etc. Moreover, notwithstanding Raynaud's remark already alluded to (p. 48), Petit and Verneuil cite numerous writers to show that gangrene does occur in malarial subjects. Thus they quote from Huguier (1855) a case of spontaneous gangrene of the prepuce and part of the glans penis which set in in an attack of intermittent fever and was accompanied by the formation of a small slough on the upper lip.[1] Among the parts mentioned by Petit and Verneuil[2] as liable to become gangrenous in malarial fever are the ears, nose, teeth, genitals and extremities. These writers state that malarial gangrene may or may not be preceded by ischaemia or local asphyxia (depending on telluric intoxication); but while recognizing that it closely resembles the symmetrical gangrene of Raynaud, they do not admit the identity of the two conditions.[3] We may, however, safely regard those cases that manifest Raynaud's phenomena as examples of Raynaud's disease, whereas cases that manifest gangrene alone ought not to be so designated. Though the penis almost invariably escapes altogether in Raynaud's disease, a case recorded by Puzey[4] shows that it may succumb to a combination of influences of which one or more are recognized causes of Raynaud's disease. The patient was a man who had a chancre followed by a suppurating bubo and sloughing of the whole prepuce in 1869, and secondary symptoms in 1870. From September 1870 till May 1873, he resided in India where he was frequently laid up with intermittent fever. In November 1873, sexual intercourse was soon followed by a serpiginous ulcerating sore which gradually involved all the old cicatricial tissue. Towards the middle

[1] No. 139, p. 167.   [2] *Loc. cit.*, p. 171.
[3] *Loc. cit.*, p. 185.   [4] *Brit. Med. Jour.*, 1874, ii., 274-275.

of January the glans was wrinkled and shrivelled, and in a few days more, dusky and evidently dead. Then the skin of the whole penis became cold and dusky, and the organ shrank in size. By the end of January, there was a line of demarcation at the junction with the scrotum. In another month the penis, which was now perfectly black, dry and hard, remained attached only by a few strands of necrosed tissue which were cut by scissors. There was no glycosuria, albuminuria, or other evidence of visceral disease. It was noted that the patient had a very feeble circulation, and was wasted and sallow. His fingers tapered much, and his nose often became blue at the tip.

The combinations in which susceptible parts may suffer are so various that it is needless to attempt to enumerate them. Often the necrosis is limited to the epithelium so that only desquamation results. Frequently a blister forms; this occasionally dries in, so that the ultimate issue is almost the same as in the last case, but much more commonly it bursts, and it is then very apt to leave behind it an ulcer involving the true skin and so giving rise to a scar. The contents of such a blister may be serous, sanguineous, or purulent. Another minor lesion is loss of the nails; these may reappear after a time. Even if the nails do not fall, their growth may be arrested for a considerable time, especially during the continuance of intense pains. Raynaud calls attention to a particular variety of blister—a large bulla which becomes deep brown in colour as it dries, and he points out that this does not consist merely of epidermis raised by serum, but that it is associated with a true superficial gangrene of the papillary layer of the derma.[1] The soft tissues may die to any depth, and one or more phalanges of the digits, or portions of them, may undergo

[1] *Thesis*, p. 20.

G

necrosis. A considerable part of one or both feet may be lost. Begg's patient not only lost the tip of the nose and part of each ear, but had to undergo amputation of both hands and both legs. In Dayman's patient, a line of demarcation appeared on the right forearm and left hand, and there was coarse desquamation on the calves, in addition to gangrene of the tip of the nose, ears, and lips. In one of Barlow's cases, amputation was performed at the middle of the thigh. Gangrene of the nose is generally limited to the point, and gangrene of the ear to the upper part of the helix, but the helix, antihelix, and intervening fossa may be involved.

Since gangrene is the culminating point to which local cyanosis tends, and since many cases of local cyanosis do not advance so far as a stage of gangrene, we are quite prepared for the facts, which are almost corollaries to these others, first that the gangrene is by no means as a rule even approximately co-extensive with the asphyxia, and second, that gangrene and local asphyxia are often present simultaneously in one person. The three stages, syncope, asphyxia, and gangrene, have indeed been noted simultaneously in different digits, but this is by no means common. It is at times quite surprising to observe how trifling is the actual necrosis of tissue in a part which at one period threatened to be the seat of a much more extensive gangrene.

The distribution is generally in a rough way symmetrical, though this rule is far from absolute; the reservation applies to digits, ears, and cheeks. Raynaud still adhered in 1872 to the element of symmetry as the special feature of that variety of gangrene which he had first described; and in accordance with this attitude, he had great hesitation in admitting to the same nosological group the sixth case in the *New Researches.* This patient began to suffer, eleven years before Raynaud saw him, from cyanosis and partial gangrene of the right toes and trifling asphyxia of the left foot, the whole attack lasting for about a year. Seven years afterwards a second attack began, in which the left great toe was invaded by gangrene and the right foot by asphyxia. Twenty months before he came under Raynaud's observation the surviving portions of the right toes began to succumb to gangrene, and sixteen months later, while the right foot was cicatrizing, the left toes in their turn became cold, blue, and then black and dead, the process being accompanied by agonizing pain. Latterly, too, the second and third left fingers became cold at times, and a minute slough developed at the tip of the index finger. But this that Raynaud calls an alternation rather than symmetry of the phenomena on the two sides is not enough to exclude the case from the group that deserves to be styled Raynaud's disease.

We may admit with Raynaud that in genuine cases of this disease, the gangrene is always *dry*; the process is a mummification. And Raynaud claims that the conditions under which symmetrical gangrene occurs always imply either absence of blood, or presence of blood unsuitable to nutrition.[1] But very often the necrosis is so trifling as not to amount to what is called dry gangrene; it may, for instance, be only a small blister. And this introduces us to another departure from apparent symmetry in the lesions, since we may meet with severe and extensive gangrene on one side of the body, and a very insignificant lesion on the other.

A part that has undergone mummification may in course of time drop off almost unnoticed, but if it be of some size, a line of demarcation of the usual kind may appear, and

[1] *Thesis*, p. 145.

surgical interference is sometimes necessary to obtain a satisfactory amputation.

Different groups of cases may be recognized. In one type, with or without a preliminary stage of local syncope, certain digits become subject to attacks of local asphyxia. After a time the cyanosis instead of passing off becomes constant, and it persists for days or weeks, the colour deepening until the part is almost or perfectly black. Of this dark area, a portion, which may be considerable, but is often very small, retains the black colour and becomes dry and hard, while the remainder gradually regains a more normal appearance. If, as often happens, the dead tissue is on the pulp of the digit, it may become constricted at its base, and at this line of constriction blisters may appear. The necrosed part is ultimately cast off and the cicatrix that remains may be very slight.

In a second type, the patient suffers for years from paroxysms of local syncope and local asphyxia, and in course of time small blisters develop on the affected digits and burst, or definite ulceration takes place, or small masses of tissue become gangrenous. This variety may become associated with sclerotic changes in the soft tissues (scleroderma); it may be regarded as more definitely neurotic than the other, and as more characteristic of the female sex.

In both of these types the occurrence of gangrene is commonly associated with pain. This is often very severe, and may, especially in cases of gross necrosis, amount to agony. Tissue that is actually dead is of course devoid of sensation, but it would appear that the maximum of cyanosis, which is attained immediately before necrosis, is capable of giving rise to the most intense stimulation of the sensory nerves. While absence of every kind of sensation is a characteristic feature of gangrene, we need not expect the patient to recognize this, since, though a certain mass of tissue is dead, the underlying and immediately adjacent tissues are the seat of intense cyanosis, of whose subjective aspects the unfortunate victim is only too conscious. Moreover, the slightest pressure upon the dead part will influence the abnormally sensitive neighbouring tissue. The patient suffers, therefore, from the symptoms of local asphyxia in their most severe form. It has been repeatedly noted that whenever a part becomes frankly gangrenous the pains are relieved. This doubtless means that when sufficient time has elapsed for the observer to recognize that one part is dead, whilst the neighbouring part is still alive, the latter has already begun to recover.

In a third type which may be recognized, necrosis of tissue is brought about indirectly. The extremities are in a state of chronic asphyxia throughout the colder months of each year, and at various points over the cyanotic area blebs and ulcers appear, and after a time give place to cicatrices. The necrotic foci are not so definitely "acroteric" in this case; they may be situated about the ankles, for instance, or over the knuckles. Some of them closely resemble "broken" chilblains, and are perhaps identical with these pathologically. Their situation over prominences and moving parts suggests that influences acting locally are the immediate cause of necrosis, the vitality of the tissues having been reduced to a low ebb by the persistent local asphyxia. Cases of this kind are not paroxysmal, and the ulcerative process does not give rise to the terrible suffering witnessed in the more characteristic cases of symmetrical gangrene, though there may be some pain in the neighbourhood of a blister for a time. There may, however, be a considerable degree of uneasiness or even pain in the whole of the affected extremity attributable to the cyanotic state.   On the other hand, spontaneous pain may be completely absent throughout.

In a fourth type of case, which has but a doubtful right to be called Raynaud's disease, local asphyxia invades the extremities, generally without a preceding stage of syncope, and passes rapidly or slowly, but steadily, without paroxysms, on to gangrene.   When the gangrene is recovered from, the whole disease is at an end.   This type occurs spontaneously or after acute fevers, and in either case may affect more than one member of a family (Makins, Richard).   Gangrene may occur in one member of a family, while in another the process stops short at local asphyxia.

However small the individual focus of necrosis be, the occurrence of a considerable number of such foci, either about the same time or in slow or rapid succession, must obviously modify the aspect of the affected parts.   A digit whose pulp is partly destroyed tapers towards its extremity. The nail may be normal, or deformed in various ways.   The scars may be white or dark.   Raynaud calls attention[1] to the tendency which the ends of the digits have to get hard and shrivelled as well as slender as a consequence of symmetrical gangrene ; and in differentiating local asphyxia from congenital cyanosis, he remarks on the clubbing of the finger-ends which is so often found in association with the latter.   It must be borne in mind, however, that if ulceration takes place about the bases of the nails in Raynaud's disease, the finger-ends may come to assume a bulbous aspect, and the nails may at the same time be curved. In a given case, some finger-ends may be bulbous, and others attenuated.   Losses of tissue at the extreme tips of the digits will cause shortening.   The results of the more serious forms of gangrene are too obvious to need mention.

[1] *Thesis,* p. 103.

The reported cases do not show that after an attack of this kind of gangrene healing is particularly tardy. It naturally depends greatly on the depth of the lesion whether a sore will take one or many weeks to heal. The time necessary for the spontaneous detachment of a slough also varies much. If amputation takes place at an interphalangeal joint, a few months may suffice; whereas if the separation is in the middle of a phalanx, more than a year may be required if the surgeon leaves the matter to nature.

Though the general health may be unimpaired, it is apt to suffer, if the pains are severe and prolonged, through the loss of sleep and its consequences. It may also be impaired by the suppurative process and fever associated with the separation of large sloughs.

The temperature is not necessarily disturbed in symmetrical gangrene, but under certain circumstances, such as the co-existence of chronic Bright's disease, it may be subnormal. On the other hand, the usual daily febrile elevation is observed during the separation of a massive slough. The separation of a number of small pieces of dead tissue may also be associated with fever in young or debilitated subjects.

As a rule the pulse is normal, but exceptions to this are frequent. It may be simply accelerated (say to 100), while its rhythm and volume are normal. Or it may be still more rapid (say 120) in connection with a febrile temperature. Or it may be feeble, small and intermittent under the influence of the malarial cachexia or of some other debilitating agency. In all this there is nothing characteristic of symmetrical gangrene. But in a certain proportion of cases, the pulse in the medium-sized arteries (radial, tibial, etc.) leading to the seat of lesion is either lost or greatly reduced in volume. In a few such cases, the persistence of this condition throughout the whole period of illness, and even after recovery, suggests a congenitally abnormal distribution of the vessels, but in other cases, the arterial pulsation is restored as the patient recovers.

The red corpuscles or the haemoglobin of the blood may be somewhat reduced. An increased proportion of white corpuscles has been noted in a case that followed diphtheria (Powell). Blood taken with suitable precautions from affected parts and put into nutrient gelatine has proved to be sterile (Radziszewski).

There is no definite period in the history of a case at which gangrene supervenes upon the earlier stages. The liability to attacks of local syncope or asphyxia may exist for days, or for one or more winters, or for many years before gangrene sets in. Or necrosis may only occur at rare intervals in parts which are liable to frequent attacks of local syncope. Frequently, however, Raynaud's phenomena, with symmetrical gangrene as their culmination, present themselves as the symptoms of a single definite illness, instead of the manifestations of a constitutional susceptibility. In cases of this kind, we not only encounter diagnostic difficulties, but have to consider the serious question how broad we are prepared to make the designation "Raynaud's disease." This class of case is especially apt to occur in children and after acute febrile diseases. If during a period of weeks or months a patient suffers from a series of paroxysms of local asphyxia which then come to an end altogether, we have no hesitation in calling this Raynaud's disease. If a boy who has hitherto enjoyed excellent health acquires well marked cyanosis of the fingers, toes, nose, and ears, which after several days passes off altogether, can we refuse to this the same designation?

And if a single attack of local asphyxia be present for some days, not in the midst of perfect health, but in the course of enteric fever, is its pathology different?

Similarly if local asphyxia, with occasional paroxysmal exacerbations and relaxations, becomes on the whole more severe until it culminates after some months in tissue necrosis, after which it gradually disappears, we have clearly to do with Raynaud's disease. But how are we to classify a case in which a single attack of local asphyxia increases almost continuously till it passes into gangrene, and which, after elimination of the dead tissue, ends in complete recovery? Such cases may be primary, or secondary to acute disease. We are strongly tempted to regard them as distinct from Raynaud's disease, and yet a case not very different from such may be associated with paroxysmal haemoglobinuria,—a circumstance that may be relied upon as indicating a generic if not specific affinity with Raynaud's disease.

Another question that must be raised is whether repeated attacks of acrosphacelus (as in the cases quoted by Raynaud from Bocquet and Molin[1]) have the same meaning as repeated attacks of local syncope or of local asphyxia; are all alike manifestations of paroxysmal disturbance of the vasomotor mechanism? And another question, closely allied to this, is: does acrosphacelus take place without preceding local asphyxia or syncope? For manifestly if we are prepared to recognize a form of Raynaud's malady characterized by gangrene without cyanosis or syncope, we may at once admit that repeated attacks of acrosphacelus are analogous to repeated paroxysms of local asphyxia.

It is a matter of common knowledge that the disease

[1] *Thesis,* Cases xxiii. and xxiv.

often fails to exhibit any stage of local syncope. Doubtless in some cases such a stage is overlooked because it is so brief, but it is certain that in many instances it does not exist. It is far less common for syncope to lead up to gangrene without any stage of local asphyxia. Scarcely any conclusive and sufficiently detailed reports of such cases exist, though a few of the cases collected by Raynaud from other writers may belong to this category. One of those that most nearly answer the requirements was reported by Rognetta in 1834. The fingers and toes were white and cold as ice, and the condition was described as one of "white gangrene." It certainly seemed as if necrosis would take place, but after it had continued for four months and resisted all other remedies, Dupuytren cured it in a week by bleeding.

The most puzzling cases of this kind are those in which widespread symmetrical gangrene occurs in those who have not been hitherto the subjects of circulatory disturbances, and who afterwards regain complete health. Mr. Hutchinson has reported[1] the case of a bookbinder, aged 37, who lived and worked under favourable conditions, and who began in warm weather to suffer pain in his feet. Soon he was confined to bed by an illness which proved to be both long and severe, and was associated with great debility and pain in the chest, as well as gangrene of the ends of all the fingers and toes, the borders of the ears, and the tip of the nose. Apart from some duskiness of the extremities at the commencement, there were no premonitory symptoms of circulatory disorder, and apart from the actual loss of tissue, good health was regained. Mr. Hutchinson fully admits the difficulty of

[1] No. 80, pp. 8-9; No. 86, pp. 99-100; No. 89, pp. 74-75; No. 92, p. 202.

classifying a case like this. He thinks it highly improbable that the peripheral arteries should suddenly pass into a state of spasm sufficient to cause gangrene of the extremities and yet passing off completely and permanently, and he is disposed to think that the heart's action was at fault, the disorder being neurotic or more probably inflammatory, and connected with the simultaneous pain in the chest. The case is of great interest as a typical example of symmetrical gangrene, without any marked paroxysmal features, and only doubtfully akin to Raynaud's symmetrical gangrene.

To me it seems impossible to accept Mr. Hutchinson's explanation as satisfactory. It is difficult to see how the central organ of the circulation could fail so seriously as to cause gangrene of the extremities without causing at least lividity of the general surface. Moreover, the fingers suffered more than the toes, whereas even when a patient is confined to bed, the feet constantly suffer more than the hands do from cardiac disability. The whole distribution in fact points to the peripheral vasomotor arrangements having at least a considerable share in the production of the symptoms. An alternative theory mentioned by Mr. Hutchinson is that some poison in the blood (coming from within or from without) had temporarily closed the peripheral arteries and thus led to gangrene. This, I think, is the only theory that will account for the facts, and it has the advantage that it can be applied to a considerable number of cases which are very difficult to understand in the light of Raynaud's theory by itself.

PROGRESS AND TERMINATION OF
RAYNAUD'S DISEASE.

RAYNAUD'S disease in its more characteristic forms practically never causes death, and seldom shows any manifest
tendency to shorten life. Some of the less typical cases,
such as those that follow acute diseases, end in complete
and apparently permanent recovery. Patients with Raynaud's disease may die from some other affection such as
phthisis or chronic nephritis, with which the former has
associated itself. Yet, though Bright's disease is a cause of
Raynaud's disease, the tendency to gangrene in a case
where the two are associated may pass away years before
the patient's death from the consequences of renal inade-
quacy. Cases where Raynaud's disease resembles a single
attack of a definite illness following some fever, or setting
in acutely in the midst of apparently perfect health, are
linked to the more characteristic cases by others in which
two attacks occur, the interval between these varying from
a few weeks to several years. An undoubted case of Raynaud's disease recorded by Taylor illustrates this connection.
There was an obviously neurotic element in it, though there
was but a single attack. A nervous woman, aged 28,

suffered from numbness of the finger-tips, which made it
difficult to thread a needle or to grasp small objects. The
fingers gradually became pale and cold, and then black,
and in about six weeks part of the pulp in all the fingers
became gangrenous. In other six weeks the dead tissue
fell off. The finger-ends cicatrized slowly and acquired
a conical shape. Similar lesions occurred in the nose and
ears. Several years later there had been no recurrence.
The general health was good all along, and there was no
history of exposure. In other cases again, the symptoms
(including gangrene) must be regarded as the expression of
a very enduring or life-long tendency. The cases that go on
to scleroderma are allied to this category. And of yet other
cases—probably numerous, but how numerous cannot be said
until many reports have been published giving the histories
of the patients to the time of death—we may say what has
been remarked of the Homeric Epos, and by Carlyle of
Universal History : they do not conclude, but simply cease.
And why they should cease is sometimes quite as mysterious
as why they should begin. The child whose case I have
detailed at page 77 recovered in a couple of years from
the local asphyxia and gangrene, and lived for more than
two years without any return of the symptoms, though in
the course of this time she passed through a severe attack of
erysipelas. Long after the gangrenous parts have separated,
the extremities may be cold and cyanotic or may become
dead in cold weather. Liability to occasional local syncope
may persist after cyanosis has ceased. Even a patient
who has suffered from gangrene in several winters may
entertain a reasonable hope that in the years to come,
even in the winter season, she may escape with nothing
worse than local syncope. The following case from
Defrance illustrates how terribly persistent a neurosis this

disease may be.[1]   A female was subject from the age of 8
years to a sense of suffocation on slight effort, and in
consequence of such effort, or of emotion, her whole body
would become white and pervaded with a feeling of intense
cold, though there was no actual shivering.   At the end
of three or four days she would pass into a state of cyanosis,
characterized by violet marbling over the whole body, with
spots of deep blue on the fingers and toes, the lips being
violet.   Sensation at this period was normal, whereas in
in the stage of syncope she was not conscious of "her
own body."   These alternations of syncope and asphyxia,
without any pain, continued for 31 years, until (7 years
before her admission at the age of 46) excitement caused
by a fire was followed by the occurrence of ulceration on
both little fingers.   After an interval of two years, the
middle and ring fingers of both hands were attacked by
painful ulceration.   During the two years preceding her
admission there was further damage to the fingers, and
at the last report, five months after admission, she had
lost one complete phalanx and portions of others.   The
toes were much less affected.   In this patient it was possible at one period to see local syncope on some digits,
local asphyxia on others, and gangrene on others.

[1] *Considérations sur la gangrène symétrique, etiologie et pathogénie,*
Paris, 1895, p. 44.

RELATIONS BETWEEN RAYNAUD'S DISEASE AND OTHER MORBID CONDITIONS.

Typhus fever is sometimes complicated by symmetrical gangrene which is due to arterial thrombosis, as in a case recorded by Murchison [1] where the iliac and femoral arteries of both sides were obstructed, and portions of both lower limbs became gangrenous. The same writer states that he has also observed the nose, penis, scrotum, and pudenda to slough in this disease. [2]

Occasionally, however, a case is met with which is very like Raynaud's disease. Thus Fischer tells of a man, aged 34, who, while under treatment for exanthematic typhus, suffered from blueness of the ears, tip of the nose and toes, with anaesthesia and coldness. Whilst the nose and ears were recovering, the toes became gangrenous, and the anterior part of each foot had to be amputated. Fischer accepts Raynaud's theory that there was a cramp of the small arteries.

[1] *Continued Fevers of Great Britain*, 3rd ed., edited by Cayley, 1884, pp. 199-201.
[2] *Op. cit.*, p. 214.

Estlander, in 1871, remarked on the striking resemblance between Raynaud's symmetrical gangrene and spontaneous gangrene as seen in those cases of typhus where no evidence of thrombosis can be detected, and where at the commencement of the fever the heart is not weak.[1]

There is a history of **Enteric fever** in a small number of cases of Raynaud's disease, but antecedent, as a rule, to the latter by so many years that any question of an etiological relationship is excluded. In one case, however (recorded by Hastreiter), the connection was closer. A soldier who had had enteric fever in the preceding autumn began to suffer in the middle of December from a slight catarrh of the bladder, without any sign of urethritis. The urine soon became clear again, and the man was dismissed at the end of January. The vesical catarrh recurred in a few days, and he was re-admitted. Five days later, he was seized with a cold feeling all over his body, and his feet became numb and in great part livid, though partly pale. Within a week he was well again. Both his hands and his feet had been frostbitten three years previously.

Arterial obstruction is occasionally met with as a complication of enteric fever, generally in the second or third week. This is almost invariably due to thrombosis, affects most frequently the femoral artery, leads to gangrene of the part, and is generally fatal. But numerous other arteries besides the femoral are liable to obstruction which brings about gangrene, and we may admit the claim of some writers that embolism may explain some cases, since thrombi may grow in an enfeebled heart and be partly detached. The importance for our present purpose of arterial obstruction in enteric consists in the fact that the gangrene brought

---

[1] " Ueber Brand in den unteren Extremitäten bei exanthematischem Typhus," *Arch. f. Klin. Chirurg.*, 1871, xii., 499-500.

about in this way may be symmetrical, as for instance in both upper arms (Petri),[1] or in the four limbs and the breast (Schulz).[2] And when the extremities of the limbs are involved, the question of Raynaud's disease may have to be considered. Thus Richard reports the case of a boy, aged 16, who was admitted about seven weeks from the commencement of the fever. He had sloughs on several parts exposed to pressure. The four outer toes of each foot were deep red, cold and insensible. The pedal arteries beat strongly, but the posterior tibials could not be felt. The affected parts became gangrenous, and several phalanges were lost, almost symmetrically. Pulsation returned to the tibial arteries, and the boy made a good recovery. Several other members of the family had enteric about the same time, one of them being a brother who was admitted on the tenth day. His feet were pale and cold as ice. Later on, violet spots appeared on the toes and feet symmetrically, in the territories of the external planter arteries. The posterior tibial arteries beat feebly. The violet spots became black and some of them became replaced by serous blebs. In this case gangrene was almost confined to the epidermis. A young sister of these lads had a slaty blue tint with coldness of both feet for some days, but did not suffer from gangrene. Another brother, aged 20, remained free from such phenomena. In the first of these cases it was found on examination of one of the toes that brownish, homogeneous, non-stratified clots were present in all the small vessels, and that there was no endarteritis. Richard claims that the coagulation was secondary, and that the primary disorder in

[1] " Ein Fall von symmetrischer Gangrän," *Berliner Klin. Woch.*, 1879, xvi. 509-510.
[2] " Typhus abdominalis mit symmetrischer Gangrän," *Deutsches Archiv f. Klin. Med.*, 1884, xxxv., 183-190.

H

the vessels depended upon the spinal cord as explained by Raynaud's theory.   Without at present committing ourselves to this view of Richard's, we may note in passing that the characters of the coagula and vessel walls are consistent with it, and that the mere fact of so rare a complication as local asphyxia of the extremities occurring in three members of a family suffering from enteric fever is in favour of the neurotic theory of Raynaud rather than the theory of primary thrombosis.   In any case we see how difficult the diagnosis may be.   The common family susceptibility manifested by these patients is itself of great interest and finds a parallel in that shown by the two brothers mentioned by Raynaud, who alone, out of thirty-six children in one settlement, suffered gangrene through eating ergotized rye bread.[1]

Brünniche recorded in 1870 the case of a boy of 4, who in the third or fourth week of a typhus [? abdominalis] of medium intensity had a bluish black colour of the skin on the helix of the left ear, the tip of the nose, and the tips of the right and left toes, with red spots on the dorsa of the feet.   The affected parts were ice-cold and the seat of violent pains.   Pulsation in both radials and popliteals was normal.   Warmth relieved and cold intensified the condition. After twelve days the epidermis on the ear and nose burst, and allowed a few drops of blood to escape, whereupon the patient recovered.

Smallpox is noted in the reports of some cases of

---

[1] *Thesis*, pp. 135-136.   On the general question of gangrene in enteric fever, reference may be made to Murchison, *Continued Fevers of Great Britain*, ed. by Cayley, 3rd ed. 1884, p. 560 ; Keen, *Surgical Complications and Sequels of Typhoid Fever*, 1898 ; and Lereboullet, "Contribution à l'étude des gangrènes sèches par oblitération artérielle observées dans le cours de la fièvre typhoïde," *Gaz. hebd. de Méd. et de Chir.*, 1878, 2 sér., xv., 17-19, 24, 33-36.

Raynaud's disease, generally as a long past occurrence. One of Raynaud's patients, however (Case ix. of the *Thesis*), had an attack of the modified disease in the course of Raynaud's disease; and in a case recorded by Defrance (Obs. I.) the patient suffered from symptoms rather suggestive of Raynaud's phenomena, during, and for some time after, an attack of severe confluent and petechial smallpox.

Scarlet fever is seldom mentioned in connection with Raynaud's disease. Any relationship that exists between the two must be indirect. Thus, a girl who had scarlet fever at 7, suffered from Raynaud's disease at 19, and was then found to have slight albuminuria (H. J. Dixon). A patient who was under my observation for a short time had scarlatina at 13 and rheumatism at 16; but phthisis, which she afterwards acquired, was more probably the cause of the vasomotor malady. Another patient of my own manifested Raynaud's phenomena a year after an attack of scarlet fever and two years after the onset of chorea, from which he was still suffering at the time of his visit.

Besides this, scarlet fever is occasionally followed by a form of symmetrical gangrene of the buttocks, thighs, arms, and other parts, which has probably no kinship with Raynaud's disease. The pathology of such cases is obscure. Thrombosis, embolism, neuritis, pressure on and soiling of the parts, are among the possibilities, and another explanation is that which has been found to account for some cases at least of noma,—the invasion, namely, by virulent streptococci of tissues whose vitality has been reduced by a specific febrile process. Southey reports the case of a boy of 5, who, a fortnight from the commencement of an acute illness, supposed to be scarlet fever, had pain and discoloration in the front of the abdomen. The skin over a symmetrical area in this region sloughed. Healing took place in eight weeks from the commencement of the gangrene.[1]   Zwicke tells of a female child, aged 2½ years, whose hands and feet became swollen whilst the fingers became bluish black, eight days after the onset of scarlet fever.   Both hands became bluish red, the left forearm and hand became gangrenous, and superficial necrosis took place in the toes of both feet.   The autopsy revealed hypostatic pneumonia.[2]

The agency by which gangrene may occasionally be brought about in scarlet fever is shown by a case recorded by Pearson where it was necessary to amputate through both thighs.   An embolus was found in the popliteal artery of the leg that was dissected.[3]

Measles (with or without whooping-cough) is naturally a fact in the past history of a considerable number of patients, and as a rule it has no connection with Raynaud's disease.   Sometimes, however, the association is closer. Raynaud's phenomena have been observed to set in two months after an attack of measles which ended in a good recovery (M'Call Anderson), and on the other hand, measles has occurred shortly after the second of a series of attacks of Raynaud's phenomena (Calwell).   Hutchinson describes a case[4] where local syncope began about the same time as attacks of measles and whooping-cough; and Myers reports a case where haemoglobinuria and Raynaud's disease began soon after measles.

In the few reported cases where **Whooping-cough** has

[1] *Brit. Med. Jour.*, 1882, ii., 1094.   "Case of symmetrical gangrene of the skin of the abdomen in a child."

[2] *Charité-Annalen* (1881), viii., 1883, 466-7.

[3] *Brit. Med. Jour.*, 1896, ii., 1510.   [4] *Medical Week*, 1893, i., 97.

accompanied, or preceded by a short interval, an attack of Raynaud's disease, its influence cannot be separated from that of measles from which the patients happened to suffer at the same time.

Diphtheria, from which a very small proportion of patients are said to have suffered, appeared in one instance to be the direct cause of Raynaud's disease. The latter set in a few weeks after the throat became sore, or about the time when paralysis might have been looked for (Powell. See p. 73 for an abstract of the case).

Erysipelas appears to be an occasional cause of Raynaud's disease. Thus in a case recorded by Englisch, a woman suffered from erysipelas of the left leg in April, 1867, and in the following July blisters developed between the toes of the same foot. In January, 1869, after a considerable period of good health, blisters appeared on the toes of the right foot, and after a time erysipelas invaded the right leg. The vasomotor affection was chronic and did not assume its more serious forms until 1875. There was an exacerbation as late as 1878, the year of reporting.

A still more marked example of the connection between the two diseases is given by Defrance (Obs. I.). A washerwoman, aged 46, who was admitted in April, 1895, had suffered three years previously from a severe attack of smallpox, which was complicated with painful swelling of the extremities and loss of the nails. Her health was thereafter gradually re-established, but the menses, irregular in 1894, ceased in January, 1895. Erysipelas set in at the beginning of February of the latter year, first involving the left ear, and then invading the four limbs and the trunk, with the exception of the abdomen. On the 20th of the month, intolerable pains began suddenly in the hands, which also became swollen and blue. The patient screamed day and night. The heart and radial arteries, lungs, digestive organs, kidneys, and eyes were all normal. In fact, the pairs and commencing gangrene of the extremities appeared, when she was admitted, to constitute the whole illness. The pains which had begun suddenly in February, ceased suddenly on the 1st April at the idea of entering hospital, but they began again the same night. On the 13th April the feet were attacked. Portions of several fingers became mummified, but the thumbs and toes did not suffer much loss of tissue. There was slight cyanosis of the nose and ears.[1]

On the other hand, a patient of my own who had recovered from an attack of Raynaud's disease with gangrene, though still presenting a congenital abnormality of the cutaneous circulation generally, went through an attack of erysipelas without any return of the vasomotor affection. (See page 77.)

Influenza is mentioned by Batman in connection with a case of Raynaud's disease. The report is not sufficiently detailed, but the patient had influenza in three successive years, and made a tardy convalescence after each attack. Apparently local asphyxia began at some time in the course of these three years.

There is evidence of inherited **Syphilis** in about 3 per cent. of cases of Raynaud's disease, and of the acquired disease in 2.8 per cent., the latter figure being doubtless a good deal under the truth.[2]

---

[1] Holm, in 1872, recorded a case where, shortly after recovery from erysipelas of the face, the same disease again attacked the same part, and was associated from the commencement with local asphyxia of the four extremities. Some gangrenous losses occurred, and a cyanotic spot appeared on the front of the chest.

[2] Raynaud considered the association with syphilis to be a pure coincidence (No. 147, p. 649).

With regard to the *inherited* disease, seven out of eight recorded cases were males. The age at which Raynaud's disease set in varied from 2 to 25 years (average, 8½ years). The one female was aged 17, and suffered from haematemesis, haemoptysis, and haematuria. One male (aet. 2) had haemoglobinuria later on ; another (aet. 3) was still suffering from Raynaud's disease two years later, when interstitial keratitis set in ; another (aet. 3) suffered from Raynaud's malady (including syncope, asphyxia, and gangrene) during three months and was then treated and rapidly cured by mercury and iodide of potassium. In other instances Raynaud's disease was associated with congenital mental defect, which may have been attributable to the inherited disease (F. Marsh ; Hutchinson [1]). In Pasteur's case, though the patient was the subject of inherited syphilis, and was actually suffering at the time from chronic ulceration of the pharynx, the disease was induced by a dog-bite, so that the association may have been a coincidence. Nevertheless, it seems clear that inherited syphilis is sometimes directly or indirectly a cause of Raynaud's disease.

It is seldom that *acquired* syphilis can be recognized as a cause. Morgan (1889) could only find records of ten cases in which Raynaud's disease occurred in syphilitic subjects (congenital disease, 5 ; inherited disease, 5). Most of these ten, however, must be set aside as doubtful ; they include, for instance, the two given in Raynaud's *Thesis* (Cases xvi. and xvii.), and the case already quoted from Puzey (p. 96) in which the penis was involved. And with regard to a few of the others, the clinical histories scarcely warrant the assumption that the patients were syphilitic.

[1] No. 87, pp. 220-222.

Of five patients recorded as having suffered from the acquired disease, two had acquired it 17 years before the onset of Raynaud's disease, one 7 years before, and another 10 or 12 years before. The patients of Portal and Bernard Henry were both syphilitic, but other causes may have been operative. The case which most clearly shows a connection between acquired syphilis and Raynaud's disease is one that was recorded by Morgan in 1889. The patient was a farm labourer, aged 28, and came under observation in August, 1888. He had enjoyed good health until 1882, when he got a hard chancre, for which he underwent a six weeks' course of treatment. Secondary symptoms ensued, and went on for about a year. Patient remained well thereafter for three years and then suffered for a time from extensive ulceration of the fauces and palate. After this he had fifteen months of good health. He next began to suffer excruciating pains in various parts—lower limbs, pelvic and shoulder girdles, and spine. These made him scream and were worst at night. After he had been almost constantly in bed for some months, the pains became tolerable and at length ceased. The next symptom was severe tingling followed by icy coldness in the fingers and ears, with anaesthesia and complete analgesia in the fingers. The extreme coldness of the digits lasted for five or six weeks, and while the parts were constantly pale, there were paroxysms of still more striking pallor. At the end of the time mentioned the finger-tips became livid and after a few days black. As lividity took the place of pallor, so pain replaced numbness. The ears and tip of the nose became blue soon after the fingers. In a few days more the skin separated from the black portions of the digits. These phenomena supervened in the warm summer weather which preceded admission. Some days after admission a considerable portion of the helix of the right ear sloughed away. Treatment by iodide of potassium and perchloride of mercury produced an immediate and marked improvement. The slough separated from the fingers ; the pains gradually ceased ; the black parts that had not actually died became blue and then greenish yellow. It was noted that the tips of the toes were slightly blue. The urine once contained blood, but otherwise there was no evidence of visceral disease. The arteries of the arms were normal. Vision was good, and the retinal arteries, though narrow, did not undergo paroxysmal narrowing. Patient was dismissed after a residence of twenty-two days, with only small scars and a tapering condition of the finger-tips to testify to the loss of tissue which had been sustained. Good health persisted for three months, and was then interrupted by violent shooting pains in the forehead, with simultaneous dimness of vision. Antisyphilitic treatment brought about complete cure in a fortnight. On this occasion there was some weakness of the extensor muscles of the hands.

Though the element of paroxysm, one of the most characteristic features of Raynaud's disease, was present in this case, its obvious association with structural changes of late syphilis, and its ready response to antisyphilitic remedies, may well give rise to doubt as to its title to the name of Raynaud's disease. The following two cases, which have no claim to this designation, throw light on the question. Schuster[1] reports the case of a man, aged 37, who, several years after acquiring syphilis, had dry gangrene of the three inner toes of the right foot. The two remaining toes were anaesthetic and the whole foot felt cold.

[1] "Fussgangrän in Folge von Syphilis," *Arch. f. Dermat. u. Syph.*, 1889, xxi., 779-782.

The left foot also was cold and numb. There was no pulse
in either posterior tibial artery. After amputation of the
gangrenous foot, gummata were found on the wall of the
posterior tibial artery.

Elsenberg[1] gives the name Raynaud's disease (inappro-
priately) to the next case. A woman, aged 22, was admitted
in a subfebrile state with enlargement of the liver. Dark
spots were present on the cheeks and chin, and many
gangrenous areas of skin were found on the upper and
lower limbs. Gangrene progressed, and emaciation and
weakness led to a fatal issue. Small arteries in the neighbourhood of the gangrenous foci were found to be diseased
and gummata were present in the liver.

Gonorrhoea is rarely mentioned in the reports, and has
probably no direct influence. But it may give rise to
rheumatism, and this in its turn may favour the occurrence
of Raynaud's disease. Thus in one case a man had gonorrhoea 12 years, syphilis 7 years, and gonorrhoea again 4
years before the vasomotor disease, which set in on a warm
day in August. Both attacks of gonorrhoea were followed
by rheumatism in the wrist and fingers (Fordyce).

Tuberculosis. About 6 per cent. of cases of Raynaud's
disease are reported as being or as eventually becoming
tuberculous—not a very large proportion if 14 per cent.
of the general population actually die of tuberculosis.
Several of my own patients have suffered from tubercle at one
time or another. In about half the cases, tuberculosis takes
the form of phthisis. One of the cases collated by Raynaud[2]

[1] " Die sogenannte Raynaud'sche Krankheit (Gangraena symmetrica)
syphilitischen Ursprungs," *Arch. f. Dermat. u. Syph.*, 1892, xxiv.,
577-587.
[2] Raynaud considered the association with tuberculosis to be a pure
coincidence (No. 147, p. 649).

(*Thesis*, Case vii.) succumbed to acute phthisis, and another to phthisis (Case viii.). In Case xviii., where there was mitral stenosis, several masses of tubercle were found in the apex of the right lung. In Cases ix. and xii. there were abscesses under the sternomastoid muscle, which may have had a tubercular origin. Raynaud also describes a case of recovery from local asphyxia, diabetes, and phthisis.[1]

Raynaud's phenomena may be met with in connection with latent or active phthisis. They may supervene or become severe when the disease is advanced or when haemoptysis is practically the only evidence of its presence. Raynaud's disease occasionally occurs in those who have suffered during months or years from strumous lesions with a discharge.

Tuberculosis appears to be but rarely a cause of Raynaud's disease, and it is probable that the associated suppuration in the lungs or in diseased glands is more important than the specific tubercular process. The association is doubtless in most cases, as Raynaud thought it was in all, a mere coincidence. One of my patients was a little girl who suffered for about three months from paroxysmal local asphyxia, and who, several months after recovery, came back to be treated for glandular swellings in the neck.[2]

Malarial fever in its relations to Raynaud's disease has been considered at length in the section on Etiology.

Rheumatism in one or other of its manifestations enters into the clinical history of over 7 per cent. of cases of Raynaud's disease. The usual relationship is that the patient has had acute rheumatism many years before. In some instances, however, he has long been a sufferer from the chronic disease. Subacute rheumatism has been

[1] No. 147, pp. 649-650.   [2] No. 117, pp. 273-274.

observed to develop in a patient under treatment for Raynaud's disease (C. Beale).

Besides this, rheumatism may be operative by causing cardiac valvular disease, a lesion which seems to favour the occurrence of Raynaud's malady in susceptible subjects.

Raynaud's disease has also been seen in association with **Rheumatoid arthritis** (Hutchinson[1]) and occasionally in persons liable to **Gout** (Hutchinson; Aitken), but such cases are quite exceptional.

The following case from Colleville[2] presents certain resemblances to Raynaud's disease, though regarded by its narrator as due to phlebitis, since there was no paroxysmal element, and the illness proceeded to gangrene in a few days. A housewife, aged 23, had gangrenous tonsillitis followed by acute rheumatic polyarthritis. When the pains ceased, local asphyxia appeared in several digits of each hand, little gangrenous patches developed on several fingers, and the last phalanx of the right middle finger fell off.

Quinsy seems to predispose to Raynaud's disease by lowering the general tone and not through any specific effects.

Anaemia, either in the form of chlorosis, or secondarily to phthisis, albuminuria, lactation, rickets, etc., can scarcely be said to be more common in the subjects of Raynaud's disease than in the rest of the population, if due regard be given to age and sex.

Enlargement of the spleen has been noted in a few cases,—very few, indeed, if we set aside those specially collected to show the connection between Raynaud's disease

---

[1] No. 85, pp. 312-313.
[2] "Sur un cas de gangrène symétrique des extrémités d'origine rhumatismale," *La France médicale,* 1884, i., 126-129.

and malarial fever. (Of the latter, several examples are given by Calmette.) Thomas Smith has reported the case of a girl, aged 3, in whom the splenic enlargement was attributable to rickets. In a most interesting case reported by Thomas and Osler, the patient was subject each winter to attacks of Raynaud's disease, haemoglobinuria and epileptic convulsions. After a number of years the convulsions ceased, but the attacks of local asphyxia and haemoglobinuria continued, and two new phenomena were added to them—viz. paroxysms of colic and enlargement of the spleen.

Another case is given by Raynaud (*Thesis*, Case ix.). In this woman the red blood corpuscles were greatly diminished in number and the white corpuscles were present in the proportion of 1 to 15 or 20 red, and ultimately of 1 to 5. The patient died from asthenia, and at the autopsy the spleen was found to be enlarged, being 20 cm. long, 12 broad, and 6 thick, and 1 kgr. in weight (8″ × 4.8″ × 2.4″; 35 oz.). Its capsule was thickened and its tissue firm, elastic and cirrhotic. The liver weighed 3.5 kgr. (123 oz.). Simon described and discussed this case in his inaugural dissertation on leucocythaemia in 1861. He regarded it as an example of this disease and considered the local syncope, asphyxia and gangrene of the extremities to be symptoms of leucocythaemia. Raynaud, on the other hand, considered the lesions in the extremities, the leucocytosis, and the enlargement of the spleen to be common results of some profound but unexplained disorder of the general nutrition.[1]

It is surprising that leucocythaemia has been so very rarely noted in connection with Raynaud's disease, especially since the relationship of the latter to malarial fever has

[1] *Thesis*, p. 61. In the *Nouv. Dict.* (1872, xv., 649) Raynaud refers to the association with leucocythaemia as a pure coincidence.

come to be recognized. For the great frequency of a malarial history in leukaemia has been known for many years. Gowers found a history of ague or of residence in an ague district in 25 per cent. of the cases of splenic leukaemia which he collected.[1]

Haemorrhages of various kinds may occur in the subjects of Raynaud's disease. Uterine haemorrhages have been discussed in the section on etiology, and bleeding in connection with the urinary system will be considered hereafter. Of the remainder, epistaxis is perhaps the most frequent; it is mentioned in 6 per cent. of the clinical reports. Sometimes the connection is purely accidental, as when the bleeding took place in an attack of enteric many years before. Or a person long subject to epistaxis may have got rid of it before Raynaud's disease set in. On the other hand, there may be some manifest connection, as in one case where frequent bleedings from the nose during two weeks preceded the onset of local asphyxia of the digits (Warren); or in another, where an elderly lady became subject to Raynaud's phenomena 12 years, and to frequent epistaxis 10 years, before the report was published (J. C. Simpson). Among other instances recorded are two of Raynaud's Cases (viii. and ix. in the *Thesis*). In one of these, some drops of blood escaped from the nostrils each morning in the early stage of the disease ; in the other, the haemorrhage occurred at an advanced stage, in a series of attacks which were sufficiently severe to wear out the patient, who was also the subject of leucocythaemia.

In other instances again, epistaxis is associated with haemorrhage elsewhere. Thus one of Hutchinson's patients had epistaxis twice, and this on the second occasion was

[1] *Lancet*, 1878, i., 460, 495.

accompanied by haematuria and by haemorrhage from the gums. Another haemorrhage that sometimes occurs is haemoptysis, which may or may not be definitely referable to phthisis and may be associated in different cases with epistaxis, haematuria, or purpura. In a case recorded by Bland, where Raynaud's disease was added to acute mania, there were haemorrhagic extravasations on the buttocks and thighs, and blood was present for three days in the expectoration and urine. Extravasations into or under the skin have been reported in one or two other cases. Raynaud's disease has also been met with in association with the return of a haematemesis which had been absent for years (Solis-Cohen). Solis-Cohen tells of a man who had phthisis with haemoptysis and local asphyxia of the hands. The hands of his mother, of one brother, and of one sister younger than himself, were said to resemble his own, whilst those of his father and older brothers and sisters were normal. The sister and brother who had blue hands were subject to bleeding from the nose. This sister got rid of the epistaxis with her first pregnancy.

Cerebral haemorrhage may, of course, occur in a subject of chronic Bright's disease with Raynaud's phenomena.

Suppurative processes may possibly predispose to Raynaud's disease. Quite exceptionally little abscesses in the tips of the digits may complicate the progress of local syncope and asphyxia in the same parts. Raynaud's disease with haemoglobinuria has been observed in a patient with suppurating cervical glands (Southey[1]), and in another with a suppurating bursa of the hip (Wilks). In Landry's case (Case viii. in Raynaud's *Thesis*), the affection of the extremities supervened on an abscess of the breast and a tertian intermittent fever which followed a

[1] No. 172.

confinement. In Case ix. of the *Thesis,* a large abscess formed, in the course of the illness, under the sternomastoid muscle and healed quickly after evacuation. In Case xii., a little boy who had had a suppurating gland a considerable time before the onset of local asphyxia, suffered in the course of Raynaud's disease from glandular abscesses under the left sternomastoid.

It is rarely that gangrene in this disease gives rise to metastatic abscesses. These were observed, however, about the hip and elsewhere in a boy who had undergone spontaneous amputation of both feet and who eventually made a good recovery (Harold). Small abscesses may, of course, occur after amputation, in consequence of exfoliation of a piece of bone.

Diseases of the lungs and pleurae have rarely any important influence in the etiology of Raynaud's disease. Phthisis has been considered under the subject of tuberculosis. A past attack of bronchitis, pneumonia, or pleurisy must generally be regarded as a coincidence. Chronic bronchitis is so frequent that it is not surprising that some patients with Raynaud's disease should suffer from it simultaneously. Occasionally, however, the relationship is more intimate. Thus in one case, a lady began to suffer from Raynaud's symptoms when she was recovering from an attack of bronchitis (Hutchinson [1]), and in another, a woman, whose right hand was already affected, became troubled with her left in the course of bronchitis (Haig [2]). In the case which Mr. Hutchinson quotes from Huguier (see p. 21), the symptoms appear to have followed on a violent cold ; and in one of Hutchinson's own cases,[3] a cold in the chest brought on the definite symptoms referable to the extremities. In a

[1] No. 86, p. 97.   [2] No. 59, p. 29.   [3] No. 86, p. 98.

case recorded by Nielsen, the vasomotor phenomena followed pneumonia and were accompanied by bronchitis. One of F. P. Henry's patients was liable to asthmatic attacks which were regarded as analogous to the other symptoms, both being due to spasm of unstriated muscle. In Case xix. of Raynaud's *Thesis*—not a typical example of the disease—hepatization of the base of the left lung was noted.

It is a question how far measles may be operative as an occasional cause of Raynaud's disease through the associated bronchial catarrh and not directly.

Pneumonia or bronchitis is apt to be a cause of death in cases of Raynaud's disease, or, more correctly speaking, in cases associated with Raynaud's phenomena. In some of these, there is also a cardiac lesion. Thus in Case xix. of Raynaud's *Thesis*, red hepatization of a portion of one lung was discovered after death, together with stenosis of both auriculo-ventricular orifices. West records a genuine instance of Raynaud's disease which continued for about a year, and was then complicated by an illness closely resembling erysipelas of the face. This in turn led on to a fatal pneumonia. In a case described by Hutchinson, a patient who had been subject for 10 years to paroxysmal local asphyxia succumbed to an attack of bronchitis at the age of 25.

On the other hand, a person who suffers, not merely from local cyanosis and gangrene, but also from haemoglobinuria, may pass successfully through an attack of acute pneumonia with pleurisy (as in Myers's case).

Diseases of the cardio-vascular system. It is a suggestive fact that some abnormality in connection with the cardio-vascular system is noted in fully 12 per cent. of cases of Raynaud's disease (22 out of 180). But this

I

statement is misleading, for a number of cases ought strictly speaking to be detached from this group. In more than one of the collated cases, the changes were the usual accompaniments of chronic Bright's disease. In others, the abnormal feature was the existence of a murmur at the base of the heart, probably haemic, and in others it was tachycardia which was present as an element in exophthalmic goitre or some allied neurosis. In another instance there was oppression in the precordial region, and in yet another an unexplained, distressing pain in the chest with great debility. Eliminating these, there still remain the following conditions: weak, irregularly acting heart, 1 ; angina pectoris, 1 ; presystolic thrill with angina-like pain, 1 ; presystolic murmur, 1 ; slight ventricular systolic murmur at the apex, 1 ; aortic systolic murmur, with or without cardiac symptoms, 5 ; aortic diastolic murmur, 2. These 12 amount to nearly 7 per cent. of the 180 cases of Raynaud's disease.

Cleeman records the case of a man who became unduly sensitive to cold when over fifty years of age in consequence of several hours' exposure to damp and cold. After he had been subject for six years to paroxysms of local syncope with occasional superficial gangrene of a finger, he was suddenly seized on a cold day in winter with agonizing pain behind the upper part of the sternum and in both upper arms. This lasted for two hours and was followed by great prostration for a day or two. A week later he was found dead in his bedroom.

Moursou mentions a case where an attack of angina pectoris followed the cold stage of an intermittent in a man who also suffered from local asphyxia of the extremities.

It is probable that in some of the cases where a valvular

murmur exists the association is a mere coincidence, and that in others the endocarditis and the vasomotor phenomena depend for their inauguration on some common cause.

Conditions that embarrass the functions of the thoracic viscera may be accompanied by Raynaud's phenomena, and opinions may easily differ on the question whether or not a given case of this kind may justly be called "Raynaud's disease." It seems clear that such conditions may in exceptional instances be, if not the sole cause, then a contributory cause of local asphyxia and symmetrical gangrene. Three of the cases collected in the *Thesis* (xvii., xviii. and xix.) may be cited by way of illustration. One of these was recorded by Bernard Henry. A syphilitic woman of middle age suffered from spontaneous gangrene of the four extremities with local asphyxia of the ears, nose and other parts. She died within three months, and it was found at the autopsy that the auriculo-ventricular orifice would scarcely admit a finger.[1] The tissue of the heart was somewhat fatty. The lungs were healthy. The brachial and femoral arteries were normal, but adherent to the bone.

Godin's patient was a woman, aged 25, who succumbed to gangrene of both feet brought on by exposure to excessive cold. Considerable stenosis of the mitral valve was discovered after death, and the heart and arterial trunks were unusually small, but the vessels were quite permeable and otherwise normal.

Topinard's patient was a woman, aged 32, who was admitted on account of epileptiform attacks. Gangrene invaded both lower limbs and local asphyxia appeared

[1] This lesion is not mentioned in the *Gaz. Méd. de Paris* (1857, xii., 323) from which Raynaud quotes, but in the English abstract of the case in the *Brit. and For. Med. Chir. Review* (1856, 254-255).

later in the upper extremities.   The post-mortem revealed stenosis of both auriculo-ventricular orifices.   There was no thrombosis or disease of the vessels.[1]

In a very complicated case described by Hale White, where cardiac lesions existed, an embolus was found in the main artery of one of the gangrenous limbs, while the arteries of the other gangrenous limbs were normal and permeable.

In 1872 Bull[2] recorded a remarkable case where a woman became blue in the face and other parts, especially in fresh air and on effort.   After a time the lividity passed off, but there were symptoms and a diastolic murmur referable to some cardiac lesion, and the patient eventually died suddenly.   Aortic insufficiency was revealed by the post-mortem, and four chordae tendineae of the mitral valve were ruptured—a lesion that was considered responsible for the sudden death.

In a case that came under my own observation, the cyanosis of the extremities, nose and ears was associated with great enlargement of the heart.   The limit of cardiac dulness corresponded on the right to the left border of the sternum, and on the left to a vertical line ten inches from the middle line.   The apex impulse was in the seventh intercostal space, $8\frac{1}{2}$ inches from the middle line.   All the nails of the hands were deformed and there was linear atrophy of the skin in front of both shoulders.   There was some aphasia in addition to cardiac symptoms.   The blueness was increased by cold, by stooping, etc., and was associated in the hands with scaliness.

In 1871 Budde[3] reported a case of Addison's disease

[1] *Bull. de la Soc. Anat. de Paris*, 1855, 523-526 ; *Thesis*, Case xix.
[2] Quoted in Schmidt's *Jahrbücher*, 1872, clv., 24-25.
[3] Quoted in Schmidt's *Jahrbücher*, 1872, clv., 25.

which was complicated by the appearance from time to time of varying degrees of cyanosis of the cheeks, lips and hands. The post-mortem did not furnish any explanation of this phenomenon.

It must be borne in mind that symmetrical gangrene occurs not infrequently apart from Raynaud's disease. It may be the consequence of symmetrical embolisms, as in a case recorded by Pearson[1] where both lower limbs were involved, or in the extraordinary case mentioned by Raynaud[2] where an obstruction of this kind was found not only in the aorta above its bifurcation but also in each brachial artery. Thrombosis appears to be an occasional cause, as in Winstanley's case of gangrene of both lower limbs,[3] where, with a normal state of the heart, lungs, and large thoracic vessels, the abdominal aorta was distended with clot for two inches above its bifurcation; or in Lehmann's case,[4] where there was gangrene of both lower limbs in a boy of nine months, with thrombosis of both common iliac arteries. Not infrequently, however, there is actual disease of the vessel walls, to which secondary thrombosis may be added. Thus Ransom and Kingdon[5] record a case of symmetrical gangrene of the face in consequence of atheroma of the aorta with great narrowing of the innominate and left carotid at their origins. Among the parts invaded by gangrene was the left ear, and there was also cyanosis of the right ear and of the dorsa of the hands and feet. Thiersch[6] reports the case of a man, aged 35, who for ten years had symmetrical gangrene which began in the toes. He died of apoplexy, and the autopsy

[1] *Brit. Med. Jour.*, 1896, ii., 1510.   [2] *Thesis*, pp. 125-127.
[3] *Lancet*, 1896, ii., 811.
[4] *Arch. für Kinderheilkunde*, 1893, xvi., 70-77.
[5] *Lancet*, 1889, i., 1037-1028.   [6] No. 183.

showed haemorrhage into the left lateral ventricle and extensive and severe arteriosclerosis, which specially involved the arteries of the legs. Or the lesion may be arteritis obliterans, a condition characterized especially by thickening of the intima of the small arteries, though the middle coat of the small arteries and the intima of the venules may also be involved. The disease is quite distinct from atheroma, calcification and syphilis, and may occur in young adults. The large arteries may become blocked by laminated clot, no doubt as a result of the more distally placed obstruction.[1]

To show how closely cases dependent upon organic changes in the vessels may simulate Raynaud's disease, two examples may be quoted. Hutchinson[2] tells of a man, almost 80 years old, whose ten digits all became gangrenous in part, the fingers, however, suffering much more severely than the toes. The gangrene was everywhere dry and it began in warm weather when the patient was otherwise in good health. The disease afterwards spread over the feet. The patient had suffered from gangrene of part of one toe two years previously. Mr. Hutchinson regarded this case as being on the whole an example of senile gangrene, though this, as he remarks, rarely attacks the upper extremities, and still more rarely is bilaterally symmetrical. Cardiac weakness probably had its influence, as well as the diseased state of the vessels.

The second case is a remarkable one recorded by

---

[1] See A. Pearce Gould, *Clin. Soc. Trans.*, 1884, xvii., 95-104; 1891, xxiv., 134-140. W. B. Hadden, *Clin. Soc. Trans.*, 1884, xvii., 105-107 ; *Lancet*, 1888, i., 268-269. W. J. Walsham, *Clin. Soc. Trans.*, 1886, xix., 304-306 ; *Lancet*, 1888, i., 571-572. Spencer, *Brit. Med. Jour.*, 1898, i., 371-372.

[2] No. 92, 206-208.

Hodenpyl[1] in 1891. The illness extended altogether over more than 20 years. A man at the age of about 45, and in the midst of apparent health, became affected by gangrene of one great toe, which was amputated. The other toes and then the legs were afterwards affected, so that in all some twenty amputations were performed. In January, 1890, the end of the penis was attacked and had to be amputated. There was good health thereafter till February, 1891, when the patient was seized with vomiting and abdominal pain, which led up in a few days to a fatal issue. The abdomen was filled with blood which came from the aorta just above the bifurcation. The gangrene was attributed to thrombosis in the aorta.

Disorders of the digestive system are not uncommon in patients who suffer from Raynaud's disease, and in a considerable proportion of cases, the presence of such every-day troubles as dyspepsia and constipation is doubtless a coincidence. Similarly the concurrence of diarrhoea or dysentery with Raynaud's phenomena in those who have been exposed to malarial infection abroad is not surprising. Vomiting may be part of an attack of megrim. Or the digestive disturbance may be secondary to Bright's disease. In a case recorded by H. H. Morton, the patient had long had chronic nephritis, and the disturbances in the extremities became much aggravated on recovery from a gastric attack. A few cases, however, deserve special notice. Thus Raynaud tells of a young woman who, a week after her confinement, had a choleriform attack of sufficient severity to threaten life. She recovered gradually, but became affected with cyanosis within three months (*Thesis*, Case xv.). In Faure's case gastric catarrh with feverishness followed the immersion of the warm hands and feet in

[1] *Medical Record* (N. Y.), 1891, xxxix., 495-496.

cold water.   This kept the patient in bed for ten days, and Raynaud's phenomena only set in a month after the immersion.   In Sainton's case, local asphyxia began when the patient was suffering from lead colic, but it recurred after the colic was cured.   *Jaundice*, or at least a yellow colour of the surface, is occasionally observed in Raynaud's disease with or without haemoglobinuria.   Porter narrates one instance where a middle-aged woman was liable, independently of exposure, to attacks of local syncope and asphyxia of the hands and feet.   These occurred three or four times a day and alternated "with paroxysmal attacks of epigastric pain and vomiting, usually followed by slight jaundice."   Albumen and bile were found in the urine after such a seizure, but no blood or blood colouring matter was detected.   Some of these symptoms referable to the digestive system are important on account of their close similarity to the phenomena of paroxysmal haemoglobinuria.   Thus Abercrombie narrates a case where there was pain in the stomach when the hands were cyanosed and the urine normal, though subsequently the boy became subject to haemoglobinuria. In another case recorded by the same writer, haemoglobinuria and cyanosis of the extremities were both induced by cold and were associated with epigastric pain.   In one of Barlow's cases with normal urine, the patient was sometimes sick, and might vomit, at the onset of the attack of cyanosis ; and in another, in which some of the attacks were accompanied by haemoglobinuria, there was sometimes pain in the stomach without nausea before or after the attack, but without relation to the appearance of dark urine.   Slight icterus (regarded as haematogenous) was noticed on the days following several of the attacks.   Nausea, vomiting and epigastric pains may occur without jaundice or haemoglobinuria (Renshaw).

Diabetes insipidus has been associated with Raynaud's disease in rare cases. One was Case ii. in the *New Researches*. A man of 22 was admitted to be treated for excessive hunger and thirst which had troubled him for several months. He ate four to six rations daily, drank 4 or 5 litres (say 7 or 8 pints) of liquid, and passed about as much urine.

Another case is recorded by Defrance (Obs. I.), the patient being a woman of 46, in whom Raynaud's disease followed erysipelas. She had suffered from thirst and moderate polyuria (3 litres or 5 pints of urine daily) since early life.

An unusual quantity of urine ("nervous urine") may be passed before an attack of Raynaud's phenomena even in childhood. In adult life such temporary polyuria may be more definitely related to hysteria.

Glycosuria, though itself uncommon in Raynaud's disease, is met with more frequently than diabetes insipidus. It will be remembered that some authorities regard malarial infection as a cause of glycosuria if not of diabetes itself. Thus Petit and Verneuil insist on the relationship between glycosuria and gangrene, and between glycosuria and paludism, and they quote several cases to illustrate the co-existence of glycosuria and gangrene in paludic subjects.[1] Gangrene is well known as a complication of diabetes in persons who have reached or are approaching the degenerative period of life; it frequently affects the lower limbs, and where it is not secondary to a traumatic or inflammatory lesion, appears to be more immediately induced by atheroma or peripheral neuritis. Moreover, there is some reason to believe that temporary glycosuria may occur in connection with boils and other suppurations. All these

[1] No. 139, pp. 706, 707-709.

considerations, therefore, leave abundant room for doubt as to the significance of glycosuria in a case of supposed Raynaud's disease.

Raynaud himself gives us an interesting case in the *Nouveau Dictionnaire* (1872).[1]   A woman, aged 31, who for eight years had been liable, especially in winter, to local asphyxia of the extremities, began to suffer from asphyxia of the nose in 1868.   At the same time the general state became rapidly impaired and she suffered from great thirst, polyuria and insomnia with rapid emaciation.   She thereupon consulted Raynaud who noted perfectly symmetrical gangrene of the extremities, intense glycosuria, and undoubted signs of early phthisis.   He enjoined a strictly nitrogenous diet, gave alkalies internally, and sent the patient to Vichy for three years in succession.   She improved rapidly, the mortified parts separated, the evidences of phthisis subsided, and the glycosuria diminished, and after being present for three years disappeared.   Several phalanges were lost, but otherwise cure was complete. Raynaud put the probable sequence thus : several years of recurring local asphyxia ; then diabetes which, added to the other, brought on gangrene and tuberculosis.

Colcott Fox refers to a man, aged 51, who was seen on account of symmetrical sores on his shins.   It was found that he had marked glycosuria (of which he had not been aware), and that a brother 10 years younger had also diabetes.   The sores healed, but in the following year he had blisters on the lower limbs.   He was said to have been subject for years to local syncope and to occasional asphyxia of the fingers.   He died of diabetes with albuminuria and other complications, five years after his first visit.

[1] Pp. 649-650.

Changes in the minute vessels were perhaps the immediate cause of gangrene in a case recorded by Radziszewski where glycosuria was associated with alcoholism and albuminuria in a woman of 57 years.

The glycosuria was regarded as "secondary to the gangrenous affection" in a case recorded by Fabre. A girl of 18 suffered from local asphyxia of the nose, cheeks, chin, ear, fingers, toes and other parts. Then she had fever, glycosuria, and gangrene of most of the fingers. Several relapses occurred during some months. There was a history of intermittent fever. The sugar disappeared from the urine before the gangrene was recovered from.

Setting aside cases of diabetes insipidus, cases of glycosuria, and one or two others, some abnormality of the urine is reported in nearly 17 per cent. of cases of Raynaud's disease. This statement applies only to cases where the two are closely associated in point of time. Such cases may be conveniently, though it must be confessed somewhat arbitrarily, classified as follows :—

	Males.	Females.		M. and F.	Percentage.
Albuminuria, -	- 4	4	=	8	4.4
Bright's disease,	- 3[1]	3	=	6	3.3
Haematuria, -	- 6[2]	2	=	8	4.4
Haemoglobinuria,	- 4	4	=	8	4.4
	17	13	=	30 (in 180 cases)	16.6

With regard to one of the eight cases of **Albuminuria**, this symptom was probably of no importance; only once was a faint trace of albumen detected, and the urine other-

[1] In one of these cases the urine frequently contained haemoglobin.

[2] In one of the 180 cases, not included in this number, there was once blood in the urine when the patient was suffering from malarial fever, long before Raynaud's disease set in.

wise was normal (Power). Slight albuminuria was associated with Raynaud's phenomena in a case following diphtheria (Powell). In a case recorded by Porter, albumen and bile, without any blood, were detected in the urine, and sometimes jaundice was observed after attacks in which local syncope and asphyxia of the extremities alternated with paroxysms of epigastric pain and vomiting. Another patient who had slight albuminuria was the subject of inherited syphilis (Penny). In Van der Hoeven's case, the albumen varied greatly in amount, but ultimately disappeared; this intermittent albuminuria was attributed to spasm of the renal capillaries. In another case, the urine was said to contain albumen to half the total quantity, and, as the symptoms in the extremities followed an exposure, there was probably concurrent nephritis (Atkin). The slight albuminuria was not easily to be accounted for in a case recorded by Dixon, but was more readily intelligible in one reported by C. Beale, where the patient had suffered from phthisis for several years, and had, moreover, whilst under observation, an attack of subacute rheumatism.

It would appear then that albuminuria in Raynaud's disease may be the result of changes in the kidney (nephritis, amyloid degeneration, etc.), and that the blood-state consequent upon the renal disease may be the immediate cause of Raynaud's phenomena. Possibly, however, exposure to cold and damp may cause both nephritis and Raynaud's disease directly, or the one directly and the other secondarily. Similarly the morbid blood-state due to the presence of the toxin of diphtheria accounts for albuminuria directly, by its action on the kidney, and for Raynaud's phenomena, directly or indirectly. Cases where albumen, with or without bile, is present in the urine only at times, and in obvious relation to other paroxysmal phenomena, require another explanation, and will be discussed later.

Bright's disease as met with in association with Raynaud's disease is generally of some standing, and may usually be regarded as being in some way the cause of the vasomotor affection. Roques describes the case of a woman whose renal symptoms dated from her second confinement, a year before admission. When she came under observation, she was suffering from failure of the heart with congestion of the viscera and severe albuminuria. She had been liable to attacks of local syncope of the fingers several times daily for three months, and she now began to have local asphyxia of the fingers and toes. A fortnight after admission, there were small dry sloughs on two toes. In another fortnight she was dead. The autopsy revealed splenization of the right lung and great enlargement of the heart. Vegetations were present on the aortic curtains and the kidneys were granular. The radial and pedal arteries were normal. There were no infarctions and no emboli in the arteries.

Haig reports[1] the case of a woman, aged 47, whose vasomotor symptoms were of three years' duration. Her urine was found to be always of low specific gravity with a trace of albumen, but how long her kidneys had been diseased is not plain. The left ventricle was enlarged and there was also chronic bronchitis.

In a case recorded by Henry H. Morton, the patient had suffered from chronic interstitial nephritis for a number of years. Among her symptoms were local syncope and sometimes cyanosis of the fingers. Gangrene only supervened on recovery from a gastric attack.

[1] No. 59.

Garland tells of a lawyer, previously healthy, in whom Raynaud's phenomena began after a severe exposure. He died from Bright's disease within four years, and during practically the whole of that period he was suffering from asphyxia or necrotic lesions in the extremities. In this case no mention is made of local syncope, but in the preceding cases, the three stages of syncope, asphyxia and gangrene were all observed.

Jacoby describes the case of a man, aged 42, who was seen early in December, 1884, on account of the trouble in his fingers. Repeated examinations of the urine gave negative results. At the end of January, 1885, however, there were renal symptoms, with a condition of the urine pointing to chronic interstitial nephritis. A year later, hypertrophy of the left ventricle was noted, and in February, 1888, the patient died of apoplexy. Not only did this case present the three stages of Raynaud's malady, but it had gone on to gangrene before any other disease could be detected. Accordingly Jacoby discards his original diagnosis of Raynaud's disease, and looks upon the syncope, cyanosis and gangrene in this case as the earliest symptoms of the renal affection.

A very important case recorded by Aitken was that of a man, aged 43, who, when seen in October, 1894, had been subject for many years to occasional gouty attacks, and had been found as early as 1889 to have chronic interstitial nephritis. The ears became liable to attacks of paroxysmal cyanosis in 1887, the fingers in 1888, and the toes in 1892. Cyanosis was always preceded by syncope, and eventually gangrene occurred and involved numerous phalanges of the fingers and toes. There was frequently a small amount of haemoglobin in the urine, and the retinae presented the characteristic changes of chronic Bright's disease. Aitken found that the excretion of urea was diminished during the attacks, and he thinks that vascular spasm took place not only in the extremities but also in the renal vessels. The following are some of his data :—

Date of Attack. 1895.	Average Daily Excretion of Urea.		Remarks.
	Between Attacks.	During Attack.	
March 2	—	280 grs.	
,, 20	320 grs.	200 ,,	
April 12	260 ,,	140 ,,	Twitching marked. Two fits.
May 9	280 ,,	200 ,,	Do. do. do.
,, 21	320 ,,	240 ,,	No twitching.
,, 31	280 ,,	160 ,,	One fit.
June 13	280 ,,	200 ,,	Do.
,, 20	260 ,,	180 ,,	Do.
,, 28	240 ,,	120 ,,	Do.
July 26	200 ,,	120 ,,	Several fits. Coma.

Early in July, the association was noted of (i.) diminution of the proportion of urea in the urine, (ii.) spasm of the vessels of the extremities, (iii.) spasm of the retinal vessels, and (iv.) uraemic convulsions. In the end of July, there were intense cyanosis of the digits and ears, uraemic fits occurring in rapid succession, a fall in the excretion of urea to 120 grains daily, and finally death from coma. Aitken's opinion is that the uraemia could scarcely be the cause of the vasomotor phenomena; he regards the diminished excretion as a result of the vasomotor spasm.

In addition to the cases in the classified list, there is one given by Debove, where the primary disease was a nephritis, probably of the subacute parenchymatous type, originating in pregnancy. The woman was seized with anasarca and acute renal symptoms in September, 1878, at the third month of her first pregnancy. She was somewhat better two months later, but aborted at the sixth month. Renal symptoms became severe again early in 1879, and in May symmetrical gangrene of the fingers set in. It is admitted that for 20 days in March she was taking 25 cgr. (barely 4 grains) of ergot daily, but as the black colour did not appear till two months later, Debove claims that the ergot was not responsible for the gangrene. The heart was unaffected. The patient succumbed in August.

Haematuria. Of the eight patients who had haematuria, one was a girl of 17, whose "urine contained a few red corpuscles," and who also had haemoptysis or haematemesis. The report does not exclude the possibility that the blood was menstrual. Another patient was a lad of 16, who had haemoptysis. Red corpuscles were only once detected in the urine (Solis-Cohen). The urine in Morgan's case once contained blood. In a case recorded by Hutchinson, there was simultaneous haematuria, epistaxis, and bleeding from the gums.[1] Bland's maniacal patient had blood in the sputum and in the urine for three days. The three remaining cases ought properly speaking to be added to the group of haemoglobinuria. In one of Southey's patients the haematuria was intermittent, was provoked apparently by cold impressions, and recurred from time to time during a long period, and so resembled haemoglobinuria, though blood corpuscles were found in the urine. In one of F. P. Henry's cases, the urine when presenting the colour of blood, sometimes contained a few red corpuscles, and sometimes contained none at all—a feature well known in connection with paroxysmal haemoglobinuria. The same remark applies to the case recorded by Wilks.

[1] No. 91.

If we consider these three last cases of haematuria (all of the male sex) as being really examples of haemoglobinuria, we then find **Haemoglobinuria** occurring in 11[1] out of 180, or in 6.1 per cent. of cases of Raynaud's disease.

This association does not appear to have come within Raynaud's experience. In 1871 Mr. Hutchinson reported the case of a woman who had gangrene of the tip of the nose and part of the ear, with iridoplegia, and who during the preceding winter had suffered from frequent shivering-fits after exposure. On being asked, she said the urine had often been dark. Although it was never observed to contain blood colouring matter during the patient's stay in hospital, Mr. Hutchinson thought at the time of reporting that the morbid state was allied to "intermittent haema-tinuria." There was no evidence of malaria. [2]

In 1879 Wilks reported a case of "haemoglobinuria, gangrene of the fingers, etc., associated with prolonged suppuration." Red corpuscles were sometimes but not always associated with the haemoglobin.

In a case of Raynaud's disease published by Southey in 1880 there was a history of blood-coloured urine having been passed on several days in succession. Since then the observations of Southey (1883), Barlow (1883) and later writers have made it clear that the association is by no means so rare as to be a curiosity.

Raynaud's disease and paroxysmal haemoglobinuria, in typical instances, possess many features in common. Both are paroxysmal rather than periodic. In both, exposure to

[1] In addition to the 11 cases, there was one in which the patient, a malarious subject with gangrene of the ears, reported that he had some-times passed dark urine, though the specimens examined contained no blood colouring matter.

[2] This early case is not included in the 180 used for statistical purposes.

K

cold is the most important exciting cause of an attack. The attack in either case may commence with shivering. Both are predisposed to (and in some cases possibly directly caused) by malarial fever. Over 8 per cent. of cases of Raynaud's disease have had malarious antecedents, as against 16 per cent. free from them (76 per cent. of the reports making no statement on the subject). Dickinson found that of the 21 cases on which his elaborate study of paroxysmal haemoglobinuria was based,[1] 15 (or 71 per cent.) had a history either of ague or of a probable exposure to malaria. Of the 11 cases in which the two affections were met with together, there is only one (equal to 9 per cent., however) with a definite history of ague,—a man who had malarial fever at 8, and began to suffer from the diseases under consideration at 55 (F. P. Henry). With regard to two or three of the others, it is probable that a malarial history can be excluded. As to the remainder, no history of the kind is given, though it is quite likely that some had resided in ague districts.

With respect to the sex of the patient, the combined affection seems to occupy an intermediate position between the other two. Thus :

	Males (per cent).	Females (per cent).
Raynaud's disease, - - - -	37.4	62.6
Paroxysmal haemoglobinuria (Dickinson),	71.4	28.6
Raynaud's disease with haemoglobinuria,	63.6	36.4

With regard to the age at which they commence, the separate and combined diseases seem to be almost alike.

While cold is the usual excitant of an attack of Raynaud's phenomena, these may be called forth in exceptional cases by the local application of warm water. Similarly Dickinson

[1] *Renal and urinary affections*, Part iii. (1885), 1162.

describes a case where a patient passed black urine after a warm bath, though she was dried before the fire and carefully protected from cold.[1]

Urticaria is an occasional complication of Raynaud's disease,[2] of paroxysmal haemoglobinuria,[3] and of the combined affection.[4]

Epilepsy is not uncommon in the subjects of Raynaud's disease. Boas has recorded[5] a case of paroxysmal haemoglobinuria, in which the patient when at his work would, under the influence of severe cold, be seized with a fit of complete insensibility, accompanied by "epileptoid phenomena." A patient of Southey's who had Raynaud's disease, and also passed blood-coloured urine ("intermittent haematinuria (?)"), is reported to have taken a fit, in which she was insensible for an hour.[6]

A yellow colour of the skin is sometimes seen in either disease or in the combined affection. This is generally regarded as haematogenous and not biliary, but in Porter's case bile was found in the urine whilst blood colouring matter was absent. The liability to attacks, as well as the onset of individual attacks, may be determined, in the case of paroxysmal haemoglobinuria as in the case of Raynaud's phenomena, by exposure to cold,[7] or by severe effort,[8] or by violent emotion.[9]

[1] *Renal and urinary affections*, Part iii. (1885), 1200.

[2] S. Taylor.

[3] *E.g.* case recorded by R. W. Forrest, *Glasg, Med. Jour.*, 1879, xi., 421-424.

[4] Southey, No. 173.

[5] *Deut. Arch. f. Klin. Medicin*, 1883, xxxii., 371-372.

[6] No. 172.   [7] Fraser, *Edin. Med. Jour.*, 1897, ii., 315.

[8] Grawitz, *Klinische Pathologie des Blutes*, 1896, 154.   [9] *Ib.*

W. G. Spencer tells of a boy of 13 who had been liable to paroxysmal

The liability to the combined affection may, like the liability to either separately, persist for years.

Cases in which the phenomena of Raynaud's disease and of paroxysmal haemoglobinuria co-exist differ much from one another; sometimes the one and sometimes the other type predominates. For instance, the prevailing type in a given case may be one characterized by paroxysms of Raynaud's phenomena, but after some of the attacks, haemoglobinuria may occur. Or the two sets of symptoms may be more nearly on the same plane. Or they may occur alternately and never simultaneously (Tannahill). On the other hand, the prevailing features may be those of haemo-globinuria, but with some of Raynaud's phenomena super-added at times. Thus the late Dr. Druitt, in describing his own case, tells how blue spots would appear on his face like patches of incipient gangrene.[1] And Dickinson[2] records a case of paroxysmal haemoglobinuria in which, on one occasion, after the child had been washed with warm water, the digits and part of the dorsum of the left hand became purple and cold without any discoloration of the urine taking place.

In the eleven cases here collected, Raynaud's phenomena were, of course, the prevailing feature. The ages at the time of onset of these phenomena varied from 2 to 55 years (males, 2 to 55; females, 2 to 39), the average being 18½ years (males, 22; females, 12½). The dark coloration

haemoglobinuria from the age of one year, though the circulation in his extremities had always been good. He suffered frostbite in consequence of sleeping out two nights in a van in a stableyard, while the other boys who were with him escaped without injury. (No. 174.)

---

[1] *Med. Times and Gaz.*, 1873, i., 408-411; 461-462.

[2] *Op. cit.*, p. 1199.

of the urine may be first observed about the same time as the first attack of Raynaud's symptoms, or some months earlier, or a short time later, or more than a year later. A man who had local syncope of the fingers and lost several toe nails in one winter, kept fairly well throughout the following summer, but suffered next winter from local syncope and haemoglobinuria (Bristowe and Copeman). A woman who was liable for a time to attacks of local syncope afterwards became subject to local asphyxia, and along with this, to haemoglobinuria. A typical arrangement is that the haemoglobinuria is noticed about the same time as, or shortly after, the cyanosis, and continues thereafter to occur after some, but not after all, of the attacks of cyanosis.

The morbid changes in the blood and urine in connection with haemoglobinuria appear to be of the same order whether this is associated with Raynaud's phenomena or not. The urine passed after the attack is red, brown, or still darker in colour, and on standing, deposits blood-colouring matter, which is recognizable by the spectroscope and by the characteristic reaction with guaiac. The spectroscope reveals haemoglobin or oxyhaemoglobin, and sometimes methaemoglobin. As a rule, no red corpuscles are seen, but in certain cases a small number can be detected on some occasions and not on others. It may be only the stroma of the corpuscle that remains recognizable. Albumen is generally recognizable by the ordinary tests. Tube casts of different kinds and oxalates may constitute part of the deposit.

Myers found that in a case of liability on exposure to both haemoglobinuria and local cyanosis, the red corpuscles obtained from cyanosed parts were generally normal in form, though sometimes crenated; but they always manifested an abnormal disinclination to form rouleaux. Sometimes "bloodflakes" were observed, light red or dark red in tint, and four to ten times the size of red corpuscles.

In such cases, attacks may be induced experimentally, as by immersing the hand for a time in cold water. A paroxysm may or may not be followed by a slight elevation of temperature. Myers's patient went through an attack of acute pneumonia, in which the temperature rose to 104.5°. The disease ended by a favourable crisis, and throughout its course there was no blood or even albumen in the urine.

Haig found, in a case of local asphyxia where some of the attacks were followed by haemoglobinuria, that the blood showed a great diminution of red corpuscles after an attack (*e.g.* one hour before an attack, 3,800,000 ; one hour after the attack and during the haemoglobinuric period, 2,990,000 per c.m.). In a specimen obtained in the course of the paroxysm, disintegrating red cells and an increased number of white cells were observable. In this as in other cases, attacks could sometimes be induced experimentally, and the corpuscles formed rouleaux badly.

Vesical catarrh has been alluded to (in connection with enteric fever) as being possibly a rare cause of Raynaud's phenomena.

Diseases of the Nervous System. Nearly a fourth of all patients with Raynaud's disease are reported to suffer, or to have suffered in the past, from phenomena related to disturbance of the nervous system. The true proportion· must, as usual, be greater than that reported. Some nervous symptoms, however, must be regarded as secondary,—for instance, the drowsiness that may follow the paroxysm, and perhaps the urticaria that may be associated with the vasomotor disorder. Fits and coma in Bright's disease, apoplexy resulting from cerebral haemorrhage, and sciatica have no neccessary connection with

Raynaud's disease. Five per cent. have had **Convulsions** at one time or another, besides cases that have had a single convulsive attack or have suffered from diseases such as "congestion of the brain," general paralysis, etc., in which seizures of this kind are likely to occur. The convulsions may have occurred in infancy, many years before the onset of Raynaud's disease (as in Case viii. of the *Thesis*). Or the patient may be a regular epileptic in whom Raynaud's phenomena began about the same time as, or many years after, the fits. Case xix. of the *Thesis* came under treatment for epileptiform attacks. Or there may be a tendency to Raynaud's phenomena all through life, the patient having convulsions in infancy and becoming epileptic at puberty (Féré and Batigne). A remarkable case has been reported by Thomas and Osler of a man who, at the age of 23, became subject to paroxysms of local asphyxia of the four extremities, ears and nose, with some necrosis of the ear-tips. The attacks occurred in winter only, and were associated with severe epileptic convulsions and with haemoglobinuria. The fits occurred only in winter (except a very few which took place in cold wet weather in summer) and were preceded by local syncope and followed by haemoglobinuria. Occasionally local syncope or asphyxia would come on for a time without a convulsion. After three winters of this, the convulsions ceased, but the other two symptoms continued. After other three years, there was still the liability to discoloration of the nose, ears and fingers and to haemoglobinuria, and he was now subject in addition to paroxysms of abdominal pain and had his spleen considerably enlarged. In a case recorded by Féré, epilepsy and Raynaud's disease were believed to date from about the same time, and it was noted that both sets of phenomena were aggravated during the cold season.

Insanity is occasionally associated with epilepsy in the subjects of Raynaud's disease. For instance, a person who has always been weak-minded and occasionally takes fits may be attacked by Raynaud's disease; or an epileptic is seized with acute mania and exposes himself to such severe cold that local asphyxia and gangrene ensue. In Case xix. of the *Thesis* there was intellectual impairment as well as epilepsy. Apart from such cases, mental alienation is present in about 4½ per cent. of cases of Raynaud's disease. The type of insanity varies in different cases. Thus Macpherson tells of a girl in whom the vasomotor symptoms set in four days after her admission with acute mania. At the outset, however, a week before admission, there had been depression with suicidal impulses instead of exaltation. Shaw describes a case that occurred in a woman who suffered from delusions of persecution and poisoning, and who had frequently attempted suicide and was often violent. Targowla tells of a man who at the age of 36 began to suffer from melancholia with suicidal impulses and insomnia. Raynaud's phenomena began about a year *earlier* than the mental symptoms. The attacks of melancholia and of local asphyxia did not appear to exert any influence on one another. Ritti has recorded two very interesting cases of circular insanity in which syncope and asphyxia of the extremities appeared in the stage of depression. Iscovesco describes the cases of three women with confirmed general paralysis who had local asphyxia of the extremities. In one of Hutchinson's patients, Raynaud's phenomena developed in connection with an aggravation of a congenital mental defect.

Hysteria is occasionally associated with Raynaud's phenomena. In Case viii. of the *Thesis*, the pains, when at their greatest intensity, were accompanied by hysterical convulsions. In Case ix., the patient was the subject of chlorosis and hysteria from the time of puberty, or for some ten years before the other illness commenced. On the other hand certain hysterical phenomena which were observed in Case xv. seem to have been due to the exhaustion and pain caused by the vasomotor disorder in one who had not previously been neurotic. Case ii. was an example of frequent local syncope in a highly hysterical young woman.

Chorea and Raynaud's disease were observed together in one case by myself.[1] A boy began to suffer from chorea at the age of 7. In the following year he had an attack of scarlet fever, and in the year after that asphyxia of the extremities set in. Both the chorea and the local cyanosis were said to improve in summer.[2]

In a few cases the subject of Raynaud's disease is liable to **Headaches,** which may resemble attacks of migraine. On the other hand, such headaches may trouble a patient in the course of Raynaud's disease less than they had formerly done. A case is reported of a man who suffered from attacks of localized pain in the head similar in character to the pain felt in the fingers. It sometimes accompanied and sometimes alternated with the pain in the extremities, and was supposed to be due to "localized meningeal congestion."[3]

Solis-Cohen has described as examples of "vasomotor

[1] No. 118.

[2] Brünniche tells of a boy who suffered for some days from cyanosis of the digits, nose and ears, and, on one of those days only, suffered from slight chorea-like twitchings (No. 24). Another writer, who does not give further details of his case, speaks of the right hand of a "choretic" patient remaining "dusky purple" for some weeks (No. 61, p. 357).

[3] H. C. Wood, *Trans. Coll. Phys. Philad.*, 1892, xiv., 166.

infiltrations—*e.g.* about the shoulder and upper arm; (*b*) palsy of the vascular and oculopupillary fibres of the left cervical sympathetic and superficial gangrene of the left cheek—most of the phenomena of this group being transitory; (*c*) acute atrophy of the left half of the face; (*d*) superficial gangrene of the buttock and sacral region; (*e*) disturbances of speech—beginning suddenly in October. Patient became pale at the same time, her lips were blue and the retinal arteries were narrowed to a striking degree. She had difficulty in finding familiar words and she transposed words or syllables and used wrong ones. Voluntary movement was not affected in this seizure. The attack was at an end in 15 or 20 minutes, speech being quite restored. A similar attack occurred four weeks afterwards. Soon after this, in November, local cyanosis invaded the toes, and sometimes ischaemia of individual toes would precede or follow the asphyxia. In March, 1882, there was partial gangrene of the right great toe and of the outer surface of each labium majus. Throughout the whole course of this illness the general health remained fairly good, menstruation was regular and the circulatory organs and the urine were normal. Patient was not syphilitic.

Another curious case which also shows the association with aphasia is described by Osler.[1] A woman, who had suffered during five or six years from occasional attacks of numbness and mottling of the fingers, was seized in April, 1891, when aged 47, with dizziness and transient obscuration of consciousness. A month later she had a similar attack with pain and local asphyxia in the two inner fingers of the right hand. In January, 1892, there was a third attack of dizziness with asphyxia and superficial gangrene of the second and fifth right finger-tips. In a fourth attack,

[1] No. 134, p. 524 ff.

at the beginning of February, there was aphasia, paralysis of the right hand and paresis of the right foot, from all of which she soon recovered. Four weeks later she was seized with complete motor aphasia and had spasm in the right hand, but was well again in less than a day. In February, 1895, there was local cyanosis of the distal portion of the right middle finger, unaccompanied, however, by any cerebral symptoms. Early in April there was an attack of headache, left hemiparesis, and discoloration and tenderness of several digits of the right hand. In July there was a third attack of aphasia, with right hemiplegia, and local syncope and asphyxia in the right hand and fingers. About this time the tip of the nose was slightly blue—the only occasion on which the face was affected. In January, 1896, she was seized with giddiness and vomiting, followed by intense pain in the right hand. The fingers became blue and the hand anaesthetic. Speech was retained. Gradually the limb became cold and purple up to the elbow, with mottling still higher. The patient died comatose in a couple of days.

Bramann has described a curious illness which, if not actually Raynaud's disease, presents many points of resemblance to it. He met with it in three brothers aged 7, 10 and 13 years. Their parents and sisters were quite healthy. The disease began in each of these three boys in the fourth year of life. Violent pains with great redness and swelling attacked almost exactly symmetrical spots on the extremities. Most of these lesions proceeded to gangrene. The attacks recurred at varying intervals and involved sometimes the hands alone, sometimes the feet only, and sometimes all four extremities. The pains ceased when the dead tissue began to be separated. When the boys came under observation, the second had suffered most, and the youngest least severely. The former had lost almost all the terminal phalanges of the fingers. The stumps were clubbed and there was recent ulceration of the little fingers. The great toes had lost their distal phalanges. There was impairment of sensation in the four limbs, especially in the two older patients, and altogether Bramann considers the symptoms to point not to vascular but to spinal disease. He suggests syringomyelia as most likely.

Morgan's case, which has been given in summary in connection with the subject of syphilis, presented features which strongly suggest a lesion involving the roots of the spinal nerves.

In a few cases **Peripheral neuritis** has been found to be present in association with symptoms closely resembling those of Raynaud's malady. One of the best examples is a case which was recorded by Wiglesworth in 1887, where an epileptic and insane woman, who suffered from chronic Bright's disease with secondary hypertrophy of the heart, lost considerable portions of her fingers and one great toe by gangrene. She died rather suddenly after a fit, and the autopsy revealed degeneration of nerves in all four limbs. In a case recorded by Rakhmaninoff in 1892, where pleurisy, hepatization of an entire lung, and peripheral neuritis were demonstrated after death, the symptoms were by no means characteristic of Raynaud's disease.

A case recorded by Collier in which peritonitis was present may be mentioned here, since it was suspected that the inflammation in the region of the great abdominal plexuses had something to do with the vasomotor symptoms. The three stages of Raynaud's disease were observed during life, but though all four extremities became pale at times, severe gangrene was confined to the toes of the left foot.

It is worthy of note that intrathoracic tumours, apparently

by pressure on nerves, may induce local asphyxia (Fagge [1]), and even partial gangrene (B. O'Connor [2]) of the fingers. Russell Reynolds [3] tells of a lady in whom pressure on the lower cervical spinous processes induced pallor of the face, duskiness of the lips, and enfeeblement and speedy loss of the right radial pulse. Beaven Rake [4] has reported the occurrence of local asphyxia in the areas between the anaesthetic patches of non-tuberculated leprosy in a case where the nerves were found after death to be diseased.

Articular lesions, not unlike the arthropathies of various nervous diseases, are occasionally met with in cases of, or allied to, Raynaud's disease. In Case i. of the *New Researches* there were fibrous indurations in the skin of the palms, which became much less marked under treatment. Effusion into joints, ankylosis, etc., have been recorded, but the cases were not all typical. **Muscular atrophy** has been repeatedly observed, chiefly in complicated cases, and diminution or loss of muscular response to electricity has been noted.

Ocular symptoms. Inasmuch as the fundus oculi is the one situation in the uninjured living body where blood-vessels can be actually examined by inspection, we cannot wonder at the importance Raynaud attached to the cases he recorded in 1874 as lending support to the theory he had enunciated a dozen years before. In one instance [5] a man became subject, at the age of 59, to paroxysms of local asphyxia of the extremities, and a few weeks later to **paroxysmal impairment of vision**.

[1] Fagge and Pye-Smith, *Principles and Practice of Medicine*, 3rd ed., 1891, ii., 118. See also a case recorded by Treves; No. 185.

[2] *Brit. Med. Jour.*, 1884, i., 460.

[3] *Brit. Med. Jour.*, 1868, ii., 655-656.

[4] *Lancet*, 1887, ii., 958; 1889, i., 301. [5] Case i., in *New Researches*.

During the period of asphyxia, he could see quite well, but as the digits were recovering their normal colour, the sight, especially of the left eye, became dim. Vision was restored at the moment when a new attack of asphyxia supervened. Ophthalmoscopic examination in the period when the discoloration of the extremities was at a minimum revealed narrowing of the arteries and pulsation of the veins. During the period of cyanosis the arteries did not regain their normal calibre as might have been expected, at least in their whole extent, and the venous pulsations persisted. Yet the cyanosis of the extremities and the visual troubles alternated so regularly that the diminution of one " infallibly announced the appearance of the other, and this many times in the same day." This went on for several months and then recovery took place. Before the patient left hospital he was free, not only from local cyanosis, but also from the abnormal ocular phenomena, subjective and ophthalmoscopic.

The second case in the *New Researches* was that of a young man who was liable to paroxysms of cyanosis in the hands and face. At the moment when such a paroxysm commenced, he experienced a notable obscuration of sight, but when the cyanosis passed off, vision was restored. The ophthalmoscope revealed narrowing of the arteries of the fundus in the cyanotic period with restoration of calibre when reaction set in. The retinal veins were not observed to pulsate.

A few other cases are on record in which vision was temporaily impaired in connection with Raynaud's disease. Thus in Bland's patient—a maniac who brought on an attack of local asphyxia and gangrene by exposing himself to cold—there was for a time dimness of vision and inability to read, with unusual pallor of the fundus, and the vessels were "blanched and almost indistinct." In Morgan's case the retinal arteries were narrow though vision was good, but after recovering from Raynaud's phenomena and enjoying three months of good health, the patient suffered for a time from severe headache and simultaneous dimness of vision. Stevenson has reported a case where the patient suffered on one occasion from complete loss of sight for some minutes, and on several occasions from dimness of vision, but there is no report of an ophthalmoscopic investigation. Calmette (1877) mentions three malarious patients who were subject to attacks of local asphyxia and also to ocular troubles. The ophthalmoscope revealed in two of them narrowing of the papillary arteries, and in the other pulsation of the veins. In the last, and in one of the former cases, it is reported that the ocular phenomena coincided with the others. The phenomena in the remarkable case recorded by Weiss included marked narrowing of the retinal arteries.

Among other ocular symptoms occasionally noted in Raynaud's disease is **iridoplegia.** This was present in Hutchinson's earliest case (1871). Both pupils were quite immobile, though the left was larger than the right. The nose and the left ear suffered from gangrene. In a case of my own where the left ear became partly gangrenous, the right pupil was larger than the left. Nystagmus has been observed in a mentally weak patient with inherited syphilis (F. Marsh). Either interstitial keratitis or albuminuric retinitis may be associated with Raynaud's phenomena, probably because either inherited syphilis or Bright's disease may be a cause of both vasomotor and ocular symptoms.

Conjunctivitis is sometimes present, but is probably a mere coincidence.

Numerous **Diseases of the skin** are mentioned in the clinical histories of patients with Raynaud's disease. In

L

some instances, the presence of the cutaneous affection (ringworm, molluscum contagiosum, etc.) must be regarded as a mere coincidence.   Other facts, such as the liability in numerous cases to chilblains in early life, point to a constitutional tendency or constitutional weakness.   In a few cases, the patient has been subject to eczema, but it is not at all clear that this association has been other than accidental.   The same is true of bromidrosis.   Hyperidrosis of the extremities has been noted as ceasing in connection with a severe cold, from which the vasomotor affection dated (Mills).   Localized purpura and other cutaneous **Haemorrhages** have occasionally been observed.   West reports a case where a rash, at first scaly and afterwards like erysipelas, appeared on the face.   **Urticaria** is an occasional complication of Raynaud's disease as of its congener paroxysmal haemoglobinuria.   Solis-Cohen reports under the designation " vasomotor ataxia," a series of cases characterized by somewhat widespread phenomena, including not only local asphyxia, but also dermographism (a red streak produced on the skin by very light stroking, and lasting for several or for many minutes), factitious urticaria (produced by a firmer stroke, the reddened part becoming elevated like a wheal in nettlerash), and sometimes teleangiectases on the trunk or limbs.

Cavafy reported in 1883, under the title of "Symmetrical Congestive Mottling of the Skin," two cases which may have been akin to Raynaud's disease.   The patients were unmarried females, aged 22 and 21.   The first had noticed three years previously a reddish mottling which began on the left shoulder, spread down the arm, and afterwards involved the other arm, cheeks, and thighs.   She had rheumatic fever a year before the onset of this condition, but had no cardiac lesion.   She suffered from dyspepsia at

times, and one or two fingers would get numb in cold
weather, but otherwise she enjoyed good health. The
cutaneous markings disappeared on pressure and diminished
with warmth and exercise. They became more conspicuous
under the influence of cold and of menstruation. Ten
months after the original note of her case, she was readmitted
with rheumatic polyarthritis. The mottling of the skin was
present as before, and the patient reported that on two
occasions one of her fingers had suddenly become pale and
numb, and afterwards bluish red and very painful, the
attack lasting about half an hour.

The second patient had suffered for a year and a half
from a similar affection which, beginning at the ankles,
spread to the legs and thighs, and after a year to the arms,
and still later to the trunk. The face was still unaffected
when she came under observation, and for at least nine
months afterwards. The condition varied with the temperature, as in the first case, but was not influenced by
menstruation. Raynaud's phenomena were never noticed,
and the general health was perfect.

But by far the most important cutaneous complication of
Raynaud's disease is **Scleroderma.** Raynaud, in his pathological history of symmetrical gangrene,[1] speaks of the small,
white, hard cicatrices left on the fingers, the slender form
acquired by the digits, the hardness of their tissue, their
shrivelled aspect, and the parchment-like appearance which
may supervene without preceding vesication. In 1872[2] he
says that he has observed the perversion of the capillary
circulation to become associated in course of time with a
condition of skin resembling sclerema, in which case the
normal colour is never restored. " In the space of an hour
one sees the fingers change colour several times. The

[1] *Thesis,* p. 103.   [2] *Nouv. Dict.,* xv., 645.

prevailing tint is a pale greenish gray, which at times gives place to black. The sclerotic thickening involves the fingers and the dorsal aspect of the hands. . . . The fingers remain constantly semiflexed. . . . In a case of this kind which I communicated to P. Horteloup (*Thèse sur la Sclérodermie,* 1865), there was at the same time some thickening and rigidity of the skin of the face."

One of the earliest recorded cases illustrating the connection of the two diseases was that published by Ball in 1872, and regarded by him as a special variety of scleroderma. In the discussion which followed the introduction of this case at the Société Médicale des Hôpitaux, Raynaud claimed it as an example of the disease that now bears his name.

Numerous cases which have since been published in France and Britain abundantly demonstrate the frequent coexistence in one person of the phenomena of the two diseases.[1] It is to be noted, however, that some cases were recorded in France under the title of scleroderma which we should certainly consider to belong rather to Raynaud's group. The following is an example. A girl of 21 began to suffer at the age of 18 from coldness of the hands, which became cyanotic, and were covered with abundant perspiration.

[1] See Brochin, "Sclérodermie et asphyxie locale des extrémités," *Gaz. des Hôpitaux,* 1878, li., 250-251 ; Finlayson, *Glasg. Med. Jour.,* 1881, xvi., 454 ; *Manchester Med. Chron.,* 1885, i., 315-318 ; Colcott Fox (who says that in two of his undoubted cases of generalized scleroderma affecting the hands, both women had long been subject to dead fingers, while one of them continued to have mild attacks of asphyxia of the fingers after the onset of scleroderma), *Clin. Soc. Trans.,* 1885, xviii., 300-306 ; Hutchinson, *Brit. Med. Jour.,* 1887, i., 1149 ; *Arch. of Surg.,* 1891, ii., 30-32 ; *Medical Week,* 1893, i., 100 ; Goldschmidt, *Revue de Méd.,* 1887, vii., 401-419 ; E. Mendel, *Deut. Med. Woch.,* 1890, xvi., 763-764 ; Chauffard, *La France Méd.,* 1895, xlii., 425 ; J. A. H. White, *Lancet,* 1896, i., 1136 ; Fuchs, *Wiener Klin. Woch.,* 1896, ix., 872-877.

Numbness and then pains in the fingers followed. Even if the patient was not exposed to cold, if she experienced any nervousness or emotion, the local asphyxia of the extremities would immediately appear, like the tingling of the fingers felt in the cold of winter. Later on, rigidity of the fingers, with hardening of the skin, set in. Similar phenomena appeared on the face. Phlyctens appeared on the fingers, and the tissues of the latter, even to the bones, underwent atrophy.[1]

It will be understood, then, that either Raynaud's disease or scleroderma may exist by itself for an indefinite time, and that either may be complicated after a time by the supervention of the other. Scleroderma rarely occurs in that form of Raynaud's disease which consists simply in repeated paroxysms of local cyanosis.[2]

A more or less marked tendency to scleroderma was manifested by 13 of the 180 collated cases of Raynaud's disease (7.2 per cent.).[3] These 13 cases were all in females. Whilst both Raynaud's disease and scleroderma affect by preference the female sex, the occurrence of the latter as a complication of the former appears to be relatively still more closely restricted to females.[4] The average age of the 13 cases at the time

[1] Vidal, " De la sclérodermie spontanée," *Gazette des Hôpitaux*, 1878, li., 939.

[2] See Hutchinson, No 89, p. 75. R. Hingston Fox reports a case where scleroderma developed on the face as a sequel to long continued congestion without pallor (No. 52).

[3] Of course other examples of the association are on record, but in these cases Raynaud's phenomena did not predominate to such a degree as to justify their being included in the collection used for statistical purposes.

[4] For cases in males, see Vidal, *Gaz. des Hôp.*, 1878, li., 940 ; Hutchinson, *Arch. of Surg.*, 1891, ii., 30-32.

of reporting was 39 years (maximum 64, minimum 15). But Raynaud's phenomena had begun to show themselves at the average age of 29 (1 to 35 years before publication). One of the patients at least (and perhaps another) was malarious. ·The vasomotor phenomena included local syncope in 12 of the cases if not in all, local asphyxia in 12 or in all, and gangrene in 7. In cases of the kind now under consideration, namely, where Raynaud's phenomena constitute the prevailing type, the sclerotic changes may begin about the same time as the vasomotor symptoms, or a number of years later. They may be confined to the fingers (sclerodactyly), or may extend up the forearms, or may affect the face also, or the face without the limbs; and in time they may become more general. The tendencies to haemoglobinuria and to scleroderma in Raynaud's disease appear to be entirely distinct from one another; I am not aware that they have been observed together.

MORBID ANATOMY.

THOUGH Raynaud's disease does not cause death, and can seldom be regarded as even shortening life, it has been possible to study the morbid anatomy of the disease, partly by the examination of limbs or other parts which have been amputated, whether spontaneously or by the surgeon's art, and partly by autopsies on the bodies of persons who have died from some other disease with which Raynaud's phenomena were associated. And, while it may at once be said that there is no anatomical condition whatever, either gross or minute, that can be looked upon as peculiar to the disease in question, it is nevertheless important to state briefly the appearances that have actually been observed in cases of the kind.

As portions of the extremities undergo dry gangrene, they tend slowly to lose in volume. They become rigid and inelastic, and are of course insensible. Incisions may show that the tissue is yellowish and bloodless, and possessed of a faint cadaveric odour. Firm compression may cause a small quantity of pale bloody fluid to exude, and the microscope may reveal in this fluid white and red corpuscles in various stages of alteration from the normal. Blood taken from such parts and inoculated in gelatine cultures has been found to be sterile (Radziszewski).

(A) *Typical cases of Raynaud's disease, and cases which resemble that affection clinically.*

The following points were noted after death in the case recorded by Solly (1839 and 1840). Sympathetic in the neck, chest and abdomen normal. Both femoral arteries much shrunken, but otherwise the arteries of the stumps normal. Large arteries and veins and the four cavities of the heart filled with dark clotted blood. A small quantity of clear serum in pericardium. Heart somewhat pale, but otherwise normal. Lungs pale. Anaemic but otherwise normal condition of the abdominal viscera. A few small subcutaneous haemorrhages. Great emaciation.

Case ix. in Raynaud's *Thesis* (1862; described in 1861 by Jules Simon in his inaugural dissertation on leucocythaemia) occurred in a woman who also suffered from leukaemia, and who died from exhaustion. The post-mortem revealed enlargement of the spleen, liver, and mesenteric glands. There was a good deal of fat over the heart and in the subcutaneous tissue. The pericardium and pleurae contained small quantities of fluid. The heart was pale and soft. The lungs were healthy and non-adherent. The intestine and the brain were healthy in appearance, and with the exception of a small subserous fibroid, the uterus also was normal. The capsule of the spleen was thickened, and the organ itself was firm and elastic. Microscopically there were observed scanty, deformed red corpuscles, very abundant white corpuscles, and numerous fusiform fibres, cells, and nuclei indicative of connective tissue overgrowth. The arteries were healthy and patent. Raynaud detached one of the upper limbs, injected the brachial artery, and carefully dissected the branches arising from this vessel, but could find nothing either in their calibre or in their shape to account for the symptoms from which the patient had suffered.

In Begg's case (1870) there was no ossification of the arteries, arteritis, venous obstruction, disease or weakness of the heart, want of nervous energy or cachexia. The tibial arteries in the mortified and amputated lower extremities were (contrary to expectation) pervious. The vessels of the upper limbs were not examined. Begg attributed the disease to " organic changes in the capillaries."

In one of the cases recorded by Richard (1880), where Raynaud's phenomena supervened in connection with enteric fever, pulsation was absent for a time from the posterior tibial arteries, and the boy lost several phalanges from his toes. In one of these toes, brownish, homogeneous, non-stratified clots were found in all the small vessels, but there was no endarteritis. Richard, accepting Raynaud's doctrine of symmetrical gangrene, inferred that the coagulation was secondary, and that the primary condition depended upon the spinal cord.

Roques (1883) described a case where the vasomotor symptoms were superadded to those of Bright's disease, which appeared to date from a confinement. The postmortem revealed splenization of the right lung, great enlargement of the heart, a normal state of the mitral valve, vegetations on the aortic curtains, granular kidneys, a normal condition of the radial and pedal arteries, and absence of emboli in the arteries and of infarctions of the viscera.

One of Affleck's patients (1888) had her foot amputated by Syme's operation two months from the onset of the symptoms. The anterior half was mummified. The vessels were found to be healthy. The internal plantar nerve at the part furthest removed from the seat of gangrene had suffered extensively from neuritis, and was now degenerating.

In Collier's case (1889) symptoms akin to those of Raynaud's malady, and others which might be accounted for by subacute peritonitis, set in about the same time, and led up to death in the fourth month of the disease. Portions of the four inner toes of the left foot had become gangrenous. The heart was found to weigh only 4 oz., but its muscle was firm and healthy, and its valves were normal. A few old pleuritic adhesions were present on both sides. The lungs, stomach and duodenum were healthy. The small intestine was found to be slightly stenosed in three places, viz., (1) six inches from the duodenum, (2) in the lower jejunum, and (3) in the ileum. At the first of these situations the mucous membrane was smooth and devoid of valvulae conniventes over a length of four inches. There was no ulceration, and no cicatrization could be detected to account for the narrowing. The great bowel was healthy. The peritoneum presented numerous old, firm adhesions. The serous coat of the small intestine was hyperaemic, and in the abdominal cavity, especially about the origin of the coeliac axis, there were about 8 oz. of yellow pus. The uterus was healthy. Recent superficial haemorrhages were seen in the ovaries. The pelvic cavity and its remaining contents were normal. The liver was pale. The spleen weighed 1 oz., and was surrounded by old adhesions. The kidneys weighed 3½ oz. each, but were otherwise normal. The brain and cord appeared healthy to the unaided eye. The vessels of the left leg were healthy and pervious, and the tibial nerves were also healthy. Microscopic examination showed that the muscle of the heart, sections of the spinal cord taken at various levels, and longitudinal and transverse sections of the left tibial nerves all presented healthy characters. The skin near the gangrenous toes was normal, with the exception of slight endarteritis of the small vessels nearest the dead tissue; but this condition, Collier remarks, was " probably a result of the thrombosis of vessels at the so-called line of demarcation." He thinks that the clinical and post-mortem evidence showed that gangrene in this case was not due to disease of the vessels or to embolism or thrombosis. He suggests that the irritation of the great abdominal sympathetic system caused the arterial spasm which called forth the paroxysmal symptoms in the extremities and the gangrene of the toes.

In one of Barlow's cases (1889),[1] amputation was performed at midthigh. The anterior and posterior tibial, the plantar and the muscular nerves of the amputated limb were free from disease (axis-cylinders well marked, no segmentation of myelin, and no increase of connective tissue in perineurium or endoneurium). The arteries were thrombosed, but it was difficult to say whether this condition had arisen previously or subsequently to the gangrene. There was some thickening of the outer and middle coats, but this appeared to be recent, and there was no ordinary atheroma or calcification. The thickening of the walls was at least as great in the case of the veins as in that of the arteries.

A patient whose case was recorded by Colcott Fox (1885 and 1889) suffered from diabetes and eventually also from albuminuria and general anasarca. There was hypertrophy of the heart, enlargement of the liver, pulmonary emphysema, chronic bronchitis and pleurisy, together with general atheroma of the medium sized and larger arteries, including the arteries at the base of the brain.

A girl of 17 came under the care of Samuel West after being subject for about a year to attacks of local syncope

[1] No. 12, p. 125.

of the four extremities. During the latter half of that
period local asphyxia followed local syncope, and the
patient suffered besides from a scaly eruption on the face.
There was some superficial gangrene of the digits. About
a fortnight before admission, the rash on the face assumed
an appearance closely resembling that of erysipelas.
Several weeks later there was considerable fever, and she
died in the third week after coming under observation. So
far as the vasomotor disease was concerned, the post-mortem
results were negative. Pneumonia was found to involve
the upper half of the right lung. The other organs were
healthy. The radial artery and radial and median nerves
at the wrist were all normal microscopically, and nothing
abnormal was discovered in the medulla.

A case recorded by Dehio is of particular interest since
the narrator, with apparent justice, claims that it offers
a striking proof that Raynaud's symmetrical gangrene can
occur as an independent and typical disease in persons
otherwise perfectly healthy. The patient was a woman
of 31, and the disease followed a severe fright due to an
assault at night by several men. There was extensive loss,
by gangrene, of phalanges of the fingers, and the dead
parts were amputated seven months after the onset of the
disease. In the living soft parts removed by operation
from the left ring and right index fingers close to the
dead parts, and accordingly influenced by the process of
elimination, the *epidermis*, including the Malpighian layer,
was unaltered. The *cutis* and subcutaneous fatty tissue
showed a slight inflammatory small celled infiltration,
especially in the lymph sheaths of the larger and smaller
vessels, and also, though in a less marked degree, in the
neighbourhood of the nerve twigs. The *vessels* themselves
were the seat of a fibrous endarteritis and endophlebitis.

The veins on the whole were less changed than the arteries, but even the former had their intima so thickened in some instances as to reduce the lumen by about a half. The lumen in some vessels was completely obstructed by partially organized thrombi, but here, too, the fibrous thickening of the intima was distinct. The digital *nerves* were also much changed. Most of the fibres had perished, so that only isolated axis-cylinders and medullary sheaths were recognizable, and even these were narrowed. Their room was occupied to some extent by spaces, but principally by connective tissue thickening of the endoneurium. The perineurium of single nerve bundles and of the whole nerve trunk was thickened. A few nucleated round cells were seen in the supporting connective tissue, but these were not sufficiently numerous to constitute an infiltration of the nerves.

Hale White's case has but a doubtful right to be ranged alongside the group now under consideration. A girl who had suffered for some years from cardiac symptoms and occasional cyanosis of the extremities was seized with gangrene of portions of the right upper and both lower limbs. She died from failure of the heart, and the conditions observed after death included not only serious cardiac, pericardial, pulmonary and pleural lesions, but also embolism of the right brachial artery. On the other hand, the posterior tibial artery and the dorsal artery of the foot on both sides contained no emboli and were otherwise normal. The plantar and posterior tibial nerves were found on microscopic examination to be free from any primary neuritis, any slight changes that they showed being accounted for by the proximity of the gangrene.

Durante reports two cases of fatal symmetrical asphyxia of the extremities (one ending in extensive gangrene) in children of syphilitic parents. A post-mortem in one of these cases revealed nothing particular. Durante considers the disease to be not syphilitic but purely neurotic.[1]

(B) *Non-typical cases of Raynaud's disease, and cases which, though not resembling Raynaud's disease clinically, have been adduced in support of a theory of that affection different from the one proposed by Raynaud himself.*

An epileptic and insane woman, aged 26, who was under the care of Wiglesworth, suffered from chronic Bright's disease with secondary hypertrophy of the heart. She had lost by mortification considerable portions of the digits of the hands and the entire right great toe. There was atrophy of the thenar, hypothenar and interosseous muscles of the hands. Spontaneous ulceration of various digits took place under observation, commencing with dry scabs, which were always accompanied by burning pain, and left slowly healing ulcers; one slough formed over the right olecranon. This patient died rather suddenly after a fit within a year and a half of her admission to the asylum, and the autopsy furnished the following facts :—The pia mater was slightly thickened. The cerebral cortex, cerebellum, pons, medulla, spinal cord and peripheral nerves were all normal to the unaided eye. The kidneys were granular; the valves of the heart were normal. Microscopically, nothing noteworthy was detected in the spinal cord. Thirteen nerves in all were examined from all four limbs, and no one of these was quite normal. Most of them showed well-marked changes in the shape of overgrowth of fibrous elements and degeneration of nervous elements. The epineurium and

---

[1] Quoted in *Brit. Med. Jour.*, 1898, ii. *epit.*, 285.

perineurium were greatly thickened, the latter often encroaching on the nerve bundles. The perineural lymph space was often broadened. The endoneurium was overgrown and contained an undue number of nuclei. The nerve tubules were partly degenerated, the myelin sheaths being atrophied. The posterior tibial was the nerve most affected in each lower limb. The left median nerve was the one most damaged in the upper limbs. It could not be positively said whether the degeneration of nerve tubules or the interstitial growth was primary. The walls of many of the vessels were thickened,—no doubt, as Wiglesworth remarks, in connection with the renal disease.

Another interesting case is recorded by Rakhmaninoff (1892). A joiner, aged 17, was admitted with gangrene which in the course of three days had involved both feet and the lower parts of the legs. He had never recovered complete health after an attack of exanthematic typhus two years before. He had suffered from anaemia and frequent false sensations of cold in the hands and feet, and occasionally for several minutes at a time from numbness in the fingers and toes. This numbness was followed by convulsive agitations of the muscles of the hand and forearm with lancinating pains. The attacks came at irregular intervals,—it might be several times a day, or only once in a week or even in a month. He suffered for a time also from thoracic and abdominal pains with severe general sweating. Three days before admission, he felt cold and pain in the upper limbs, the cold being replaced after some hours by intolerable heat. At the same time the dorsa of the feet became red and swollen ; this condition extended upwards, the lowest parts became livid, and by the next day sensation in the toes was lost and walking was impossible. Shivering and fever followed, and gangrene was soon definitely established. The legs were amputated four weeks later, but though the wounds did well, the patient suffered from high fever with pain in the side and cough, and he died in coma a fortnight afterwards.

At the post-mortem, the brain and cord were found to be oedematous, but otherwise normal even to the microscope. Fibrinous pleurisy, grey hepatization of the entire right lung, oedema of the left lung, and enlargement of the spleen, were among the other conditions noted. The great nerve trunks of the extremities, as well as the muscular and cutaneous branches, were examined microscopically and were all found to be the seat of degenerative neuritis. The myelin was broken up, and the sheath of Schwann was empty at some places. Some axis-cylinders had undergone segmentation; others had disappeared. In the nerve trunks, the interstitial tissue was increased in amount and infiltrated with cells. The small vessels outside and inside the perivascular sheaths had their walls much thickened, and some were quite obliterated. The changes observed were more marked in the lower than in the upper limbs, and were greater in the small twigs than in the large trunks. Rakhmaninoff regarded this case as an infectious multiple neuritis starting from the typhus fever.

A good deal of attention (more perhaps than the circumstances now warrant) has been attracted by a case recorded by Mounstein in 1884. A man, aged 51, had his right leg amputated for gangrene which, beginning two months previously, had brought about loss of the first, second, and fifth toes, as well as patches of skin on the remaining toes and on the heel, instep and dorsum of that foot. The patient died a week after the operation. The vessels of the limb had no abnormal contents; only at the border of the lesion were microscopic hyaline thrombi found in the capillaries.

The posterior tibial artery presented several calcareous or bony patches which, however, had not induced thrombosis. The posterior tibial nerve was much thicker in its lower than in its upper part, and had a translucent appearance from loss of myelin. The peroneal nerve was in the same state. The microscope revealed loss of myelin and increase of connective tissue, especially near the gangrenous part, with a great increase of nuclei in the accompanying small vessels. The nerves of the healthy leg were altered in a similar manner though to a less degree. The nerve-roots connected with the lumbar region of the cord were inflamed on the left side only. The brain and cord were anaemic. Nothing noteworthy was detected on examination of the other viscera.

In a second case reported by Mounstein, a man, aged 47, had senile gangrene of the left foot. Thrombosis of both tibial arteries was the cause of the gangrene, and yet the nerves of the affected part were inflamed. And so, says Hochenegg (from whose essay these two cases are quoted), we must distinguish primary neuritis causing gangrene from secondary neuritis due to extension of inflammation along the nerves from the line of demarcation.

Hochenegg narrates the case of a man, aged 51, who at the age of 45 had been suddenly seized with weakness of the right lower limb, which gradually became worse. Some time after this, but still long before admission, the sense of touch became impaired, and at length he could not manipulate small objects. Latterly there was great loss of general strength. A few days before admission, the left hand and forearm became swollen and reddish blue, without pain and without apparent cause. On admission it was noted that he had marked scoliosis and enlargement of the head. The right leg was not so strong as the left. The upper half of

M

the body, from the neck downwards, was completely anal-
gesic, and was almost devoid of the sense of temperature.
The upper limbs, too, were in great part anaesthetic.
The patient died of collapse three days after admission.
The post-mortem revealed enormous distension of the
cerebral ventricles. Cavities were found in the cervical
and upper half or more of the dorsal region of the spinal
cord. The right lateral column was degenerated as
far down as the commencement of the lumbar enlargement. In the medulla there was degeneration of the
gracile and cuneate columns and of most of the right
lateral cerebellar tract. The pyramids and grey matter
were unaltered. No change was found in the nerves
of the brachial plexuses or of the arms, except atrophy of
a few nerve fibres, secondarily, it was supposed, to the
spinal lesion. Certainly there were no inflammatory or
recent degenerative changes. There was no atrophy or
degeneration in the left supinator group, and the vessels
were normal and without thrombi.

Pitres and Vaillard (1885) report the case of a woman,
aged 24, who, never able to learn reading or writing,
became still feebler intellectually when she reached the
age of 18. Speech became hesitating, tremors and stiffness involved the limbs, walking became impossible, and
she became demented and bedridden. A week before
admission, the feet were observed to be cold, blue and
insensible, but the patient made no complaint. Both feet
became gangrenous. Sloughs formed on the buttocks
and afterwards in many other parts. Death occurred two
months after admission. Great thickening of the cranial
bones, the presence of abundant clear fluid in the lateral
ventricles, intimate adhesion of the pia to the cortex,
especially in the sphenoidal and fronto-parietal regions,

and enlargement of and fatty change in the liver were the gross morbid appearances detected at the necropsy. The spinal meninges, lungs, heart, spleen, kidneys, genitals, stomach and intestines, aorta, and the arteries and veins of the lower limbs were normal. The nerves of the lower limbs appeared healthy to the naked eye. The microscope revealed a slight diffuse sclerosis in the dorso-lumbar region of the cord involving the antero-lateral columns in their entirety, and the posterior columns, with the exception of their anterior fifth. The commissures, canal and anterior horns were normal. On the right side, the median, cubital, crural, great sciatic and internal and external popliteal nerves were normal; but the peroneal cutaneous nerve was much altered. It contained a number of healthy fibres, but many also that presented varicosities filled with droplets of myelin and of protoplasm, and also nerve sheaths completely empty. The anterior tibial nerve in the middle of the leg had suffered still more profoundly; it did not contain a single healthy fibre. The nerve fibres had all lost their medullary sheaths, and were represented by sheaths furnished with numerous nuclei and varicose dilatations, containing granular protoplasm and drops of myelin. Between the fibres there were numerous leucocytes and fat droplets. The posterior tibial nerve near the gangrenous part was altered in a similar fashion and did not show a single normal fibre. On the left side, the median, cubital, crural, great sciatic and internal and external popliteal nerves were healthy. The anterior tibial was but slightly affected at its upper end, but at its lower part most of the fibres were degenerated. The posterior tibial, as on the right side, was quite destitute of healthy fibres.

In a second case reported by Pitres and Vaillard, a woman, aged 56, whom poverty had driven to rag-picking, began to suffer from anorexia and insomnia, was easily fatigued, and ceased to feel the ground with her feet. Four months later, after she had been walking during part of the night, her soles became blistered, and at the same time troublesome diarrhoea set in. Two months after this, and a few days before her admission, the feet were swollen and painful, and covered on the dorsa with reddish spots. In the course of some days the feet became frankly gangrenous, and death ensued from asthenia. Nothing remarkable was found in the brain, cord, lungs, liver, kidneys, or heart. The arteries and veins of the lower limbs were normal. The nerves of the lower limbs were normal to the naked eye, except that both internal plantars were somewhat violet in colour, whilst the vessels accompanying these nerves were greatly dilated. Microscopically the left internal plantar nerve was found to be destitute of normal fibres; some were represented simply by sheaths with scattered nuclei, but many were less severely damaged. The lower ends of the left posterior and anterior tibial nerves were also severely affected. The internal and external popliteal and external saphenous nerves on the same side were but slightly altered. The lower end of the right posterior tibial contained nó normal fibres. The right anterior tibial was seriously diseased. The external popliteal was but slightly, and the internal popliteal and sciatic nerves were not at all affected.

Legrain[1] (1896) mentions the case of a male patient who suffered first from pain for several weeks, and then from a violet and blackish discoloration of the feet and lower third of the legs. The limbs were amputated at an interval of a month. In the amputated portion, above

[1] "Gangrène massive symétrique des extrémités inférieures," *Ann. de dermat. et de syphiligraphie*, 1896, vii., 1090, 1091.

the level of the gangrene, there was found arteritis obliterans in one leg, and mesoperiarteritis in the other. The peripheral nerves were reported as being in a state which almost amounted to the neuritis described by Pitres and Vaillard.

Two cases reported by Déjérine and Leloir in 1881 may be briefly alluded to here, though they have no relation to Raynaud's disease. The purpose of the research conducted by these investigators was to demonstrate anatomically that cutaneous gangrene may be due to primary peripheral neuritis. In one case, a woman aged 49, who had suffered from chronic rheumatism, died from cachexia with diarrhoea, sloughing over the sacrum, etc. The cutaneous nerves in the region of the slough, and also, though in a much less degree, the intramuscular nerves, were the seat of atrophic parenchymatous inflammation. The spinal cord and its anterior and posterior roots were healthy. The other patient was a woman, aged 44, who had locomotor ataxy, and suffered from sloughing of the buttock. The cutaneous nerves of the region bordering on the slough were diseased.

Three cases quoted in Raynaud's *Thesis* (Cases xvii., xviii. and xix.) have been already mentioned in connection with cardio-vascular disease, and need not be further discussed here. The original reports were published very many years ago, and details that would now be regarded as most important are unfortunately not available.

PATHOLOGY.

RAYNAUD, it will be remembered, setting aside structural diseases of the heart and vessels, embolism, diabetes and ergotism as inadequate to explain the facts, though admittedly capable of operating as contributory causes or modifying influences, supposed (1) that local syncope and asphyxia are due to spasm of the small vessels, this spasm if sufficiently prolonged leading to gangrene of the part deprived of blood; and (2) that this spasm of the vessels depends upon an abnormal excitability of the vasomotor centres in the spinal cord. With regard to the first of these propositions, the dependence of local syncope and local cyanosis upon a disordered innervation of the vascular system has scarcely ever been seriously questioned, for O. Weber's view that local syncope was due not so much to spasm of the vessels as to contraction of the smooth muscle of the skin has obtained practically no support.[1]

Fortunately we are able to set out with a few propositions

[1] Quoted by Hochenegg, *op. cit.* p. 16. Hochenegg himself thinks that local syncope is brought about in the manner indicated by Raynaud, but that frequently there is also simultaneous contraction of the musculature of the skin, the latter accounting for the subjective feeling of cold (*ib.*, p. 57).

which correspond either to actual fact or to universally accepted theory. Thus we may postulate that (1) local syncope, in its simple forms, if not in every case, is the result of contraction of the small arteries; for section of a vasoconstrictor nerve causes loss of arterial tone and flushing, whilst stimulation of the peripheral portion of such a nerve causes contraction of the vessels and bloodlessness of the part. (2) In exceptional cases of Raynaud's disease, the spasm may extend to the larger arteries; for in such cases the pulsation of the radial at the wrist may be almost imperceptible, and, moreover, contraction of the central artery of the retina has been actually seen in connection with this disease. (3) Contraction of the larger superficial veins may occur, for this has been actually seen. It was repeatedly noticed in a case described by Weiss (see p. 83), and if anything could make this assertion more incontrovertible, it would be a comparison of the passage quoted on pp. 83, 84 from Barlow, describing what he saw in one of his patients, with the following which is taken from a recent text-book of physiology: "Stimulation of the peripheral end of the cut sciatic nerve, the crural artery being tied, causes the constriction of the superficial veins of the hind limb. The contraction begins soon after the commencement of the stimulation, and usually goes so far as to obliterate the lumen of the vein. Often the contraction begins nearer the proximal portion of the vein and advances toward the periphery. More commonly, however, it is limited to band-like constrictions between which the vein is filled with blood. After stimulation ceases, the constrictions gradually disappear." [1] To these three propositions we may add that (4) almost certainly the small veins are the seat of spasm in many cases of Raynaud's phenomena; for not only

[1] *American Text-book of Physiology*, edited by Howell, 1896, p. 485.

would analogy lead us to believe this, but the occurrence of cyanosis, without syncope and without apparent contraction of the larger veins, can scarcely be accounted for in any other way.

Raynaud's sketch of what happens in the paroxysm is a good starting-point for the discussion of the modern doctrine of the disease. " It commences by a spasm of the capillary vessels. . . . In the simplest cases, those in which the malady remains, if I may so say, in a rough state, the exaggerated peristaltic contraction of the capillaries drives the blood before it, the extremities become pale, withered looking, and insensible. This is the ' dead finger.' But this phenomenon does not persist long enough for gangrene to follow. To contraction succeeds relaxation, the circulation is re-established, and everything returns to the normal state after a period of reaction more or less painful. Such is *local syncope*, in which the venules participate in the contraction of the arterioles.

" Local asphyxia is only a more advanced condition. After an initial period of capillary spasm there occurs a period of reaction, but it is incomplete reaction. The vessels which return first to their primary calibre, or even beyond, are naturally those which present in their structure the fewest contractile elements, namely the venules. At the moment when these are opened, the arterioles being still closed, the venous blood, which had been at first driven back into the great trunks of the dark blood system, flows again into the finest vascular divisions, and then the extremities will take on that tint varying from blue to black, which is a certain index of the presence of venous blood in the capillary network. This explains two phenomena to which I have called attention in speaking of the symptoms. The first is that the cyanotic tint of the extremities succeeds in general to an extreme pallor, or, in other terms, that syncope precedes asphyxia. The second is that, at the outset at least, the asphyxiated parts have not that very deep tint which one observes following on a violent constriction of a limb; in this last case, in fact, there is venous blood extending into arteries of a calibre which is relatively considerable. In local asphyxia the venous reflux does not go beyond the capillary network properly so-called; it results therefrom that the colour which is observed has a certain transparence; it is a mixture of cyanosis and pallor."

"In the meantime the *vis a tergo* having ceased its action on the venous side, the return circulation is no longer favoured, except by the causes which in the physiological state are limited to the part of accessory conditions; such are the muscular contraction of the limbs, the play of the valves, the aspiration exercised by the thoracic cavity, etc. Consequently the blood stagnates even in the great venous trunks, and then are produced along with a very slight oedematous suffusion those subcutaneous livid venous markings which have been rightly compared to those which the prolonged use of warming pans produces."[1]

In local syncope, then, there is undoubtedly contraction of the arterioles. Probably there is often simultaneous contraction of the venules, particularly in cases where the ischaemia persists for a considerable time. For if the venules were not contracted, venous blood would soon flow back into the capillaries, as it does in a haemorrhagic infarction, and make the affected part cyanotic. Even in the state of local syncope, the pallor is apt to be dusky —a fact which is to be accounted for in two ways; first,

[1] *Thesis,* pp. 143-145, *Nouv. Dict.* xv., 651 sqq.

by reflux of venous blood, as just described, and second, by the presence in the capillaries of a small quantity of blood, which, being either stationary or in extremely sluggish movement, is sufficiently long in contact with the tissues to become de-oxygenized. Raynaud's theory as to the manner in which syncope is replaced by asphyxia, namely, by relaxation of the venules occurring sooner than that of the arterioles, is the best available, and has the merit of accounting for the facts in cases where a well marked stage of syncope leads up to a well marked stage of cyanosis.

The frequent cases where local cyanosis sets in almost suddenly without preceding syncope, are to be accounted for by spasm of the venules. This does not absolutely exclude the participation of the arterioles in some feeble degree, but if there is from the outset lividity without pallor, we must assume a cause acting distally to the arterioles, and contraction of the venules is not only the simplest, but in itself a highly probable explanation. This theory is supported by the fact that superficial veins large enough to be examined by the naked eye have been actually seen to contract in a few cases of local cyanosis ; naturally the contraction of the larger veins will accentuate the asphyxia brought about by spasm of the venules. To show how unsafe it is to exclude the arteries, it may be mentioned that in one case of Barlow's, where there was cyanosis without syncope, and where the dorsal veins of the hands could be seen to undergo constriction in a characteristic fashion, the radial pulse became almost imperceptible during the paroxysms, although in the intervals it was normal. The way in which the phenomena vary in course of an attack—syncope leading up to asphyxia, or asphyxia leading up to syncope—suggests that a wave of contraction may pass along the vessels in the peripheral field of the circulation (arterioles, capillaries, venules), just as Barlow saw a wave of contraction pass along the veins of the hands.

The natural consequence of these vascular spasms is the cutting off of the *vis a tergo* from the venous side of the circulation, and this, as Raynaud rightly observes, accounts for the stagnation in the large veins, the livid marbling of the surface, and the oedema that is sometimes noticeable.

An occasional variety of local asphyxia is that characterized by redness instead of lividity of the parts. In this case the small vessels are full—a result, perhaps, as Weiss suggests,[1] of overaction of the dilating mechanism.

Local syncope, asphyxia and gangrene have been considered in such detail in an earlier part of this essay, that little remains to be added with regard to their phenomena. The defects of sensation—tactile, painful, thermic and muscular—are manifestly due to the imperfect nature of the blood-supply to the nerves concerned with such functions in the affected parts. Raynaud asks whether the spontaneous pains of local syncope and asphyxia are directly due to the vascular contraction,—a painful cramp of the vessels.[2] The pain would then be comparable to that of colic. But the frequent absence of pain in local syncope makes this explanation unsatisfactory, and a much more likely one is that the pain results from the influence exerted locally upon the nerves by the blood, which is defective in quantity or in quality, or in both respects. The local temperature naturally falls as the stagnating blood cools. The meaning of the changes that have been observed in the blood itself will be best considered in connection with the subject of haemoglobinuria.

[1] No. 196, p. 391. [2] *Thesis*, p. 145, note.

If we accept the theory that local syncope and asphyxia are due to vascular spasm, we need have little difficulty in admitting that the cause of asphyxia, if its operation be sufficiently prolonged, will also produce gangrene. This is not denying that the trophic influence of the local nerves may be perverted by the morbid state of the parts, and may thus take a share in the production of tissue necrosis; but the astonishing manner in which extremely asphyxiated parts may regain their normal health suggests that all that is wanted for this is a restoration of the calibre of the blood-vessels.

It scarcely needs to be stated that the phenomena of Raynaud's disease must be brought about through the agency of the nervous system. The widespread and often symmetrical distribution of the symptoms; their frequent association with other neuroses; the readiness with which they respond to emotional conditions; the frequency with which they depend upon causes acting either generally, or on the nervous system in particular; and the fact that these phenomena may sometimes be removed or otherwise influenced by agencies acting upon remote parts of the body, together with what we know of the normal physiology of the vasomotor system, preclude us from regarding the disease as limited to the parts in which its principal phenomena are manifested. It might be wrong—and for our present purpose it is quite unnecessary—to deny that when the vessels in a given limited area change their calibre on the local application of heat or cold, this result is due directly to the muscular walls of the vessels, or to the minute nerve-ganglia in or beside these walls; but a local change of this kind is a phenomenon of perfect health, and does not constitute Raynaud's disease. There can be no doubt that even in those cases of Raynaud's malady where the phenomena are of but limited distribution, the nervous system comes into play. Phenomena almost exactly the same may be induced by lesions involving vasomotor nerves, as for instance compression by a tumour; but in such a case we should expect the vasomotor disturbance to confine itself to the territory belonging to the nerves involved, though it must be admitted that vasomotor disturbances appear to be capable of radiating widely just as sensory ones are well known to do.

In most cases, however, and in practically all characteristic examples, the combination of symptoms compels us to look for a cause more general or central than such a lesion as that just indicated ; and so we come to the second proposition implied in Raynaud's theory, one that has not been accepted with as little demur as the first. At first sight several possibilities appear to lie open to us. There is first Raynaud's theory that the spasm of the vessels depends upon an abnormal excitability of the vasomotor centres in the spinal cord. Overaction of these centres, he said, might be confined to a particular region of the cord. The marked symmetry of the lesions suggested that they originated in a discharge which started from the cord, either spontaneously or reflexly, and radiated thence to the extremities by the vascular nerves. The disease therefore was a neurosis, and the abnormal discharges of the spinal centres might, Raynaud suggested, be called forth by the immediate action upon these centres of the phlegmasic state, poisons in the blood with an elective action upon such centres, etc. ; or they might be called forth reflexly by irritation of the generative organs in the female, but more frequently by impressions upon the cutaneous nerves of temperature.[1]   Raynaud found

[1] *Nouv. Dict.*, 1872, xv., 655, 656 ; *New Researches*, 1874, pp. 155, 181-3.

strong support for his theory in the striking improvement undergone by several of his patients who were treated by the application of continuous electrical currents to the spinal cord, with or without galvanism of the affected limbs.

It will be seen that this doctrine of Raynaud's is a comprehensive one, recognizing as it does at least three factors: (1) overexcitability of the vasomotor centres; (2) stimulation of these centres by poisons in the blood, and (3) stimulation of these centres reflexly by agents acting on the periphery. Some writers, however, have considered it insufficient, and have suggested that **peripheral neuritis** is one, if not the principal, element in the gangrene of Raynaud's disease. The evidence is both anatomical and clinical. The *anatomical evidence* has been given in detail but without discussion in the preceding section. The first of these writers referred to was Mounstein (1884). His patient was a man of 51, who had gangrene of the right leg; there was neuritis in both legs, and this was more advanced on the side of the gangrene. As detracting from the importance of this case it must be noted that the clinical history is incomplete; that the gangrene, being unilateral, did not conform to Raynaud's type, and that the posterior tibial artery of the affected limb was diseased.

Pitres and Vaillard (1885) are utterly opposed to the theory that vascular constriction leads to gangrene, and say that in reading the cases collected by Raynaud one is struck by the constant presence of signs whose relationship with true neuritis is well known; and they instance pains, phlyctens, trophic changes in the skin, and loss or dystrophy of the nails. Their argument is far from convincing, but they cite two cases in support of it. Gangrene of both feet occurred in a young woman who was found

after death to have ventricular dropsy, chronic perien-
cephalitis, slight diffuse sclerosis of the spinal cord, and
peripheral neuritis in the gangrenous limbs. In the second
case, a woman of 56 suffered from gangrene of both feet,
and neuritis was found after death in the affected limbs. But
neither of these cases resembled Raynaud's disease clinically. Pitres and Vaillard hold that the neuritis preceded
and determined the gangrene, but they practically admit
that this is merely a presumption. They anticipate the
objection that the neuritis may have been secondary to
the gangrenous process, by saying that in cases of gangrene
of vascular origin, severe neuritis is not found in the peripheral nerves above the mortified parts, and they instance
the case of a man, aged 72, who died on the day following
an attack of hemiplegia and insensibility. Portions of
both feet were cold, blue and insensible on admission, a
day before the fatal attack. The anterior and posterior
tibial and the peroneal arteries were obliterated on both
sides by clots which came, it is said, from the aorta. The
nerves of the affected parts were normal. Obviously the
duration of the gangrene (if it amounted to that) was too
short in this case to entitle us to conclude that gangrene
does not lead to neuritis in the region of the affected
part. Besides, we may set against this argument the actual
facts from a second case recorded by Mounstein.[1] A man
had gangrene of the left foot in consequence of thrombosis
of both tibial arteries ; the nerves of the affected part were
inflamed. Legrain's case, quoted in the last section (p. 180),
also shows that the vessels and nerves are liable to suffer
together.

Hochenegg (1885) agrees with Pitres and Vaillard that in
their two cases the gangrene was the result of the changes

----

[1] Quoted by Hochenegg, *loc. cit.*, p. 39.

in the nerves, but he fully recognizes that the theory of constriction of arterioles and venules accounts for local syncope and asphyxia, and that even symmetrical gangrene may be a functional disorder, as a classical illustration of which he quotes the case recorded by Weiss.

So far, therefore, we may say that it is by no means demonstrated by the cases quoted that neuritis is a cause of gangrene, but even if we admitted that it were, the argument is not relevant, except as an analogy, to the case of Raynaud's disease, inasmuch as the cases quoted were not fair examples of that malady.

In the case recorded by Wiglesworth in 1887, there was peripheral neuritis, but the walls of many of the vessels were thickened, and there was also muscular atrophy, which is not usual in Raynaud's disease. Rakhmaninoff's case was another where gangrene occurred in connection with peripheral neuritis, but some small vessels had their walls much thickened and others were obliterated. Manifestly the nerves may have suffered in consequence of the vasa nervorum being diseased and obstructed.[1] But neither of these two cases was a typical example of Raynaud's malady from the clinical point of view.

Dehio's case appears to have been a genuine example of the disease, but as the dead parts were amputated as late as seven months after the onset, it is not surprising that changes were found in both vessels and nerves close to the dead tissue. In any case, Dehio himself declines to accept the theory of Pitres and Vaillard; he regards the nerve degeneration as secondary to the gangrene, and

---

[1] Defrance mentions a case of (non-symmetrical) gangrene with pains and paresis. The only degenerated nerves were those in the territory of diseased nutrient vessels, and the most degenerated nerve was distributed to the slough (*op. cit.*, p. 34).

believes in the "nervous central origin" of the disease in his own case as in that of others.

It is certain, however, that gangrene may occur in Raynaud's disease without neuritis. Thus in one of Barlow's cases, the nerves of the amputated limb were free from disease. The arteries were thrombosed, but whether this took place before or after the gangrene was not clear, and there was no atheroma or calcification. In Collier's case there was slight endarteritis near the dead tissue—a result probably of the changes at the line of demarcation—but the vessels otherwise and the nerves of the limb were healthy. In West's case (where, however, the gangrene was but superficial) no disease was discovered in either vessels or nerves.

In short, Raynaud's gangrene may occur without neuritis, and apparently without either arterial disease or neuritis. Sometimes neuritis is found in connection with gangrene, but a large proportion of those cases are not characteristic cases of Raynaud's disease, and, whether or no, it has not been proved that the neuritis is not secondary to, or part of, rather than the cause of, the gangrene.

But, it may be urged, Raynaud's disease may be a neuritis of the vasomotor nerves. The answer to this is that in those cases resembling Raynaud's malady where neuritis was actually observed, we cannot suppose that the inflammation was confined to the vasomotor nerves, whilst with regard to cases where neuritis was not found, anatomical evidence is awanting.

The *clinical evidence* in favour of neuritis is that vasomotor phenomena are observed in cases where neuritis is known to be present. Thus in the early stage of alcoholic paralysis there may be paroxysms of local syncope and local axphyxia ; and, in severe cases, gangrene

N

of tissue may actually occur. In leprosy and perhaps beri-beri, neuritis appears to be an important factor in the production of gangrene, which may moreover be symmetrical. But even if the vasomotor phenomena of alcoholic neuritis depend upon the neuritis—and it is quite possible that they depend either on nutritional changes in the central nervous system, or on the action of the morbid blood-state upon the central nervous system —the two diseases, if characteristic examples are taken, bear no comparison with one another. The muscular wasting and paralysis of neuritis are rarely met with in Raynaud's disease, and when they do occur are attributable to some associated condition. Raynaud's disease may occur in characteristic form without pain, and may for long be represented by a series of paroxysms of vasomotor disturbance with complete health in the intervals. We can scarcely imagine neuritis setting in as the result of a severe fright, and, although persisting indefinitely, only manifesting itself at longer or shorter intervals by paroxysms of local syncope or asphyxia, with apparently complete health between the paroxysms. The characteristic features of neuritis are, as a rule, absent in Raynaud's disease, and the tendency presented by the latter, at least in its milder forms, to persist during many years in a strictly paroxysmal form, the symptoms being completely absent in the intervals, separates it altogether from neuritis. The frequent association of Raynaud's malady with neuroses, such as epilepsy and mania, and with paroxysmal haemoglobinuria, is strongly in favour of Raynaud's theory as opposed to that of neuritis. At the same time, Nature rarely makes a broad line of demarcation between diseases, and it may be freely admitted that some chronic cases of local asphyxia, with or without necrosis of tissue, characterized by an almost constant state of vasomotor disorder, which may undergo paroxysmal exacerbations but never gives place to a condition of complete health, associated it may be with impaired or perverted sensation, muscular weakness or wasting, and possibly with other evidences of structural change in the central or peripheral nervous system—it may be freely admitted that some cases of this kind depend on peripheral neuritis (primary neuritis), though this is as yet little more than theory. It may further be admitted as highly probable that frequent and prolonged attacks of vasomotor disorder, at first of a strictly functional nature, will in some cases ultimately impair the integrity of the tissues involved, including nerves as well as vessels. Almost any change that can overtake the vessels will lead to thickening of their walls, and so tend in the long run to obstruct the blood current, either directly or by promoting thrombosis, and this will increase the damage sustained by the nerves (secondary neuritis). As the nutrition of the nerves deteriorates, their trophic influence over the tissues with which they are connected will be influenced unfavourably, and this may intensify any tendency to gangrene caused by the imperfect blood-supply. But to account for the purely paroxysmal—the most characteristic—cases of the disease, no theory can hold its own against that proposed by Raynaud; and when such cases proceed to gangrene, the one theory that satisfactorily explains such gangrene is Raynaud's, the theory of vascular spasm.[1]

[1] It would serve no useful purpose to mention all the modifications of Raynaud's theory that have been proposed by subsequent writers. The curious are referred for this to the literature of the subject. One of the more generally accepted views is that local syncope and asphyxia are neuroses, whilst symmetrical gangrene is a trophoneurosis.

Accepting then the theory of an increased excitability of the vasomotor centres in the cerebro-spinal axis, allusion must be made to the situation of the unduly sensitive centres. Raynaud is doubtless correct in saying that the part of the cord affected varies in different cases. The varied distribution and the occasional unilateral character of the symptoms suggest that the disturbance is in the subordinate vasomotor centres of the cerebro-spinal axis. This is doubtless specially true of cases that originate in consequence of severe exposure. On the other hand, cases that are due to emotion have their source in cortical disturbances, and these will no doubt operate through the principal centre in the medulla. If a sub-ordinate centre in a given limited area has once been rendered overexcitable through exposure or otherwise, cortical discharges, such as those connected with emotion, may at any time call forth paroxysmal overaction limited to the oversensitive region. The theory of a cortical starting-point for the vasomotor discharge is favoured by the frequent association with such functional disorders of the cortex as insanity, epilepsy, etc.

In Raynaud's disease, as Dr. Barlow has truly remarked, we see the influence of **habit**. The vasomotor mechanism, having once under excessive stimulation by cold responded in excessive degree, is apt in the future to respond with undue readiness to slight stimulation. The explanation may be difficult, but the fact is only one illustration of a familiar experience. An overstrained heart is liable to palpitate too easily. The first epileptic discharge of the cerebral cortex prepares the way for the second and succeeding ones, which are induced by comparatively trivial and often by inappreciable exciting causes. But one of the best parallels is the way in which a tendency

to morbid blushing in the subject of neurasthenia is per-
petuated and increased, the emotion that is required to
call it forth becoming less and less, until the dread
that this most distressing symptom will appear is of itself
enough.

The influence of emotion on the vascular system, in-
tensifying or arresting the heart's action, making the face
red or pale, etc., is so well known as to need no description. Since, apart from emotion, local syncope is most
apt to occur in the extremities, it is not surprising that
in an individual who is subject to local syncope any
emotion which causes vasoconstriction should manifest itself
specially in those parts.

The nature of the connection of Raynaud's disease with
malarial fever is an interesting question. An attack of
local syncope or asphyxia of the extremities is by no means
unlike the cold stage of an intermittent, though it is not, as
a rule, associated with the pyrexia and severe constitutional
symptoms of fever. The resemblance was noted long ago.
Calmette (1877) tells of one case where the asphyxia of the
extremities ceased when the initial shivering of the fever
began and returned when the hot stage set in; he puts it in
another way thus: dilatation of vessels in the extremities
with general vasomotor excitation (that which caused the
rigor); then, contrariwise, local constriction in the extremities with general dilatation (of the hot stage). Calmette thinks the vasomotor phenomena of telluric infection
point to great excitability of the grey axis, and he supposes
that the paludic poison (in common with some other
poisons) has an elective action on the vasomotor centres.[1]

Moursou (1880) remarks that cold and heat have the
same occasional influence on the onset of attacks of local

[1] *Loc. cit.* (1877), p. 50.

asphyxia and of intermittent fever.[1] As early as 1873, in connection with a case of local asphyxia occurring immediately after an attack of intermittent fever, this observer had suggested that the vascular spasm in the extremities is due to irritation of the vessels of the cord by melanaemic deposits. In 1880 he still thought that this theory accounted for a certain proportion of cases, whilst in others the lesion that disturbed the vessels of the cord was congestion or inflammation.

So, too, Durosiez[2] (1874) was of opinion that local asphyxia was but one of the manifestations of intermittent fever, and that both depended on a neurosis of the great sympathetic. Bréhier[3] suggested that local asphyxia was but a masked form (" une forme larvée ") of intermittent fever.

Petit and Verneuil (1883) say we may regard palustral ischaemia as a simple prolongation or exaggeration of the ordinary cold stage of the febrile attack.[4]

Local asphyxia, then, is closely related to the intermittent attack, alternating with, accompanying, replacing or following it, and may so closely resemble it that different writers have concluded that they are practically the same thing. Accordingly, the agent that excites vascular spasm in the cold stage of fever may well be the immediate cause of the attack of local syncope or asphyxia. No doubt it acts upon the vasomotor centres. It is easy to understand how attacks of fever, which often occur long after the individual has left the fever district, may be replaced by attacks of local asphyxia. But in addition to this the violent vascular spasm occasioned by the first attack of fever probably makes an impression upon the vasomotor centres similar to that caused (reflexly) by severe exposure to cold,

---

[1] *Loc. cit.*, pp. 446, 447.   [2] Petit et Verneuil, *loc. cit.*, p. 13.
[3] *Ib.*   [4] *Loc. cit.*, p. 23.

whereby the vicious habit is acquired of responding to unduly slight stimulation.

The ocular phenomena occasionally witnessed in Raynaud's disease, give strong support to the theory of vascular constriction. Raynaud first showed—in a man who had been free from malarial attacks for 35 years—that contraction of the retinal arteries in this disease may be witnessed by the ophthalmoscope. Ramorius (1877) has recorded cases of malarial poisoning complicated with paroxysmal amblyopia and narrowing of the retinal vessels, the fundus in the intervals being normal;[1] and Calmette has been already quoted to show that patients who have recently suffered, or are still suffering, from malarial fever or cachexia, and who are subject to local asphyxia, may also suffer from paroxysmal narrowing of the papillary arteries.

The occurrence of gangrene in malarial as in other cases of Raynaud's disease is to be accounted for by the prolonged vascular spasm; but where there is a considerable degree of cachexia, thrombosis in the small constricted vessels may render the necrotic process much more extensive than it would otherwise have been.

In a good many cases, Raynaud's phenomena appear to be the external manifestation of a **morbid blood-state.** The prejudicial agent may be the toxin produced in a specific febrile process such as typhus, enteric, diphtheria, and perhaps measles and syphilis; or the products absorbed from suppurating foci in the lungs or elsewhere; or lead (acting either directly or by its power of checking the elimination of uric acid by the kidneys); or uric acid; or the urinary constituents which, when present in excess, give rise to uraemia; or possibly the poison underlying the rheumatic and gouty blood-states.

[1] Quoted by Gowers, *Medical Ophthalmoscopy* (3rd ed.), 1890, p. 287.

Although alcohol causes dilatation of the cutaneous vessels, it is doubtful if it gives rise to Raynaud's phenomena, except in a very inferior degree and through the agency of early multiple neuritis.

The benefit accruing to some of the syphilitic cases from antisyphilitic treatment makes it doubtful if in these examples the vasomotor disorder was purely functional. Yet in a case reported by Krisowski, where a child of three years was the subject of inherited syphilis, the local syncope and asphyxia of the fingers and ears were characteristically paroxysmal. After the paroxysms had come and gone for two months, partial gangrene of each ear ensued. Antisyphilitic treatment is reported to have brought about a speedy cure. In such a case as that reported by Morgan, where there was evidence of a lesion involving the spinal nerve-roots, it is quite likely that the vasomotor fibres in the anterior roots were themselves involved, and the lesion may in this or some other similar manner have interfered with the blood-supply to the adjacent vasomotor centres in the cord.

Haig points out that many symptoms of Raynaud's disease resemble those of "uric acidaemia," and in one severe case he found great excess of uric acid in the blood and urine. He believes that uric acid causes contraction of the arterioles, and he mentions the case of a little girl who had 42 attacks of local asphyxia in 52 days. When she was treated by salicylate of soda (which augments the excretion of uric acid), with an acid (which causes the accumulation of uric acid in the joints, liver, etc., and clears it, for the time, out of the blood) and nux vomica, the attacks suddenly ceased for 20 days, and then appeared 3 times in 11 days.

Albuminuria appears sometimes to be the result of

haemoglobinaemia which is not sufficiently severe to give rise to haemoglobinuria; but it may also be an evidence of Bright's disease, which is to be looked upon as an occasional cause of Raynaud's disease. The case quoted from Aitken (page 142) shows that a very striking relationship may exist between the amount of urea excreted and the paroxysms of cyanosis and syncope. The arterial constriction of early Bright's disease, at first unaccompanied by structural changes in the vessels, and due to the morbid blood-state, may be regarded as representing the first stage of Raynaud's disease from the point of view of pathology, just as attacks of dead finger may, as Dieulafoy pointed out in 1882,[1] be one of the early clinical manifestations of renal sclerosis.

The subjects of Raynaud's disease and of **paroxysmal haemoglobinuria** are alike in possessing a circulatory system which is abnormally susceptible to the influence of cold. A slight chill is sufficient to produce, in the one case, local syncope or asphyxia, and in the other, destruction of red corpuscles in the blood-vessels of the chilled part. The haemoglobin of the dissolved corpuscles is set free in the blood, and so a general haemoglobinaemia results. The haemoglobin is partly excreted by the kidneys, but if there is not much of it in the blood, there may be simply albuminuria, and even this symptom may be awanting. The haemoglobin not removed by the kidneys is disposed of by the liver. The red corpuscles have, no doubt, less than the normal powers of resistance in individuals who are liable to paroxysmal haemoglobinuria, so that if they come under the influence of causes that induce Raynaud's phenomena, attacks of these latter will naturally be associated with haemoglobinaemia. In any case, whether we

[1] *Gaz. hebdom. de méd. et de chir.*, 1882, xix., 323.

have to deal with haemoglobinuria, with Raynaud's phenomena, or with a combination of the two, there is reason to believe that the immediate cause of the attack is spasm of the peripheral vessels. Even though in paroxysmal haemoglobinuria the direct action of cold on the red corpuscles may commence to break them up, this process must be greatly accelerated by the cooling of the blood, which necessarily results from the stasis in the periphery due to the speedy contraction of the vessels.

We cannot suppose that the haemoglobinuria of Raynaud's disease is due to spasm of the renal vessels, for manifestly if the latter were severe enough to allow bloodcolouring matter to escape, the haemoglobin would still be contained in red corpuscles ; the symptom would be, not haemoglobinuria, but haematuria. And as a matter of fact, red blood-corpuscles, as well as haemoglobin, are sometimes present in the urine ; but this is to be attributed to the intense renal hyperaemia which the haemoglobin induces as it is being eliminated. The occurrence of a few corpuscles, or of a trace of albumen, at times in the urine may possibly be explained on the theory of transient spasm of the renal blood-vessels.

Haig has suggested that haemoglobinuria in Raynaud's disease is due to destruction of red corpuscles by excess of uric acid in the blood.

The **jaundice** occasionally noticed in connection with attacks of Raynaud's disease has been attributed to spasm of the hepatic vessels. It is much more likely that this jaundice is haematogenous. When bile and albumen are found in the urine without blood or blood-colouring matter, we may indeed assume a spasm of the hepatic and renal vessels, but even here it is better to suppose that the albuminuria represents a degree of haemoglobinaemia insufficient to produce haemoglobinuria, whilst the icterus may be related to the increased amount of haemoglobin which the liver has to convert into bile pigment.

With regard to the association of attacks of Raynaud's phenomena with **diminished excretion of urea** in Bright's disease, the order of events is not certain, but the presumption is that what happens here is comparable to the cumulative action of drugs such as digitalis and strychnine. The urea or the drug, constantly present in considerable quantity in the blood, causes at length contraction of the renal arteries sufficient to interfere with its own elimination.

It is to be noted that the characters possessed in common by Raynaud's disease and paroxysmal haemoglobinuria constitute a powerful argument for the neurotic as against the neuritic theory of the former. The causation of an attack in either case by changes of temperature, by effort, or by emotion, the occasional complication of either disease by such a neurosis as urticaria, and the tendency of both to manifest a paroxysmal, and yet non-periodic, character, testify strongly to the functional nature of both ailments.

Haemorrhages, purpuric and other, are probably due, alike in Raynaud's disease and in paroxysmal haemoglobinuria, to the altered state of the blood.

Diseases of the respiratory organs are not very important on the ground of frequency in Raynaud's disease. They may, however, accentuate the disorder in the periphery by hampering the circulation in the chest, or by causing constitutional debility, or by giving rise to poisonous products which may be absorbed. Thus phthisis may be effectual as a cause in various ways. Whether measles acts by producing a specific toxin, or through the agency of the associated bronchitis, is not clear.

Cardiac lesions seem to be influential chiefly by embarrassing the circulation. Angina pectoris, however, has been observed to bring a case of Raynaud's disease to a fatal termination, and it has been suggested that this might be through spasm of the coronary arteries of the heart (Cleeman). As the patient had been subject for years to attacks of dead fingers, it is quite possible that the fatal spasm was not confined to the peripheral arteries.

It is not surprising that some of the more familiar **neuroses** are occasionally found in the subjects of Raynaud's disease. Diabetes insipidus, another vasomotor disorder, is a rare complication. Insanity and epilepsy are more common, and theories have been based on such relationships. Thus Ritti, commenting on his cases of alternating insanity, with local syncope and asphyxia of the extremities in the period of depression, suggests that the depression is due to cerebral anaemia, the result of vascular spasm similar to that witnessed in the extremities, whilst the mental exaltation depends on the reaction following the re-establishment of the cerebral circulation.[1] And Targowla suggested, with reference to a case of local syncope and asphyxia of the extremities associated after a time with melancholia, that local vasomotor disturbance accounted for the mental symptoms as it did for the disorder in the fingers. Theories of this kind are simple and easily constructed, but not so easily proved true. They imply that the primary fault is in the vasomotor mechanism. In Targowla's case, we are told, the cyanosis began before the mental disease, so that presumably the neurosis involved for a time the part of the vasomotor

---

[1] The pial arteries are muscular, and have been shown microscopically to be surrounded by nerve plexuses, but the vasomotor function of these nerves has not yet been demonstrated experimentally. (*Kirkes' Handbook of Physiology*, 15th ed. by Halliburton, 1899, p. 272.)

system concerned with the digits, and afterwards spread to that part which regulates the circulation in the mental area. This seems reasonable enough, and has perhaps its analogue in the way in which temporary lack of in- hibition in neurasthenia causes simultaneous vasomotor relaxation in the face and mental confusion. In insanity and in neurasthenia, the highest centres of all, including those that are concerned with will, are enfeebled and allow lower centres to act with undue readiness. The fact that disorder of a portion of the vasomotor centre may flush a cortical centre with blood does not, of course, imply that the former is of a higher grade than the latter.

Similarly, Bernstein concluded that his patient, who suffered from epilepsy, from Raynaud's disease, and from paroxysms resembling those of intermittent fever (originally due to a severe mental shock, and not influenced by quinine, though yielding to valerian and belladonna), was the victim of morbid excitability of the vasomotor centres, which at one time manifested itself in local syncope and asphyxia of peripheral parts of the body, at another pro- duced local anaemia in those parts of the brain which determine the occurrence of epileptic fits, and at yet another time gave rise to intermittent-like paroxysms.

And again Weiss, whose case is adduced by Hochenegg as a classical example of a functional disorder, explains the aphasia that occurred as a result of spastic ischaemia of the speech centre, the oculopupillary phenomena as due to ischaemia of the cilio-spinal region, the nutritive changes in the muscles as a consequence of spastic ischaemia of the anterior cornua, and the cutaneous lesions as due to a similar ischaemia of the posterior columns of the spinal cord.

The part taken by **structural diseases of the nervous**

system in the evolution of Raynaud's disease is not yet fully elucidated. Hydrocephalus may by pressure irritate, or alter the nutrition of the medullary vasomotor centre; or the alteration may be a result of the pathological process that caused the hydrocephalus. The occurrence of Raynaud's phenomena in peripheral neuritis is doubtless due to involvement of the vasomotor nerves running in the affected mixed nerves. Similarly syringomyelia may, by damaging fibres that emerge from the cord in the anterior roots, modify the vasomotor condition of the extremities, just as pressure exerted on vasomotor nerves by an intrathoracic growth may do.

The relationship of **scleroderma** to Raynaud's disease is quite obscure. Some writers assert that the two are simply varieties of one morbid process. Scleroderma is generally understood to be a trophoneurosis, but the trophic centre which is involved in the disturbance is as yet purely hypothetical. The principal fact revealed by a study of the diseased skin is endarteritis of the terminal vessels. There may also be endophlebitis. The nerves may be diseased or may be perfectly healthy. Accordingly the changes in the arterial walls have been regarded as the immediate cause of the sclerosis of the cutaneous tissues, the lesion of the arterial wall being a trophic one resulting from disturbance of the corresponding trophic nerve centre. Lewin and Heller, in their recent elaborate monograph,[1] describe scleroderma as an angiotrophoneurosis which may depend upon disorders of the peripheral nerves as well as of the central nervous system. Goldschmidt has suggested that the endarteritis is microbic.[2]

It is possible that as the cells of the anterior cornua of

[1] *Die Sclerodermie,* Berlin, 1895, p. 207.
[2] *Revue de médecine,* 1887, vii., 417, 418.

the cord preside over both the function and the nutrition of the related muscular fibres, so the cells of the subordinate vasomotor centres in the cord may preside over the nutrition as well as the function of the walls of the arterioles. Is it possible to regard the vascular spasms of early scleroderma as analogous to the fibrillary twitchings of the early period of progressive muscular atrophy?[1]

SOME CASES OF SYMMETRICAL GANGRENE OF UNCERTAIN NATURE.

In studying the literature of Raynaud's disease, we encounter a considerable number of cases of symmetrical gangrene, whose true pathological relationships are quite uncertain. Among the most important of these are cases where the gangrene sets in rapidly or suddenly, and sometimes leads in a few days to a fatal issue. A considerable proportion of such cases occur in children, and, as might be expected, grave constitutional symptoms may appear; yet, even though coma has set in, the patient may regain good health. The gangrene may be widespread, and not confined to the extremities; it may even avoid the distal whilst attacking the more proximal portions of the limbs. It may be associated with some other illness, such as diarrhoea. In a case recorded by Czurda, both upper arms of a child were bitten by a large spider. The arms became greatly swollen; the patient suffered severely for

[1] The cutaneous lesion is the same in scleroderma and in facial hemiatrophy, another disease whose pathological nature cannot yet be regarded as proved. In a case recently recorded by Lindsay Steven (*Glasg. Med. Jour.*, 1898, l. 401-408), where hemiatrophy was associated with scleroderma of both face and limbs on the right side, degenerative changes were found in the right anterior horn of the cord.

some weeks, and finally both hands became gangrenous and dropped off.

It is to be noted that in the cases referred to, the vessels, so far as they have been examined, have been normal. The morbid anatomy therefore in no way excludes Raynaud's theory, and the acuteness of the process might be suggested as an explanation of a distribution less regular than in Raynaud's malady. Some writers indeed regard these cases as examples of this affection. Thus Southey, who recorded a striking case in 1883, adopted the theory of arterial spasm. Atkinson, who published a case in 1884, set aside neuritis, thrombosis and embolism, and looked upon the disease as a neurosis. He thought that temporary vascular spasm could produce gangrene only if the parts had their powers of resistance diminished by arrest of their trophic nerve influence or otherwise. Professor Osler also admits these cases to the category of Raynaud's disease. He says "the climax of this series of neuro-vascular changes is seen in the remarkable instances of extensive multiple gangrene. They are most common in children, and may progress with frightful rapidity." [1]

If, however, we are to adhere to the position which is accepted in this essay, that Raynaud's disease is essentially paroxysmal, at least in its early stages, we must exclude such cases as have just been described.[2] Their etiology is

---

[1] *Principles and Practice of Medicine*, 1898 (3rd edit.), p. 1138.

[2] The following references to illustrative cases may be given : Czurda, *Wiener Med. Woch.*, 1880, xxx., 655-657 ; Southey, *Trans. Path. Soc. Lond.*, 1883, xxxiv., 286-289 ; Atkinson, *Amer. Jour. Med. Sc.*, 1884, lxxxvii., 57-65 ; Valude, *Gaz. Hebd. de Méd. et de Chirurg.*, 1885, xxii., 109, 110 ; Murray, *Brit. Med. Jour.*, 1886, i., 70 ; Bellamy, *Clin. Soc. Trans.*, 1887, xx., 195-198 ; Smith-Shand, *Brit. Med. Jour.*, 1888, i., 343-345 ; Brown, *Lancet*, 1891, ii., 292.

probably complex, including a debilitated condition of the body generally, and of the mechanisms of circulation and innervation in particular. Temporary vascular spasm, or trauma, acting especially on peripheral parts, may have a share in the production of the gangrene. But the exact mode in which the lesion is brought about is as mysterious as in the case of a far more frequent condition—the simple ulcer of the stomach.

CLASSIFICATION.

The following may be given as a provisional classification of cases :

Raynaud's disease—

    (*a*) Due to inherited peculiarity.

    (*b*) Due to acquired peculiarity.

    (*c*) Due to a morbid blood-state.

    (*d*) Part of a widespread neurosis (congenital or acquired).

    (*e*) Associated with structural disease of the central nervous system.

Raynaud's phenomena—

    (*a*) Due to a morbid blood-state.

    (*b*) Due to concussion or other lesion of the central nervous system.

    (*c*) Due to inflammation or other lesion of nerves.

The non-paroxysmal cases of rapid multiple gangrene are excluded from either group.

It is to be noted that malaria probably resembles severe exposure and emotion in causing not only the phenomena of Raynaud's disease, but an altered nutrition of the vaso-motor centres which permits these phenomena to recur with abnormal readiness. Other morbid blood-states besides malarial poisoning seem to possess this property, since during their existence paroxysms may be induced by temperature changes.

Several of the facts mentioned with regard to the vasomotor mechanism have their analogies in well known disorders of the motor side of the central nervous system. Thus in paralysis agitans we see a disorder of the nutrition and function of the motor convolutions, which, once acquired, is apt to persist. In chorea, under the influence of a morbid blood-state, there is a less permanent functional disorder of the motor system, and in athetosis we see a nutritional and functional disease associated commonly with structural change in the brain. The influence of emotion in diseases of this class is well known.

DIAGNOSIS.

THE diagnosis of Raynaud's disease is sometimes easy and sometimes very difficult. (1) When there are the three stages of local syncope, local asphyxia, and gangrene ; (2) when these symptoms involve symmetrical parts ; and (3) when the first two of them at any rate are definitely paroxysmal, occurring in attacks which are separated by periods of apparently complete health ;—given these three conditions and we are clearly entitled to consider the case an example of the disease in question. But there are many genuine cases of Raynaud's disease which do not conform to this type. Thus (1) the three stages may not all manifest themselves. There may be only syncope and asphyxia ; often there is only asphyxia ; and occasionally syncope of itself may be so severe as to amount to something more than an ordinary attack of dead finger. But in all these cases we must look for the paroxysmal element, and if this is awanting we are not justified in calling the case Raynaud's disease. (2) Bilateral symmetry is very important, but not essential. If this feature is lacking, the other evidence must be very strong if we are to be sure as to our diagnosis of Raynaud's disease. (3) It is well to regard the fact of paroxysm as

essential for the diagnosis.   This is the view of Dr. Barlow [1]
and of Mr. Hutchinson.[2]   A rule so absolute as this seems
at first sight very simple of application, but if we meet with
a patient who is suffering from his second paroxysm, the
first having happened several years ago, and the different
stages not being well marked, the mere question of paroxysm
does not help us much.

(4) The diagnosis of Raynaud's disease is favoured if all
the facts of the case go to show that the affection is, at least
for a time, purely functional, whether the vasomotor disorder
exist alone, or along with some other functional trouble,
or as part of a more widespread neurosis.   On the
other hand, existence of organic disease, especially if
outwith the nervous system, is not opposed to the diagnosis
of Raynaud's malady.

(5) Causation may help us.   If the illness is a result of
severe exposure, or of severe emotion, the diagnosis of
Raynaud's disease is favoured.   Other causes are each
effective in so small a proportion of cases as to be of little
value in diagnosis.

(6) The diagnosis of Raynaud's disease is opposed, but
by no means excluded, by the fact that the patient is past
middle life.

Raynaud's position was different from the one we occupy
to-day.   He had to prove that there is such a disease as
that which now bears his name—that there is a form of
spontaneous gangrene apart from that which is due to
thrombosis, arteritis, diabetes, ergotism, etc.   Its existence
is now a matter of common knowledge, and we have simply
to emphasize those aspects in which it differs from these
others.

Frost-bite may closely resemble Raynaud's disease in

[1] *Brit. Med. Jour.*, 1889, i., 359.   [2] No. 89.

respect of the parts affected, as well as the nature of the lesion, and, indeed, the difference may be merely one of degree. If there has been exposure to intense cold, and actual freezing of the part just before the attack, we call it frost-bite ; if there has been neither of these, and yet the lesions run the same course, we may call it Raynaud's disease. But exposure to intense cold may cause frost-bite which soon comes to an end, and, at the same time, Raynaud's disease, which persists much longer. So that the single fundamental distinction is that in Raynaud's disease there is an abnormal, and in frost-bite the normal degree of susceptibility to cold.

Congenital cyanosis (morbus caeruleus) can scarcely be mistaken for Raynaud's disease. There are no paroxysms of syncope or attacks of gangrene of the extremities. The dusky colour has existed practically in its present form from birth, is distributed over the general surface, and is intensified by crying or other effort. A murmur is probably audible in the cardiac region, and, as the child grows, the ends of the fingers may become clubbed. There are no pains, but there may be dyspnoea and fainting attacks.

Ergotism in its chronic gangrenous form resembles Raynaud's disease almost as closely as frost-bite does. It is distinguished by the history of the food supply, for practically its only cause is the use of ergotized rye-bread.

Senile gangrene is almost always confined to one lower limb, and generally attacks a considerable portion of the extremity. The pulsations of the artery distributed to the gangrenous area may be modified, and the wall of the vessel may be appreciably altered by disease. The age of the patient is of course an element in diagnosis.

Embolism very rarely gives rise to symmetrical lesions resembling those of Raynaud's malady, and it can be further

recognized by the existence of some disease such as endocarditis to account for it, and by the absence of paroxysm.

Arteritis obliterans, which may occur in early adult
life and lead to gangrene of one or more limbs, may present
considerable resemblance to Raynaud's disease. The non-
occurrence of paroxysms, the involvement of the limbs in
succession rather than symmetrically, and especially the
great modification or actual loss of the pulse in the vessels
of the affected limbs may prove sufficient to guide us.

Diabetic gangrene may be recognized by the glycosuria
and other evidences of diabetes. The gangrene sometimes
starts from an inflammatory or traumatic lesion. It may be
associated with, if not immediately caused by, atheroma or
peripheral neuritis, and it rarely occurs in early life.

Cardiac weakness or disease can scarcely ever give
rise to real difficulty in the diagnosis, for in any case where
it causes disturbances in the peripheral circulation it is
almost certain to be associated with distinctive cardiac
symptoms, and probably also physical signs. Occasionally,
it is true, cardiac embarrassment may accentuate, or in a
predisposed person perhaps actually give rise to Raynaud's
phenomena, but in all such cases, the safe rule is to attribute
to the cardiac condition everything that it can account for.

Hysterical gangrene, as occasionally seen in young
women, is likely to be associated with symptoms of hysteria
and anaemia. It appears chiefly on the chest and upper
limbs, but not specially on the digits. Each gangrenous
area develops suddenly, and there are no preceding
paroxysms of local syncope and asphyxia. There is reason
to suspect that many of these cases are impostures, the
gangrene being artificially produced by the application of a
caustic.

Erythromelalgia is relatively even more frequent in

males than Raynaud's disease is in females. There is no definite stage of syncope, and the colour is practically normal unless the part is allowed to hang down, whereupon it becomes dusky red or violet, and the arteries throb. Pain, unless in slight cases, is more or less constant, but it is aggravated by the dependent position and by pressure. All forms of sensation are preserved. The temperature of the affected part is elevated. The lesion is confined to, or more marked on, one side ; and, though slight ulceration may occur, it does not lead to gangrene in the usual sense of the word. The affection differs further from Raynaud's malady in being aggravated by warmth and relieved by cold.[1]

Peripheral neuritis in its characteristic form presents almost no resemblance to a typical case of Raynaud's disease. The etiology, course, and often the distribution of the lesions are quite different in the two cases. When vasomotor phenomena appear in connection with multiple neuritis, they are quite subordinate in importance to the other symptoms, such as paralysis, anaesthesia, inco-ordination, tenderness of nerves, and tenderness of muscles. These symptoms, moreover, are constantly present throughout the course of the disease ; although there may be exacerbations of pain from time to time, the disease cannot be called paroxysmal. In Raynaud's disease, on the other hand, the vasomotor phenomena are by far the most striking

[1] Weir Mitchell and Spiller report that the nerves are degenerated and the vessel-walls thickened in the affected part. Which is the primary lesion is quite uncertain, but Mitchell has recently inclined to the theory of nerve-end neuritis (No. 116, and *Amer. Jour. Med. Sc.*, 1899, cxvii., 1-13). Weir Mitchell described this disease in 1872, and named it in 1878 (*Amer. Jour. Med. Sc.*, 1878, lxxvi., 17-36). A very similar case, in a young lady, is given by Graves in his *Clinical Lectures*, 1848 (2nd edition), ii., 511 ff.

feature of the complaint, although in some cases the pains which may accompany the period of maximum cyanosis appeal to the unfortunate patient in a way that no other symptoms can. Moreover, Raynaud's disease is for a time at least a strictly paroxysmal affection. Nevertheless, as has been already pointed out, there are cases which undoubtedly present to the clinician some features of Raynaud's disease (though rarely in any typical or characteristic fashion), and yet are found anatomically to be associated with structural changes in the vessels, or nerves, or both. In such circumstances, it is well in making a clinical diagnosis to attribute to neuritis as much as the present state of our knowledge will permit, and only to regard the case as an example of Raynaud's disease when neuritis cannot account for the facts.

TREATMENT.

THE treatment of Raynaud's disease may be regarded in
two aspects: first, that which is directed against the
abnormal excitability of the vasomotor centres, or, in other
words, against the liability to paroxysms of Raynaud's
phenomena; and secondly, that which is directed against
the symptoms present during the individual paroxysm.
Treatment which is curative as regards the liability to
attacks will manifestly be prophylactic as regards the
attacks themselves. For practical purposes, however, this
therapeutic classification is not the most useful, since the
agent that is employed to cure the liability is sometimes
the best that can be given in an attack. A more suitable
division of remedies is into general and local, though
here too the distinction is not absolute.

A. GENERAL MEASURES.

It is a fortunate thing for humanity that habits, difficult
as they often are to acquire and retain, can sometimes
be broken and even got rid of. From our present point
of view, this specially applies to the habitual activity of

organs which are only partly under the control of the will. A good example is the case of the rectum, which is readily trained to call for evacuation at a certain time each day, and which is only too ready to give up this habit altogether when its demands are not regularly attended to. The bladder is another organ which can be greatly influenced by education. The vasomotor centre appears on a first consideration to be much further removed from voluntary control than the rectum and bladder, and yet by reflex stimulation great influence can be brought to bear upon it. It is probable that cold bathing with subsequent friction of the skin, going about in the open air with the head uncovered, etc., increase the resisting power of the body against catarrhs partly by educating the vasomotor system to accommodate the peripheral circulation readily to varying external temperatures. In states of debility, where the vasomotor tone is lowered, the cutaneous vessels may become relaxed and perspiration may occur in consequence of comparatively slight elevations of temperature, but by the adoption of suitable methods this objectionable condition can commonly be overcome. In Raynaud's disease, the vasomotor centres have the tendency not so much to cease acting as to act with abnormal readiness. To cure this habit, it is of the utmost importance to avoid everything that favours the occurrence of an individual paroxysm. Every prolongation of the interval between the attacks is a step towards the subjugation of the habit. As the patient learns to avoid the conditions that favour the attack, he may expect to find the paroxysms occurring, not only less frequently, but also less easily, less promptly, and less severely. Each of these is a gain, and the patient's comfort and liberty are increased. When the attack occurs less frequently, the vasomotor mechanism tends to get out of practice. When it occurs less easily, the patient can submit himself to conditions more trying than formerly, so that his liberty is increased, whilst the vasomotor mechanism, having withstood these conditions, is hardened to resist others more severe. When the attack occurs less promptly, the patient may have time before its full development to adopt measures that render it abortive; and when it occurs less severely, the patient's suffering is less, and he is encouraged to persevere in his struggle. This is true of countless neuroses, and bromide of potassium has enabled us to say it of a large proportion of cases of epilepsy. If we are able by any legitimate device to postpone an attack, and especially if we are able, as days, months, or even years pass, to greatly increase the length of the intervals, we may hope that the interval now running will be indefinitely prolonged, and that, with certain precautions which have been found in the individual case to be absolutely necessary, no further attack will occur.

The vicious habit of which the vasomotor centre is possessed is sometimes a gift of inheritance, sometimes acquired; but in either case the treatment is the same. Every precaution must be taken to **avoid undue exposure.** Those who can afford it should winter in a warmer climate. In this country, flannel ought to be worn next the skin all the year round, thin in summer and thick in winter. The feet ought to be well clothed at all times, and gloves should be worn unless in the great heat of summer. Care should be taken that the gloves, while well lined with non-conducting material, are wide enough to avoid the slightest interference with the circulation in the hands. The water used for washing ought to be as nearly as possible at blood-heat, since hot water as well as cold is capable of invoking a paroxysm. If the liability to attacks persists only during the cold season, the patient may, if he has a personal liking for cold bathing, gradually reduce the temperature of the water in a tentative way as the warm weather sets in, and may even bathe in cold water if he is judicious enough not to prolong the exposure too much, and if—which is very important—a vigorous reaction readily sets in on drying. At most, however, this is to be allowed in exceptional cases, and is not to be recommended ; since the possible benefit to be derived by the few cannot be regarded as in any way equivalent to the risk run by the many.

In severe cases, the sufferer ought to remain indoors in cold weather, and as far as possible in an airy room at a uniform temperature. If the fingers are used habitually for delicate operations such as sewing and playing, it is specially important that the atmosphere of the room be kept warm. In some of the worst cases, it may be necessary to keep the patient for a time in bed, to secure uniformity of temperature and avoid the cooling influence of displaced air.

Diet must be carefully attended to. Many of the sufferers need to have their nutrition improved. They ought to get an abundance of milk, fat, eggs, and the more valuable farinaceous foods, such as oatmeal or oatflour porridge, porridge and soups made from peas and lentils, and the various farinaceous dishes prepared with milk. Milk and eggs are conveniently given in the form of egg-flip twice daily, and milk can be taken in many other ways besides, whilst eggs can be given in custards, puddings, etc. Fat in considerable quantity can be taken in the form of cream, butter and cod-liver oil. The last is perhaps best taken in conjunction with extract of malt, which is itself an admirable nutritive and digestive agent. Another excellent way of taking fat is in the form of bacon. Butcher-meat in some form, or chicken, should be taken once a day, and fish also should be taken once or twice a day.

But persons in reduced health cannot always tolerate fattening diet, and it is necessary to assist them. To have a good appetite a man must have sufficient sleep, and accordingly if pain interferes with sleep, we must endeavour to allay it by means that interfere with digestion and appetite as little as possible. *Fresh air* promotes both appetite and sleep, and accordingly, when the day is sufficiently warm, the patient, suitably clad, should be encouraged to go out freely, his *exercise*, however, always stopping short of fatigue. In the actual paroxysm, a smart walk is the appropriate treatment for a young adult in whom the disease amounts to little more than a bad attack of dead fingers, and who otherwise enjoys vigorous health ; but little children and others who cannot be trusted, or are unable, to take vigorous exercise, and those who suffer from the disease in its more severe aspects, do better to stay in a warm room, even though the atmosphere outside be genial. The appetite may be further improved by the administration of acid and bitter tonics before meals ; and in neurotic and anaemic subjects, the exhibition of arsenic and bromide of potassium, with or without iron, after food, may prove of signal service.

In some cases *stimulants* are doubtless advisable, but the practitioner must carefully bear in mind the risk of ordering to a neurotic young subject a remedy which may very easily come to be resorted to whenever the pain becomes troublesome, for the sake of its anodyne and narcotic effects.

It is scarcely necessary to say that patients of this class should keep away from malarious influences. It is more important to discuss briefly the value of **quinine** as a remedy for Raynaud's disease. It is admittedly the best remedy for malarial fever; experience shows that it is the best drug that can be given in paroxysmal haemoglobinuria; and paroxysmal haemoglobinuria and Raynaud's disease possess a close kinship with one another in some respects, one of these being that intermittent fever is a cause of both. Analogy therefore would lead us to hope that quinine would be a remedy for Raynaud's disease.

The fact is that quinine succeeds in some cases and fails in others, but it ought certainly to be tried. Apart from drugs that appear to have an almost specific effect on some cases, the type of remedies that is indicated in a large proportion of instances is the tonic, and of this type quinine is one of the leading examples. But quinine is probably the drug which most frequently acts as a specific cure, and it is by no means clear that this applies only to malarial cases. Raynaud recommends it as the principal drug in cases where there is well-marked intermission.[1] In Case iii. of the *Thesis* (malaria not mentioned), the intermittence was destroyed by quinine, though the malady was not cured. Case v. of the *New Researches* was malarious, and derived great benefit from quinine. On the other hand, Case vi. of the *Thesis*, which was malarial, derived no benefit from this drug.

Writers who have had special opportunities of observing the connection between malarial fever and Raynaud's disease regularly prescribe quinine in the treatment of the latter, and a perusal of the cases recorded by Moursou, Calmette, and Petit and Verneuil leaves no doubt as to its efficacy. When any one of Raynaud's phenomena sets in in a malarious subject, the sulphate should be given in doses of

[1] *Thesis*, pp. 149, 150.

ten to twenty grains daily, dissolved in an acid mixture so as to make sure of absorption ; and, as in the treatment of malarial fever, it will be well to anticipate the quinine by a mercurial purge. Even when malarial gangrene has commenced, it may be hoped that quinine will prevent the necrosis from extending, or appearing in other parts, and will promote healing. In one of Vulpian's cases[1] (apparently not malarious), it was repeatedly found that when the patient took sulphate of quinine, the symptoms ceased, and that they recurred when the drug was stopped, to cease again when it was resumed. Quinine was regarded last century as a specific for gangrene. Rest in cases of threatened gangrene is an important adjuvant to treatment by this drug.

Another drug of great value is **opium** ; Raynaud speaks of " the unbounded confidence which Pott accorded to it as curative of gangrene."[2] Opium may be used in malarious or non-malarious cases, and in the young or old ; but it is, perhaps, specially serviceable in middle-aged or elderly persons who suffer from almost daily paroxysms attended by pain, and leading up to gangrene. In cases of this description, the opium should be given regularly in small doses, say thrice daily. Opium itself may be given in the form of a minute pill of a third or a fourth of a grain. Or the pill may consist of a quarter of a grain of the extract, with two grains of the extract of hyoscyamus. Or the preparation may be Battley's solution in doses of four or five drops. No doubt its narcotic influence is the most important element in the action of this drug, and by procuring sleep for the patient, it may do more than anything else to make life tolerable, or even possible.

If there is any particular reason for avoiding opium,

[1] No. 190, pp. 878, 879.   [2] *Thesis*, p. 149.

cannabis indica (m xv. of the tincture thrice daily, or much oftener) or analgesics of the phenacetin group may be tried for the relief of pain, but no substantial benefit need be looked for from these.

It might be expected that *nitrite of amyl* would be of great service in this disease, but in doses that cause vasomotor relaxation in other parts of the skin it is practically incapable of influencing the appearance of the affected part. Nitroglycerin in the usual dose also fails in the same way. Nevertheless these remedies should not be discarded altogether, since they sometimes give the patient a considerable sense of relief, although to the physician's eye they produce no good effect. Improvement has been observed under treatment by nitrite of sodium in small doses. Remedies of this class ought of course to be used when angina pectoris is associated with Raynaud's phenomena.

Haig has pointed out that attacks of local asphyxia may be caused by excess of uric acid in the blood. In such cases the excretion of this substance should be promoted by giving such agents as *alkalies*, salicylic acid and its compounds, salicin, salol, phosphate of sodium, piperazidin and quinine. For instance, ten grains of salicylate of sodium may be given thrice daily after meals, and the same quantity of bromide of potassium may be combined with it, partly to increase its sedative effect and partly to mask the taste. It may be well to increase the patient's sense of well-being at the same time, by giving a few minims of a dilute mineral acid with a vegetable bitter an hour before meals.

Improvement or cure has been noted under treatment by large doses of *ergot* (Féré, Johnston), though it is not certain that the cure was due to the ergot. It might have been thought that this drug was contra-indicated under such circumstances, but it may be noted in passing that although the cases now alluded to do not appear to have been malarious, ergot has been highly praised as a cure for chronic malaria.[1]

Short has recorded great improvement under *thyroid extract.*

It is very important to treat any morbid condition (chlorosis, anaemia, hysteria, epilepsy, insanity, diabetes, phthisis, syphilis, uraemia, etc.) with which Raynaud's phenomena are associated; the appropriate remedies for these will readily suggest themselves. With regard to syphilis, it may be remarked that antisyphilitic treatment ought to get a fair trial, since it has proved remarkably efficacious both in the acquired and in the inherited disease. But if this line of treatment does not speedily begin to show its effects, it ought to be abandoned, since recovery may take place without it.

It would do no good to enumerate all the other drugs that have been tried in Raynaud's disease; a number have appeared to cure or at least benefit isolated cases while of little or no avail in others. The most important of these are iron, arsenic, nux vomica or strychnine, digitalis, strophanthus, belladonna and valerian. Most, if not all of these, would find their place in a list of remedies that have been tried and found wanting, though this is no reason why we should not use them when other measures fail.

Raynaud[2] wisely forbids general blood-letting on the ground of its being too lowering, although in Rognetta's case which he quotes, Dupuytren employed this method with marvellous success.

[1] Jacobi, quoted in *Brit. Med. Jour.*, 1898, ii. epit., 412.
[2] *Thesis*, p. 150.

Electricity has been freely used in the treatment of Raynaud's disease.   Case vii. in the *Thesis* (recorded by Duval in 1858) was cured by the local application of the faradic current; but when Raynaud wrote his *Thesis*, he had no experience of his own upon which to found his recommendation of electricity as a therapeutic agent "to be tried with all requisite prudence."[1]   But when we come to Case i. in the *New Researches*, we find him, "guided by theoretical considerations," resolved to attempt the employment of continuous currents.   Descending currents were used for ten minutes daily, the positive pole being applied over the seventh cervical spine, and the negative pole over the lumbar region.   Steady improvement was observed from the very first, and after some weeks the patient was cured. In Case iii., the current was passed from the fifth cervical vertebra to the commencement of the cauda equina, and here, too, a steady improvement took place.   But after nine days, each application of galvanism to the spine was followed by an application to the affected upper limbs, the positive pole being placed in the axilla over the brachial plexus, and the negative pole over the ends of the closely approximated fingers.   Here again the result was perfectly satisfactory.   In both of these cases the disease had existed for several months; it manifested no tendency to disappear spontaneously, and electricity was the only therapeutic agent employed.   The next case, Case iv., was cured by the application of descending currents to the spine.   In Case v. the current was passed every morning and evening from the nape of the neck to the tips of the fingers, which were kept close together.   After improving considerably under this treatment, the condition became stationary.   As the patient was a malarious subject and had formerly derived

[1] *Thesis,* p. 148.

benefit from quinine, Raynaud now returned to this drug and had almost obtained a complete cure when she suddenly left the hospital. In the sixth and last case electricity and all other remedies proved unavailing.

Some of Raynaud's observations are worthy of attention.[1] He recommends that the positive electrode be placed on the fifth cervical vertebra, and the negative over the last lumbar vertebra or the sacrum. After a few minutes, the operator may gradually slide the negative pole up to the eighth dorsal vertebra. The duration of each application ought to be from ten to fifteen minutes, and, as a rule, once a day is sufficient. If the current employed is obtained from 25 or 30 Daniell's cells, it may after some days, though the extremities have been improving, give rise to unpleasant symptoms, such as headache and general excitement, in which case the number of cells ought to be reduced. When the current as applied over the cord begins to give trouble, Raynaud recommends that centrifugal currents should be passed through the whole length of the affected limbs. Galvanism, it may be said at once, resembles the other remedies for Raynaud's disease; if it succeeds in some cases, it fails in others.

B. LOCAL MEASURES.

The local treatment of Raynaud's disease may be summed up as aiming at (1) protecting the affected or threatened part from loss of heat; (2) stimulating the local circulation; (3) relieving pain in the part, and (4), where necessary, promoting the removal of dead tissue by surgical means or otherwise, so as to leave the surviving tissue in the best possible condition.

[1] *New Researches*, pp. 176, 177.

(1) The extremities must be kept as warm as possible by **appropriate clothing.** In severe cases, gloves of the kind described should be worn out of doors all the year round, unless the external atmosphere is as warm as that of the house, after allowance is made for the cooling effects of wind. If the attack is so severe as to confine the patient to the house, the hands or feet, if these are the parts involved, should be wrapped in cotton wool, and if the ears and face are very painful, it may be advisable to wear a mask of cotton wool.

(2) **Friction or massage** of the affected parts, with or without a stimulating lotion, is a very important remedy when it can be tolerated by the patient. Rubbing or kneading must be done gently at first, lest the skin whose vitality is reduced be abraded by rough handling and caused to ulcerate. The parts should be kept at a suitable elevation. It is allowable to keep them in a bath at blood-temperature, but this procedure is not so convenient as others which are equally or more important.

In cases where the pain is so great that the patient cannot allow the parts to be rubbed, or even touched, friction should be applied to the extremity above the level of the affected area ; though manifestly such treatment is carried out at a disadvantage, and any benefit derived must be in a corresponding degree less marked.

Electricity is a local remedy of great value. Duval (1858), it will be remembered, cured his case by local faradization, and a very striking case was recorded by Riva in 1871, where cure was brought about by the same method. At the commencement of treatment, the induced current caused no pain whatever in the affected skin of the hands, though the same parts were excessively tender on the slightest pressure. Raynaud obtained good results by sending continuous currents from the brachial plexus in the axilla to the finger tips, and more recently asphyxia of the ears has been treated by galvanization of the cervical sympathetic cords and of the ears. More than twenty years ago, Mills combined several electrical methods in the following way : (*a*) localized faradization—strong current applied by small electrode to the fingers, the large electrode being applied to the forearm, wrist, or hand ; (*b*) localized galvanization—strong current with negative pole to the fingers, the positive pole being applied to the arm, forearm, or hand ; and (*c*) galvanization of the brain and cervical sympathetic, the poles being applied in the former case to the mastoid processes, and a weak current passed for two or three minutes. As a result of his experience, Mills concluded that local faradism and galvanism are both advisable, but that galvanization of the nerve-centres is not to be recommended.

Localized electrization may be carried out with electrodes of various forms, and at various and varying positions with relation to one another. For instance, two sponge electrodes may be moved about over the affected limb at a short distance from one another. A very useful method of application is by a *bath*, since a large extent of affected skin can thus be treated at one time, and still more perhaps because it allows the current to be applied to parts which the patient could not allow to be touched by an electrode. Barlow called special attention to the value of this procedure in 1885. The affected portion of the limb is immersed in a basin of hot salt water, in which the negative pole of a constant current battery is also placed. The positive pole is applied directly to an unaffected part of the limb higher up, or, if both hands are treated simultaneously, to the neck. The current should be the strongest that the patient can comfortably bear, and should be made and broken or reversed frequently. It is well that the current should cause slight contraction of the forearm muscles, and after some minutes the patient should be encouraged to perform the voluntary movements of flexion and extension while the part is immersed and the current is being altered. This treatment should be continued, if possible, till the part becomes red, and then the limb should be dried, and if the patient will allow it, well rubbed. Galvanization and friction should be carried out once a day. The patient, or in the case of a child the parents, should be instructed to practise galvanization and shampooing every day, and ought to be encouraged to persevere with this for a long time after the attacks have ceased, in order that the liability should, if possible, be thoroughly got rid of. And if on the approach of winter, or under any other circumstances, the paroxysms threaten to return, in however mild a form it may be, diligent and persevering endeavours should be made by all available methods, local and general, to keep both the general health and the circulation in the susceptible parts as vigorous as possible. Prevention here may turn out to be very much easier as well as much more agreeable than cure.

Faradism as well as galvanism may be applied by means of the bath.

Another local method which has been found successful (Sainton), though it failed in a case where it was employed by Raynaud,[1] is the *oxygen bath*. The limb is placed in an india-rubber bag which encloses it hermetically. The bag communicates with a vessel containing oxygen, of which a fresh supply is permitted from time to time to get access to the limb. The result will naturally depend a good deal on the condition of the skin, since this may be expected to

[1] *New Researches*, Case vi.

absorb oxygen more freely if soft, moist and ulcerated, than under conditions which more nearly approach the normal.

Local bleeding is alluded to by Raynaud in favourable terms,[1] the application of leeches gave some temporary relief in Case viii. But this remedy belongs more strictly to the next class.

(3) Relief is sometimes afforded by **local applications of a sedative nature.** Warm fomentations may be medicated with laudanum, or belladonna and glycerin may be smeared over the discoloured skin. Fomentations should not be too hot, since heat may induce the vascular spasm ; and it is well to bear in mind that cold may be more soothing than warmth. In one of Raynaud's collected cases (*Thesis*, Case viii.), where the subjective sensations varied at different parts of the day, cold water was helpful at one stage and injurious at another. This patient seemed to prefer a cool atmosphere to the warmth of bed. She obtained great relief from the application to the painful fingers of compresses soaked in water and chloroform.

(4) When ulceration or gangrene occurs, treatment must be carried out in accordance with modern surgical principles. As the gangrene is dry, there is not much to do in the way of dressing. And with regard to **amputation,** we shall do well to follow Raynaud's advice and never resort to it except in the very unusual cases where a considerable part of a limb dies in mass. We may, of course, snip off portions of semi-detached slough with the scissors, and when a phalanx is partially necrosed and protrudes, resection or disarticulation, together with some trimming of the soft tissues may be required to get a satisfactory stump ; but these measures should not be carried out until the

---

[1] *Thesis*, p. 148.

surviving tissues have regained a manifestly healthy state. It ought always to be borne in mind that even when a considerable part of a digit has become quite gangrenous to all appearance, the area that actually undergoes necrosis may be most insignificant in extent.

BIBLIOGRAPHY.

THESES

(CHRONOLOGICALLY ARRANGED).

D. A. ZAMBACO.—" De la gangrène spontanée produite par perturbation nerveuse." Paris, 1857.

M. RAYNAUD.—"De l'asphyxie locale et de la gangrène symétrique des extrémités." Paris, 1862. Translated by Barlow for New Syd. Soc., London, 1888.

P. H. A. THÈZE.—" Quelques considérations sur un cas d'asphyxie locale des extrémités." Paris, 1872.

J. B. J. BRÉHIER.—"Quelques considérations sur l'asphyxie locale." Paris, 1874.

E. FOULQUIER.—"Considération sur l'asphyxie locale." Paris, 1874.

C. FAVIER.—" Quelques considérations sur les rapports entre la sclérodermie spontanée et la gangrène symétrique des extrémités." Paris, 1880.

RONDOT.—" Des gangrènes spontanées." 1880.

ACHILLE BOY.—"Essai sur l'asphyxie locale des extrémités spécialement au point de vue du traitement par le sulfate de quinine." Paris, 1881.

J. EPARVIER. — "Contribution à l'étude de l'asphyxie locale des extrémités." Lyon, 1884.

A. LAUER.—" Ueber locale Asphyxie und symmetrische Gangrän der Extremitäten mit zwei neuen Beobachtungen." Strasburg, 1884.

MOUNSTEIN.—"Ueber die Spontane Gangrän." Strasburg, 1884.

BOURRELLY.—"Asphyxie locale considérée comme symptôme." Paris, 1887.

E. GOLDSTANDT.—"Ueber symmetrischen Brand." Berlin, 1887.

G. ROSSIGNOT.—" De la gangrène symétrique des extrémités chez l'enfant." Paris, 1888.

F. DE VIVILLE.—"Contribution à l'étude des gangrènes des pieds d'origine nerveuse." Paris, 1888.

233

B. Dominguez.—"Des formes atténuées de la maladie de Maurice Raynaud." Paris, 1889.

Friedel.—"Ueber symmetrische Gangrän." Greifswald, 1889.

Bouchez.—"Asphyxie locale. Ses rapports avec les engelures." Paris, 1892.

W. Giersbach.—"Ueber symmetrische Gangrän." Bonn, 1892.

M. Zeller.—"Zur Kenntniss der Raynaud'schen Gangrän." Berlin, 1894.

L. Defrance.—"Considérations sur la gangrène symétrique, étiologie et pathogénie." Paris, 1895.

1. Abercrombie, J.—"On some points in connection with Raynaud's disease."—*Archives of Pediatrics*, 1886, iii., 567-573.

2. Affleck, J. O.—"Two cases of Raynaud's disease (symmetrical gangrene)."—*Brit. Med. Jour.*, 1888, ii., 1269-1272.

3. Aitken, C. C.—"Case of Raynaud's disease associated with uraemia."—*Lancet*, 1896, ii., 875-876.

4. Anderson, T. M'Call.—"Case of disturbance of the circulation of the left arm, the symptoms resembling those of the early stage of Raynaud's disease."—*Glasg. Med. Jour.*, 1892, xxxviii., 130-132.

5. —— *Glasg. Med. Jour.*, 1895, xliv., 417-420.

6. Atkin.—*Lancet*, 1896, i., 555.

7. Atkinson, I. E.—"Multiple cutaneous ulceration."—*American Jour. Med. Sc.*, 1884, lxxxvii., 57-65.

8. Barlow, T.—"Three cases of Raynaud's disease."—*Clin. Soc. Trans.*, 1883, xvi., 179-188.

9. —— "Sequel to paper on three cases of Raynaud's disease."—*Clin. Soc. Trans.*, 1885, xviii., 307-312.

10. —— *Appendix* to translation of Raynaud's two essays.—*New Syd. Soc.*, 1888.

11. —— *Clin. Soc. Trans.*, 1889, xxii., 413-414.

12. —— "Some cases of Raynaud's disease."—*Illustr. Med. News*, 1889, iii., 73-75 ; 97-100; 125-127 ; 176-178.

13. —— "Raynaud's disease."—Allbutt's *System of Medicine*, vi. (1899), 577-607.

14. Batman, W. F.—"Case of Raynaud's disease."—*Jour. Amer. Med. Assoc.*, 1894, xxiii., 859-860.

15. Beale, C.—*Brit. Med. Jour.*, 1887. i., 730.

16. Beevor.—*Proc. Med. Soc. Lond.*, 1889, xii., 308-309.

17. Begg, J. R.—"Idiopathic gangrene of the four extremities, nose and ears. Amputation of the extremities ; recovery."—*Lancet*, 1870, ii., 397-399.

18. BERNSTEIN.—Quoted in *London Medical Record*, 1885, xiii., 337-338.

19. BILLROTH.—*Medical Press and Circular*, 1884, ii., 453-454.

20. BJERING.—Quoted in Schmidt's *Jahrbücher*, 1878, clxxvii., 19.

21. BLAND, W. C.—"Case of Raynaud's disease following acute mania." *Jour. Ment. Sc.*, 1889, xxxv., 392-394.

22. BRAMANN.—"Fälle symmetrischer Gangrän."—*Verhandlungen der Deutschen Gesellschaft für Chirurgie*, 1889, xviii., 29-37.

23. BRISTOWE AND COPEMAN.—"Case of paroxysmal haemoglobinuria, with experimental observations and remarks."—*Med. Soc. Proc.*, 1889, xii., 256-273.

24. BRÜNNICHE, A.—Quoted in Schmidt's *Jahrbücher*, 1878, clxxvii., 19-20.

25. BULL, E.—Quoted in Schmidt's *Jahrb.*, 1878, clxxvii., 20.

26. CALMETTE.—"Des rapports de l'asphyxie locale des extrémités avec la fièvre intermittente paludéenne."—*Recueil de mémoires de médecine, de chirurgie et de pharmacie militaires*, 1877, xxxiii., 24-51.
(Preliminary note on same subject in *Gazette Médicale de Paris*, 1876, v., 529-530.)

27. CALWELL, W.—"Case of Raynaud's disease."—*Brit. Med. Jour.*, 1890, i., 1484-1485.

28. CATTLE, C. H.—"Raynaud's disease."—*Lancet*, 1889, i., 1037.

29. CAVAFY, J.—"Symmetrical congestive mottling of the skin."—*Clin. Soc. Trans.*, 1883, xvi., 43-48.

30. CHEADLE.—"Raynaud's disease."—*Brit. Med. Jour.*, 1890, i., 19.

31. CLARKE, E. W.—"Raynaud's disease."—*Quarterly Med. Jour.*, 1896-97, v., 350.

32. CLEEMAN, R. A.—"Case of Raynaud's disease associated with angina pectoris."—*Trans. Coll. Physicians, Philadelphia*, 1892, xiv., 163-166.

33. COLLIER, J.—"Symmetrical gangrene."—*Med. Chron.*, 1888-89, ix., 393-401.

34. COLMAN AND TAYLOR.—"Case of Raynaud's disease, not associated with haemoglobinuria, but in which there were local changes in the blood."—*Clin. Soc. Trans.*, 1890, xxiii., 195-200.

35. DANA, C. L.—"The acro-neuroses."—*Med. Record*, 1885, ii., 57-58; 85-87.

36. DAYMAN, H.—"Case of spontaneous dry gangrene." [Nott's case; with quaint sketch of the patient in bed.]—*Provincial Med. and Surg. Jour.*, 1846, p. 302.

37. DEBOVE.—"Note sur un cas de gangrène symétrique des extrémités survenue dans le cours d'une néphrite."—*Union Médicale*, 1880, xxix., 869-871.

38. DECK, H.—"Case of Raynaud's disease."—*Brit. Med. Jour.*, 1894, i., 187-188.

39. DEHIO.—"Ueber symmetrische Gangrän der Extremitäten (Raynaud'sche Krankheit)."—*Deutsche Zeitschrift für Nervenheilkunde*, 1893, iv., 1-13.

40. DÉJÉRINE ET LELOIR. — "Recherches anatomo-pathologiques et cliniques sur les altérations nerveuses dans certains cas de gangrène."—*Archives de physiologie normale et pathologique*, 1881, viii., 989-1015.

41. DIXON, H. J.—"Gangrene of the foot in a case of Raynaud's disease." —*Illustr. Med. News*, 1889, iii., 25.

42. DUBREUILH.—"Gangrène symétrique des doigts. Faux panaris des gaines des fléchisseurs."—*Gazette Médicale de Paris*, 1884, 316-317.

43. ENGLISCH.—"Ueber lokale Asphyxie mit symmetrischer Gangrän an den Extremitäten."—*Wiener medizinische Presse*, 1878, xix., 1085-1088; 1119-1122; 1152-1153; 1189-1191; 1213-1216; 1252-1253; 1280-1282.

44. FABRE.—"Un cas de gangrène symétrique des extrémités."—*Gazette Médicale de Paris*, 1883, 571-573.

45. FAIRLAND, E. J.—"Case of Raynaud's disease."—*Lancet*, 1895, ii., 331.

46. FAURE.—"Gangrène symétrique des extrémités."—*Gazette des hôpitaux*, 1874, 347-348.

47. FÉRÉ.—"Note sur l'asphyxie locale des extrémités chez les épileptiques, et en particulier sur un cas d'asphyxie disseminée."—*Nouvelle Iconographie de la Salpêtrière*, 1891, iv., 354-357.

48. FÉRÉ ET BATIGNE.—"Note sur un nouveau cas d'asphyxie locale des extrémités avec lésions congénitales de la peau chez un épileptique."—*Revue de Médecine*, 1892, xii., 891-897.

49. FISCHER.—"Der symmetrische Brand."—*Archiv fur klinische Chirurgie*, 1875, xviii., 335-339.

50. FORDYCE, J. A.—"Raynaud's disease of the ears."—*Trans. Amer. Dermat. Assoc.* (1895), 1896, xix., 11-13.

51. FOWLER.—"Raynaud's disease."—*Brit. Med. Jour.*, 1889, i., 80.

52. FOX, R. HINGSTON.—"Raynaud's disease."—*Lancet*, 1888, ii., 1256.

53. FOX, T. COLCOTT.—"On two cases of Raynaud's disease."—*Clin. Soc. Trans.*, 1885, xviii., 300-306; 1889, xxii., 412.

54. GARLAND, G. M.—"Raynaud's disease."—*Jour. Amer. Med. Assoc.*, 1889, xiii., 837-839.

55. GRANT, D.—"Case of Raynaud's disease."—*Trans. Intercolon. Med. Congress of Australasia*, 1889, ii., 129-135.

56. GRIFFITH, T. W.—"Three cases illustrating some of the affinities of Raynaud's disease."—*Med. Chron.*, 1891-92, xv., 89-95.

57. HAIG, A.—*Uric acid as a factor in the causation of disease*, 1892.

58. —— "Case of Raynaud's disease with paroxysmal haemoglobinuria." —*Trans. Med. Soc. Lond.*, 1892, xv., 143-156.

59. HAIG, A.—"Case of Raynaud's disease."—*St. Barth. Hosp. Rep.*, 1892, xxviii., 29-46.

60. HALL, F. DE H.—"Raynaud's disease."—*Brit. Med. Jour.*, 1891, i., 411.

61. HAMILTON, A. M'L.—"Chronic vasomotor hyperirritation."—*New York Med. Jour.*, 1874, xx., 356-358.

62. HANNEMANN, J. L.—"De manibus sphacelatis ab earum in frigidam immissione."—*Miscellanea curiosa sive ephemeridum medico-physicarum Germanicarum Academiae naturae curiosorum Decuriae* II. Annus tertius, Anni MDCLXXXIV. 1685. Obs. lvii., pp. 145-146.

63. HAROLD, J.—"Case of Raynaud's disease or neuropathic gangrenous trophoneurosis of the lower extremities."—*Lancet*, 1895, i., 341-342.

64. HASTREITER.—"Ein Fall von symmetrischer Asphyxie der unteren Extremitäten."—*Wiener medizinische Presse*, 1882, xxiii., 985-987 ; 1048-1049 ; 1093-1095.

65. HAUPTMANN, J. H.—"Case of Raynaud's disease."—*Med. Record*, 1896, l., 459.

66. HENRY, BERNARD.—Quoted in *Brit. and For. Med.-Chir. Review*, 1856, 254-255.

67. HENRY, F. P.—"Two cases of Raynaud's disease."—*Amer. Jour. Med. Sc.*, 1894, cviii., 10-19.

68. HOCHENEGG.—"Ueber symmetrische Gangrän und locale Asphyxie."—(Separat-Abdruck aus den *Medizinischen Jahrbüchern der K.K. Gesellschaft der Aerzte, Jahrg.*, 1885.) Wien, 1886.

69. V. HOESSLIN.—"Ueber locale Asphyxie."—*Münchener medicinische Wochenschrift*, 1888, xxxv., 94-96.

70. VAN DER HOEVEN.—"Lokale Asphyxie und symmetrische Gangrän der Extremitäten."—Quoted in *Centralblatt für Chirurgie*, 1885, xii., 834-835.

71. HOLM, K. A.—Quoted in Schmidt's *Jahrb.*, 1873, clix., 43.

72. HUGUIER.—Quoted by Hutchinson, *Archives of Surg.*, 1891, ii., 190.

73. HUMPHREYS, F. R.—*Lancet*, 1890, ii., 1334.

74. HUTCHINSON, J.—"Gangrene of tip of nose and part of ear—iridoplegia, etc."—*Med. Times and Gaz.*, 1871, ii., 678.

75. —— *Lectures on Clinical Surgery*, 1879, vol. i. ("On certain rare diseases of the skin"), 365-367.

76. —— *Lancet*, 1882, ii., 663.

77. —— *Med. Times and Gaz.*, 1885, ii., 35-36.

78. —— *Brit. Med. Jour.*, 1887, ii., 164.

79. —— "On certain local disorders more or less cognate with Raynaud's malady."—*Arch of Surg.*, 1890, i., 226-231.

80. —— (a) "Severe symmetrical gangrene of the extremities"; (b) "Raynaud's phenomena with thrombotic warts."—*Brit. Med. Jour.*, 1891, ii., 8-9.

81. HUTCHINSON, J.—*Arch. of Surg.*, 1891, ii., 190-191.
82. —— "Case of Raynaud's disease with acrosphacelus."—*Arch. of Surg.*, 1892, iii., 311-314.
83. —— "Acroasphyxia (Raynaud's phenomena)."—*Arch. of Surg.*, 1892, iii., Description of Plate xxxii.
84. —— "Typical and severe case of Raynaud's phenomena—maternal grief as a cause—approach to the condition of diffuse morphoea."— *Arch. of Surg.*, 1893, iv., 177-179.
85. —— "Inherited liability to Raynaud's phenomena, with great proneness to chilblains—gradual increase of liability to paroxysmal local asphyxia—acrosphacelus with sclerodermia—cheeks affected."— *Arch. of Surg.*, 1893, iv., 312-313.
86. —— "Two lectures on acropathology (Raynaud's phenomena and allied conditions)"—*Med. Week*, 1893, i., 85-87 ; 97-100.
87. —— "Congenital syphilis—fair health, but defective development of mental powers—at the age of six aggressive idiotcy—Raynaud's phenomena."—*Arch. of Surg.*, 1894, v., 220-222.
88. —— *Arch. of Surg.*, 1895, vi., 351.
89. —— "Raynaud's phenomena in an elderly woman."—*Clin. Jour.*, 1895, v., 74-75.
90. —— "Acroscleroderma following Raynaud's phenomena."—*Clin. Jour.* (1895-96), 1896, vii., 240.
91. —— "Raynaud's disease accompanied by severe haemorrhages."— *Clin. Jour.*, 1896, vii., 322-323.
92. —— "Symmetrical acrosphacelus without Raynaud's phenomena."— *Arch. of Surg.*, 1896, vii., 201-209.
93. ISCOVESCO.—"Asphyxie locale des extrémités."—*Comptes rendus hebdomadaires des séances et mémoires de la Société de Biologie*, 1894, i., 289-290.
94. ISRAELSOHN.—Quoted in *Amer. Jour. Med. Sc.*, 1894, cviii., 224-225.
95. JACOB, E.—*Brit. Med. Jour.*, 1887, i., 625.
96. JACOBY, G. W.—"Contribution to the diagnosis of Raynaud's disease (symmetrical gangrene)."—*New York Med. Jour.*, 1891, liii., 143-149.
97. JAMES, D.—*Lancet*, 1896, i., 555.
98. JOHNSTON, W. W.—"Case of vasomotor neurosis of a rare form occurring in a child."—*Amer. Jour. Obstet.*, 1885, xviii., 393-399.
99. KRISOWSKI.—Quoted in *Amer. Jour. Med. Sc.*, 1895, cx., 496.
100. LACHMUND.—"De menstruali partium in puella quadam externarum, utpote aurium, narium, digitorum, etc., mortificatione." [Schrader's case].—*Miscellanea curiosa medico-physica academiae naturae curiosorum* (1673-74), 1676, iv-v., 238-239.
101. LANCEREAUX.—"Des troubles vasomoteurs et trophiques liés à l'alcoolisme et à quelques autres intoxications chroniques (paleurs

et sueurs froides, asphyxie locale, oedème et gangrène des extrémités)."—*Union Médicale*, 1881, xxxi., 745-751; 825-828; 857-861.

102. LEGROUX.—"Asphyxie locale des extrémités. Ses rapports avec les engelures."—*Annales de dermatologie et de syphiligraphie*, 1892, iii., 184-187.

103. LELOIR ET MERKLEN.—"Syncope locale des extrémités. Eczéma de la paume des mains et des doigts."—*Annales de dermatologie et de syphiligraphie*, 1882, iii., 351-354.

104. LITTLE, J. F.—"Case of Raynaud's disease."—*Clin. Soc. Trans.*, 1897, xxx., 231.

105. LUNN, J. R.—"Case of cyanosis of feet (Raynaud's disease)."—*Clin. Soc. Trans.*, 1887, xx., 259; 1889, xxii., 426.

106. M'BRIDE, T. A.—Quoted by Mills.—*Amer. Jour. Med. Sc.*, 1878, lxxvi., 435.

107. MACPHERSON, J.—"Case of acute mania with symmetrical gangrene of the toes (Raynaud's disease)."—*Jour. Mental Science*, 1889, xxxv., 61-66.

108. MAKINS, G. H.—"Case of spontaneous gangrene of toes in a child."—*St. Thomas' Hosp. Rep.*, 1882, xii., 155-163.

109. MARFAN.—"Syncope locale des extrémités supérieures à la suite d'une commotion médullaire. Disparition rapide de l'affection."—*Archives générales de médecine*, 1887, ii., 485-488.

110. MARSH, F.—"Raynaud's disease associated with hereditary syphilis."—*Brit. Med. Jour.*, 1892, i., 1083.

111. MARSH, J. H.—"Case of Raynaud's disease."—*Brit. Med. Jour.*, 1896, i., 147.

112. MAUGUE.—Quoted in *Brit. Med. Jour.*, 1895, ii. epit., 380.

113. MENDEL, H.—"Gangrène symétrique des extrémités chez une enfant de quinze mois."—*Annales de dermatologie et de syphiligraphie*, 1893, iv., 406-409.

114. MIDDLETON, G. S.—"Case showing some of the phenomena described in Mr. Jonathan Hutchinson's articles on acropathology."—*Glasg. Med. Jour.*, 1894, xlii., 161-165.

115. MILLS, C. K.—"Vasomotor and trophic affection of the fingers."—*Amer. Jour. Med. Sc.*, 1878, lxxvi., 431-436.

116. MITCHELL, S. WEIR.—"Erythromelalgia: red neuralgia of the extremities; vasomotor paralysis of the extremities; terminal neuritis."—Chapter x. in *Clinical Lessons on Nervous Diseases*, 1897, 177-204.

117. MONRO, T. K.—"Complicated case of Raynaud's disease: local asphyxia with gangrene, occurring at a very early age—congenital disturbance of general cutaneous circulation—congenital hydrocephalus—tracheocele."—*Glasg. Med. Jour.*, 1894, xli., 267-279.

118. —— *Glasg. Med. Jour.*, 1897, xlvii., 92-93.

119. MORGAN, J. E.—"Case of Raynaud's symmetrical gangrene in a patient suffering from constitutional syphilis, with some remarks on the history, nature, and manifestations of the disease."—*Lancet*, 1889, ii., 9-11 ; 64-66 ; 107-108; 157-159.

120. MORTON, H. H.—"Raynaud's disease with report of three cases."— *Jour. Cutan. Genito-ur. Dis.*, 1894, xii., 249-253.

121. MOUILLOT, A.—"Case of Raynaud's disease."—*Brit. Med. Jour.*, 1897, ii., 806-807.

122. MOURSOU.—"Étude clinique sur l'asphyxie locale des extrémités et sur quelques autres troubles vasomoteurs dans leurs rapports avec la fièvre intermittente."—*Archives de médecine navale*, 1880, xxxiii., 340-366 ; 431-447.

123. MUSSER, J. H.—"Raynaud's disease."—*Trans. Coll. Phys. Philad.*, 1886, viii., 341-356.

124. MYERS, A. T.—"Case of Raynaud's disease."—*Clin. Soc. Trans.*, 1885, xviii., 336-338.

125. MYRTLE, A. S.—"Case of anaemic sphacelus."—*Lancet*, 1863, i., 602-603.

126. NARATH.—*Lancet*, 1895, i., 844.

127. NEDOPIL.—"Symmetrische Gangrän der Extremitäten."—*Wiener medizin. Woch.*, 1878, 623-625.

128. NIELSEN, C.—Quoted in Schmidt's *Jahrb.*, 1878, clxxvii., 18-19.

129. NOYES, A. W. F.—"Raynaud's disease (two cases)."—*Australian Med. Jour.*, 1893, xv., 265-269.

130. —— "Some notes on the conditions associated with Raynaud's disease."—*Australian Med. Jour.*, 1893, xv., 593-599; 1894, xvi., 57-64.

131. —— "Case of Raynaud's disease associated with cerebral and other phenomena."—*Intercol. Med. Jour. Australasia*, 1896, i., 544-546.

132. O'CONOR, J.—"Raynaud's disease."—*Brit. Med. Jour.*, 1889, i., 598.

133. OSLER, W.—"Case of local syncope and asphyxia of the fingers."— *Jour. Nerv. and Ment. Dis.*, 1888, xv., 207-208.

134. —— "The cerebral complications of Raynaud's disease."—*Amer. Jour. Med. Sc.*, 1896, cxii., 522-529.

135. PAGET, J.—"Case illustrating certain nervous disorders."—*St. Barth. Hosp. Rep.*, 1871, vii., 67-70.

136. PARKINSON, J. P.—"Case of local asphyxia of one hand."—*Clin. Soc. Trans.*, 1895, xxviii., 261-262.

137. PASTEUR, W.—"Case in which a transient attack of local asphyxia (Raynaud) was determined by a dog-bite."—*Lancet*, 1889, ii., 14.

138. PENNY, W. J.—"Case of Raynaud's disease."—*Bristol Med.-Chir. Jour.*, 1888, vi., 48, 49.

139. PETIT ET VERNEUIL.—"Asphyxie locale et gangrène palustres."— *Revue de Chirurgie*, 1883, iii., 1-28; 161-185 ; 432-452 ; 699-734.

140. PITRES ET VAILLARD.—"Contribution à l'étude des gangrènes massives des membres d'origine névritique."—*Archives de physiologie, normale et pathologique*, 1885, v., 106-127.

141. PORTAL.—"Gangrène sèche des premières phalanges de tous les doigts des deux pieds et des deux mains."—*Archives générales de médecine*, 1836, xi., 223-224.

142. PORTER.—*Lancet*, 1889, i., 841.

143. POWELL, A.—"Case of Raynaud's disease following diphtheria."—*Brit. Med. Jour.*, 1886, i., 203.

144. POWER, D'A.—"Case of symmetrical gangrene of the feet."—*Lancet*, 1893, i. 249-250.

145. RADZISZEWSKI.—"Une observation de gangrène spontanée symétrique des doigts de la main."—*Le Progrès Médical*, 1888, viii., 44-46.

146. RAKHMANINOFF.—"Contribution à la névrite périphérique. Un cas de gangrène symétrique et deux cas de paralysie alcoolique."—*Revue de Médecine*, 1892, xii., 321-335.

147. RAYNAUD.—Article "Gangrène" in *Nouveau dictionnaire de médecine et de chirurgie pratiques*, 1872, xv., 592-716 ; and, in particular, "Gangrène symétrique des extrémités," 636-656.

148. —— "Nouvelles recherches sur la nature et le traitement de l'asphyxie locale des extrémités."—*Archives générales de médecine*, 1874, i., 5-21 ; 189-206. Translated by Barlow for New Syd. Soc., 1888.

149. REIL.—"Ueber das Absterben einzelner Glieder, besonders der Finger."—*Archiv für die Physiologie*, 1807-1808, viii., 59-66.

150. RENSHAW, H. S.—"Multiple insular necrosis of skin and subjacent tissues."—*Brit. Med. Jour.*, 1894, i., 1238-1240.

151. RICHARD.—"De la gangrène symétrique des extrémités dans la fièvre typhoïde."—*Union Médicale*, 1880, xxix., 1025-1029.

152. RICHARDSON, B. W.—"Local syncope, or suspended life in local surfaces."—*Asclepiad*, 1885, ii., 1-7.

153. RITTI.—"De l'asphyxie locale des extrémités dans la période de dépression de la folie à double forme."—*Annales Medico-psychologiques*, 1882, viii., 36-49.

.154. RIVA.—Quoted in Schmidt's *Jahrbücher*, 1872, clv., 25-26.

155. ROGNETTA.—"Gangrène blanche. Saignées. Guérison."—*Revue médicale française et étrangère*, 1834, i., 368-370.

156. ROQUES.—"Note sur un cas de gangrène symétrique des extrémités chez une albuminurique."—*Union Médicale*, 1883, xxxv., 529-531.

157. ROSS AND BURY.—*Peripheral Neuritis*, 1893, 387-398.

158. SAINTON.—"Asphyxie symétrique des extrémités et menace de gangrène chez un saturnin. Traitement par les bains locaux d'oxygène. Guérison."—*La France Médicale*, 1881, i. 221-223.

159. SAINT-PHILIPPE.—"Asphyxie locale des extrémités."—*Mémoires et Bulletins de la Société de Médecine et de Chirurgie de Bordeaux*, (1882), 1883, 227-229.

160. V. SANTVOORD, R.—"Two cases of Raynaud's disease, with remarks."—*Medical Record*, 1888, xxxiii., 35-36.

161. SCHEIBER.—"Ein Fall von symmetrischer Asphyxie."—*Wiener Medizin. Woch.*, 1892, xlii., 1489-1492; 1524-1526; 1559-1561; 1595-1597.

162. SCHUBOE.—Quoted in Schmidt's *Jahrbücher*, 1878, clxxvii., 19.

163. SHAW, J. C.—"Raynaud's disease."—*New York Med. Jour.*, 1886, xliv., 676-679.

164. SHORT.—*Brit. Med. Jour.*, 1897, i., 1349-1350.

165. SIMPSON, J. C.—"Case of Raynaud's disease."—*Brit. Med. Jour.*, 1891, i., 800.

166. —— "Remarks on Raynaud's disease, with cases."—*Edin. Med. Jour.*, 1892-93, xxxviii., 1030-1037.

167. SKIPTON, A.—"Case of Raynaud's disease."—*Lancet*, 1893, i., 144.

168. SMITH, F. J.—*Brit. Med. Jour.*, 1892, i., 275.

169. SMITH, T.—"Case of spontaneous gangrene of the thumb and fingers of the right hand."—*Clin. Soc. Trans.*, 1880, xiii., 196-197.

170. SOLIS-COHEN, S.—"Vasomotor ataxia: a contribution to the subject of idiosyncrasies."—*Amer. Jour. Med. Sc.*, 1894, cvii., 130-147.

171. SOLLY, S.—"Remarkable case of dry gangrene occurring in a child three years and seven months old."—*Med.-Chir. Trans.*, 1839, xxii., 253-266; 1840, xxiii., 237-242.

172. SOUTHEY, R.—"Case of symmetrical gangrene, with some remarks on the disease."—*St. Barth. Hosp. Rep.*, 1880, xvi., 15-26.

173. —— "Case of local asphyxia. Symmetrical gangrene."—*Clin. Soc. Trans.*, 1883, xvi., 167-179.

174. SPENCER, W. G.—"Frost-bite in a boy, the subject of haematinuria, upon exposure to cold."—*Clin. Soc. Trans.*, 1892, xxv., 287-288.

175. STEINER.—"Ein Fall von spontaner symmetrischer Gangrän."—*Deut. Medicin. Woch.*, 1888, xiv., 65-66.

176. STEVENSON, L. E.—"Case of Raynaud's disease."—*Lancet*, 1890, ii., 917-918.

177. STURMDORF, A.—"On symmetrical gangrene."—*Medical Record*, 1891, 113-121.

178. SUCKLING, C. W.—"Raynaud's disease."—*Brit. Med. Jour.*, 1887, ii., 998.

179. TANNAHILL, T. F.—"Purple suffusion of the extremities alternating with attacks of haematinuria."—*Brit. Med. Jour.*, 1886, ii., 1213.— "Raynaud's gangrene, or local asphyxia and symmetrical gangrene of the extremities" [continuation of the preceding].—*Glas. Med. Jour.*, 1888, xxx., 425-429.

180. TARGOWLA.—" Un cas d'asphyxie locale symétrique intermittente des extrémités chez un lypémaniaque."—*Annales Médico-psychologiques,* 1892, xv., 400-403.

181. TAYLOR, R. W.—" Two cases of Raynaud's disease."—*Jour. Cut. Genito-ur. Dis.,* 1890, viii., 382-384.

182. TAYLOR, S. — " Case of Raynaud's disease."—*Lancet,* 1887, i., 208-210.

183. THIERSCH.—Quoted in *Amer. Jour. Med. Sc.,* 1896, cxii., 224.

184. THOMAS, H. M. — " Case of Raynaud's disease associated with convulsions and haemoglobinuria."—*Johns Hopkins Hosp. Reports,* 1890-91, ii., 114-118. (Report of this case continued by Osler, *Amer. Jour. Med. Sc.,* 1896, cxii., 523-524.)

185. TREVES, F.—" Case of pulsating tumour of the head, with Raynaud's disease."—*Clin. Soc. Trans.,* 1887, xx., 12-21.

186. URBANTSCHITSCH.— *Wiener Medizin. Woch.,* 1890, 977.

187. URQUHART, A. R.—" Two cases of Raynaud's disease occurring in James Murray's Royal Asylum, Perth."—*Edin. Med. Jour.,* 1895, xl., ii., 806-813.

188. VERDALLE. —"Asphyxie locale et gangrène symétrique des extrémités. Athérome artériel généralisé."—*Mémoires et Bulletins de la Société de Médecine et de Chirurgie de Bordeaux* (1882), 1883, 272-277.

189. VILLARD.—" Gangrène symétrique des extrémités."—*Lyon Médical,* 1890, lxv., 195-196.

190. VULPIAN.— *Clinique Médicale de l'Hôpital de la Charité,* 1879, 872-889.

191. —— " Asphyxie et syncope locales des quatre extrémités ; accidents cérébraux, bulbaires et cardiaques ; électrisation ; amélioration." —*Gazette des Hôpitaux,* 1884, lvii., 65-66.

192. WALDO, H.—" Case of Raynaud's disease."—*Bristol Med.-Chir. Jour.,* 1888, vi., 272-275.

193. WALSH.— *Trans. Dermat. Soc., Gt. Brit. and Irel.* (1896-97), 1897, iii., 87.

194. WARREN, J. C.—"Symmetrical gangrene of the extremities."—*Boston Med. and Surg. Jour.,* 1879, c., 76-84.

195. WEAVER, J. J.—"Case of symmetrical gangrene (Raynaud's disease)." —*Lancet,* 1888, ii., 859-861.

196. WEISS.—" Ueber symmetrische Gangrän (Raynaud's lokale Asphyxie und symmetrische Gangrän)."—*Wiener Klinik,* 1882, viii., 347-401.

197. —— " Ueber Venenspasmus."—*Wiener Medizinische Presse,* 1882, xxiii., 988-990 ; 1015-1018 ; 1045-1048 ; 1069-1072 ; 1095-1098.

198. WEST, S.—"Case of Raynaud's disease with a peculiar eruption on the face, scaly at first, subsequently like erysipelas : death from pneumonia : post-mortem negative."—*Clin. Soc. Trans.,* 1889, xxii., 146-150.

199. WETHERELL, J. A.—"Case of Raynaud's disease."—*Lancet,* 1889, i., 1302.
200. WHERRY, G.—"Case of Raynaud's disease with interstitial keratitis." —*Clinical Sketches,* 1895, ii., 38-39.
201. WHITE, J. A. H.—"Case of combined scleroderma and Raynaud's disease."—*Lancet,* 1896, i., 1136.
202. WHITE, W. H.—"Fatal case of Raynaud's disease in a girl having mitral and tricuspid stenosis, pericarditis, acute cardiac dilatation, pneumonia, embolism of the brachial artery, and atrophy of the muscles of feet."—*Clin. Jour.,* 1894, iii., 369-375.
203. WHITTON, T. B.—"Case of Raynaud's disease."—*Australasian Med. Gaz.,* 1890-91, x., 353-354.
204. WIGLESWORTH, J.—"Peripheral neuritis in Raynaud's disease (symmetrical gangrene)."—*Trans. Path. Soc. Lond.,* 1887, xxxviii., 61-68.
205. WILKS, S.—"Case of haemoglobinuria, gangrene of the fingers, etc., associated with prolonged suppuration."—*Med. Times and Gaz.,* 1879, ii., 207-208.
206. ZELLER.—"Ein seltener Fall von spontaner Gangrän."—*Berliner Klin. Woch.,* 1893, xxx., 1263-1265.

INDEX.

18 99

UNIVERSITY PRESS

GLASGOW

Catalogue of Books

Published by

James MacLehose & Sons

Publishers to the University of Glasgow

GLASGOW : 61 St. Vincent Street

1899

PUBLISHED BY

JAMES MACLEHOSE AND SONS, GLASGOW,

Publishers to the University.

———

MACMILLAN AND CO., LTD., LONDON.

New York, - - The Macmillan Co.
London, - - - Simpkin, Hamilton and Co
Cambridge, - - Macmillan and Bowes.
Edinburgh, - - Douglas and Foulis.

———

MDCCCXCIX.

CLASSIFIED LIST OF BOOKS IN

THE FOLLOWING CATALOGUE

PHILOSOPHICAL

THEOLOGICAL

MEDICAL

TOPOGRAPHICAL

A 2

UNIVERSITY AND OTHER TEXT-BOOKS

Messrs. MACLEHOSE'S

Publications

AGLEN—THE ODES OF HORACE. Translated into English
Verse by the VENERABLE A. S. AGLEN, M.A., Archdeacon
of St. Andrews. Crown 8vo. 4s. 6d. nett.

ANDERSON—LECTURES ON MEDICAL NURSING, delivered
in the Royal Infirmary, Glasgow. By J. WALLACE ANDER-
SON, M.D. Sixth Edition. Fcap. 8vo. 2s. 6d.
" An admirable guide."—*Lancet.*

ANDERSON—ON AFFECTIONS OF THE NERVOUS SYSTEM.
By T. M'CALL ANDERSON, M.D., Professor of Clinical
Medicine in the University of Glasgow. Demy 8vo. 5s.

BARR—MANUAL OF DISEASES OF THE EAR, for the Use of
Practitioners and Students of Medicine. By THOMAS
BARR, M.D., Lecturer on Aural Surgery in the University
of Glasgow. New Edition. Re-written and greatly
enlarged. Medium 8vo. 12s. 6d. nett.

BATHGATE—PROGRESSIVE RELIGION. By the late REV.
WILLIAM BATHGATE, D.D., Kilmarnock. Crown 8vo. 6s.

BIRRELL—Two Queens: a Dramatic Poem.   By C. J. Ballingall Birrell.   Crown 8vo.   3s. 6d.

BLACKBURN—Caw, Caw; or, the Chronicle of the Crows; a Tale of the Spring Time.   Illustrated by J. B. (Mrs. Hugh Blackburn).   4to.   2s. 6d.

BROWN—The Authorship of the Kingis Quair.   A New Criticism by J. T. T. Brown.   Demy 8vo.   4s. nett.

BROWN—The Life of a Scottish Probationer.   Being the Memoir of Thomas Davidson, with his Poems and Letters.   By the late James Brown, D.D., Paisley.   Third Edition.   Crown 8vo.   5s.

"A very fresh and interesting little book."—*Saturday Review.*
"This life of an unknown Scotch probationer is equal in interest to anything of the kind we have seen since Carlyle's 'Life of Sterling' was written."—*Blackwood's Magazine.*
"It is an unspeakable pleasure to a reviewer weary of wading through "A charming little biography."—*Spectator.*

BROWN—Life of William B. Robertson, D.D., of Irvine, with Extracts from his Letters and Poems.   By the late James Brown, D.D.   Fourth Edition.   Crown 8vo, with two Portraits.   5s.

"This memoir is one to have, to study, and to go to frequently."—*Cambridge Express.*

BUCHANAN—Poems by the late David Buchanan, Kirkintilloch.   Crown 8vo.   5s.

CAIRD, Principal—An Introduction to the Philosophy of Religion.   By the Very Rev. John Caird, D.D., LL.D., late Principal and Vice-Chancellor of the University of Glasgow.   Sixth Thousand.   Crown 8vo.   6s.

"A book rich in the results of speculative study, broad in its intellectual grasp, and happy in its original suggestiveness.   To Dr. Caird we are indebted for a subtle and masterly presentation of Hegel's philosophy in its solution of the problem of religion."—*Edinburgh Review.*

CAIRD, Principal—UNIVERSITY ADDRESSES on Subjects of
Academic Study delivered to the University of Glasgow.
By JOHN CAIRD, D.D., LL.D., late Principal and Vice-
Chancellor of the University of Glasgow. Third Thousand.
Crown 8vo. 6s. nett.

CONTENTS—The Unity of the Sciences—The Progressiveness of the
Sciences—Erasmus—Galileo—The Scientific Character of Bacon—David
Hume—Bishop Butler and his Theology—The Study of History—The
Science of History—The Study of Art—The Progressiveness of Art—The
Art of Public Speaking—The Personal Element in Teaching—General and
Professional Education.

"The Master of Balliol lays us under great obligation by giving to the
world this relic of his distinguished brother. It is a book, almost every
page of which we have read with unflagging interest."—*The Guardian.*

"They give evidence at every turn of courage of conviction and luminous
understanding of the trend of thought in the present age."—*Speaker.*

"The volume will be welcome to all readers who value the utterances of
a mind of a very high and rare order on themes of perennial interest to all
students of literature, science, art and religion."—*Spectator.*

"The subjects, it will be evident, are all of such a kind that an acute and
original mind could not apply itself to their treatment without producing a
distinctly happy result. These essays are full of attraction for a thoughtful
and solid reader."—*Daily Chronicle.*

CAIRD, Principal—UNIVERSITY SERMONS. Preached before
the University of Glasgow, 1873-1898. By PRINCIPAL
CAIRD. Fourth Thousand. Crown 8vo. With Portrait.
6s. nett.

CONTENTS—What is Religion?—The Likeness and Unlikeness of God's
Ways and Man's Ways—Evil Working through Good—The New Birth—
The Christian Way of Reconciling Man with Himself—Can Righteousness
be Imputed?—Is Repentance ever Impossible?—The Reversal of Nature's
Law of Competition—Corporate Immortality—Truth and Freedom—The
Guilt and Guiltlessness of Unbelief—The Relations of Love and Knowledge
—The Measure of Greatness—The Profit of Godliness—The Spiritual
Relations of Nature to Man—Art and Religion—Things New and Old—
The Temporal and the Eternal—The Law of Heredity in the Spiritual Life.

"This is perhaps the finest volume of Sermons in modern English. The
collection which most seriously challenges its pre-eminence is Dean Church's
'Human Life and its Conditions'; and we are inclined to rank the volume
before us even higher than the splendid masterpieces of the Anglican
divine."—*Record.*

CAIRD, Principal—SERMONS AND LECTURES.   In separate
pamphlet form.   Demy 8vo.   Paper covers.   1s. each.

1. CHRISTIAN MANLINESS.
2. IN MEMORIAM.   Very Rev. Principal BARCLAY, D.D.
3. MIND AND MATTER.
4. THE UNIVERSAL RELIGION.
5. THE PROGRESSIVENESS OF THE SCIENCES.

CAIRD, Edward—THE CRITICAL PHILOSOPHY OF IMMANUEL
KANT.   By EDWARD CAIRD, M.A., LL.D., Master of Balliol
College, Oxford, late Professor of Moral Philosophy in the
University of Glasgow.   2 vols.   Demy 8vo.   32s.

" It is quite the most comprehensive and maturely considered contribution
that has yet been made by an English writer to the understanding of Kant's
whole philosophical achievement.   It is the result of a study of Kant such
as perhaps no Englishman will again undertake, and is in every way a
thorough and masterly performance."—*Mind.*

CAIRD, Edward — ESSAYS IN LITERATURE AND PHILO-
SOPHY.   2 vols.   Crown 8vo.   8s. 6d. nett.

CAIRD, Edward—THE EVOLUTION OF RELIGION.   Third
Edition.   2 vols.   Post 8vo.   12s. nett.

" Professor Caird's lectures will form an epoch-making book, which more
than any other since England was startled by the sweet reasonableness of
'Ecce Homo' has given a firm, consistent, and convincing exposition, both
of the infinitely various manifestations of the earlier religions and of that
Christian synthesis which cannot die out of the human mind."—*Daily
Chronicle.*

CAIRD, Edward—THE SOCIAL PHILOSOPHY AND RELIGION
OF COMTE.   Second Edition.   Crown 8vo.   5s. nett.

CAIRD, Edward—INDIVIDUALISM AND SOCIALISM.   Demy
8vo.   1s.

CLELAND and MACKAY—The Anatomy of the Human Body, for the use of Students of Medicine and Science. By John Cleland, M.D., LL.D., D.Sc., F.R.S., Professor of Anatomy in the University of Glasgow, and John Yule Mackay, M.D., C.M., Professor of Anatomy in University College, Dundee. Profusely illustrated. Medium 8vo. 28s. nett.

CLELAND and MACKAY—A Directory for the Dissection of the Human Body. By John Cleland, M.D., and John Yule Mackay, M.D. Fcap. 8vo. 3s. 6d. nett.

CLELAND—Evolution, Expression, and Sensation. By John Cleland, M.D., D.Sc., F.R.S. Crown 8vo. 5s.

COATS—The Master's Watchword : An Essay recalling attention to some Fundamental Principles of the Christian Religion. By the Rev. Jervis Coats, D.D. Crown 8vo. 5s.

DEAS—History of the Clyde. With Maps and Diagrams. By James Deas, Engineer of the Clyde Navigation. 8vo. 10s. 6d.

DICKSON—St. Paul's Use of the Terms Flesh and Spirit. Being the Baird Lecture for 1883. By William P. Dickson, D.D., LL.D., Emeritus Professor of Divinity in the University of Glasgow. Crown 8vo. 8s. 6d.

DOUGLAS—Chemical and Microscopical Aids to Clinical Diagnosis. By Carstairs C. Douglas, M.D., B.Sc. Crown 8vo. Illustrated. 4s. 6d. nett.

[*This day.*

DOWNIE—CLINICAL MANUAL FOR THE STUDY OF DISEASES
OF THE THROAT. By J. WALKER DOWNIE, M.B.,
Lecturer in the University of Glasgow on Diseases of the
Throat and Nose. Crown 8vo. Illustrated. 6s. nett.

DUNCAN—MEMORIALS OF THE FACULTY OF PHYSICIANS
AND SURGEONS AND OF THE MEDICAL PROFESSION
OF GLASGOW. By ALEXANDER DUNCAN, B.A., LL.D.,
Librarian to the Faculty. Crown 4to. 10s. 6d. nett.

EGGS 4D. A DOZEN, AND CHICKENS 4D. A POUND
ALL THE YEAR ROUND. Containing full information
for profitable keeping of Poultry. Small 8vo. Twentieth
Thousand. 1s.

FORSYTH—A GRADUATED COURSE OF INSTRUCTION IN
LINEAR PERSPECTIVE. By DAVID FORSYTH, M.A., D.Sc.,
Headmaster of the Central Higher Grade School, Leeds.
Third Edition. Royal 8vo. 2s.

FORSYTH—TEST PAPERS IN PERSPECTIVE. 26 papers.
Full Government size. Third Edition. 1s. 6d. per set.

GAIRDNER—THE PHYSICIAN AS NATURALIST, Memoirs
bearing on the Progress of Medicine. By SIR W. T.
GAIRDNER, K.C.B., M.D., LL.D., F.R.S., Professor of
Medicine in the University of Glasgow. Crown 8vo. 7s. 6d.

GLAISTER—DR. WILLIAM SMELLIE AND HIS CONTEMPO-
RARIES. A Contribution to the History of Midwifery
in the Eighteenth Century. By JOHN GLAISTER, M.D.,
Professor of Medical Jurisprudence in the University of
Glasgow. With Illustrations. Demy 8vo. 10s. 6d. nett.

GLASGOW HOSPITAL REPORTS, 1898.   Edited by
GEORGE S. MIDDLETON, M.A., M.D., and HENRY
RUTHERFURD, M.A., M.B., C.M. With many Illustrations.
8vo. 12s. 6d. nett.

GLASGOW UNIVERSITY CALENDAR FOR THE YEAR
1899-1900. *Published annually in Midsummer*, with full
official information. Crown 8vo, Cloth. 3s. nett.

GLASGOW—THE OLD COUNTRY HOUSES OF THE OLD
GLASGOW GENTRY. Royal 4to.   [*Out of print.*

GLASGOW—MEMOIRS AND PORTRAITS OF ONE HUNDRED
GLASGOW MEN who did much to make the City what it
now is. Two vols. Royal 4to. Half Red Morocco, gilt
top. £7 7s. nett.

GLASGOW—THE UNIVERSITY OF GLASGOW OLD AND NEW
By WILLIAM STEWART, D.D., Professor of Biblical
Criticism in the University of Glasgow. With 107 Engravings. Imperial 4to, £5 5s. nett; Large Paper Copies,
£10 10s. nett.

GLASGOW—A ROLL OF GRADUATES OF THE UNIVERSITY
OF GLASGOW, from 31st December, 1727, to 31st December,
1897. With short Biographical Notes. Compiled by
W. INNES ADDISON, Assistant to the Clerk of Senate.
Demy 4to. 21s. nett.

GLASGOW—ITS MUNICIPAL ORGANIZATION AND ADMINIS-
TRATION, by SIR JAMES BELL, Bart., Lord Provost of
Glasgow, and JAMES PATON, F.L.S., President of the
Museums Associations of the United Kingdom. Crown
4to. 21s. nett.

GLASGOW ARCHÆOLOGICAL SOCIETY'S TRANS-
ACTIONS.
First Series. Demy 8vo.
    Volume I. Parts I. to V. 5s. each nett.
    Volume II. Parts I. to III. 5s. each nett.
New Series. Foolscap 4to.
    Volume I. Parts I. to IV. 6s. each nett.
    Volume II. Parts I. to IV. 6s. each nett.
    Volume III. Parts I. and II. 6s. each nett.

GRAHAM—THE CARVED STONES OF ISLAY, with descriptive
Text. By ROBERT C. GRAHAM, F.S.A.Scot., of Skipness.
Demy 4to. With 71 Engravings on Copper, Map, Plans, and
many other Illustrations. £1 11s. 6d. nett. *Sixty-five
Copies, with Proofs on Japanese, bound in Half-Morocco,
Gilt Top, £3 13s. 6d. nett.*

"This is a sumptuously printed and illustrated book, dealing in a most
thorough manner with the Christian sculptured monuments of one district
of the west coast of Scotland."—*Reliquary.*

"Mr. Graham is to be congratulated on the manner in which he has
mingled purely antiquarian lore with what is interesting historically or
picturesquely."—*Saturday Review.*

"The work, which has been a long labour of love, has been done with
patient thoroughness and complete success."—*Daily Chronicle.*

"An elaborate monograph, very handsomely printed and illustrated."—
Times.

HAMILTON, Janet—POEMS, ESSAYS, AND SKETCHES. By
JANET HAMILTON. New Edition, with portrait. Crown
8vo. 6s.

HASTIE—THEOLOGY AS SCIENCE, and its Present Position
and Prospects in the Reformed Church. By W. HASTIE,
D.D., Professor of Divinity in the University of Glasgow.
Crown 8vo. 2s. nett.

HASTIE—THE VISION OF GOD AS REPRESENTED IN
RÜCKERT'S FRAGMENTS. Rendered into English Rhyme
by W. HASTIE, D.D. Fcap. 4to. 2s. nett.

HENLEY—A CENTURY OF ARTISTS : a Memorial of Loan Collection of the Glasgow International Exhibition, 1888. By W. E. HENLEY. Extra pott folio, £2 2s. nett. Large Paper, with plates on Japanese, £5 5s. nett.

HUNTER—HYMNS OF FAITH AND LIFE. Collected and Edited by the REV. JOHN HUNTER, D.D., Trinity Church, Glasgow. New and Enlarged Edition. Fcap. 8vo. 3s. 6d. nett.

"No more catholic collection of hymns has ever been given to the world." —*The Christian World.*

"For private devotion it is above all price and praise. It should be on the same shelf as Thomas à Kempis."—*Sheffield Independent.*

HUNTER—DEVOTIONAL SERVICES FOR PUBLIC WORSHIP, including additional Services for Baptism, the Lord's Supper, Marriage, and the Burial of the Dead. Prepared by the REV. JOHN HUNTER, D.D. Sixth Edition, revised and enlarged. Crown 8vo. 3s. nett.

"It is striking for the comprehensive character of its prayers, the beauty of their expression, and the spirit of devotion which they breathe."—*N. B. Daily Mail.*

JACKS—THE LIFE OF PRINCE BISMARCK. By WILLIAM JACKS, LL.D. Demy 8vo. With many Illustrations. 10s. 6d. nett.

"The fullest and most carefully accurate biography of the Iron Chancellor yet written in English."—*Daily Mail.*

JACKS—ROBERT BURNS IN OTHER TONGUES, being a critical account of the translations of the principal poems of Robert Burns which have appeared in Foreign Languages, together with the Foreign Texts. With numerous Portraits. By WILLIAM JACKS, LL.D. Extra post 8vo. 9s. nett.

JACKS — LESSING'S NATHAN THE WISE. Translated by WILLIAM JACKS, LL.D. With an Introduction by Archdeacon FARRAR, and Eight Etchings by WILLIAM STRANG. Fcap. 8vo. 5s. nett.

JEBB—HOMER : AN INTRODUCTION TO THE ILIAD AND THE ODYSSEY. For the use of Schools and Colleges. By R. C. JEBB, Litt.D., M.P., Professor of Greek in the University of Cambridge. Sixth Edition. Crown 8vo. 3s. 6d.

"We heartily commend the handbook before us to the diligent study of all beginners and many 'ripe scholars.'"—*Athenæum.*

"A trustworthy and indispensable guide."—*Classical Review.*

JEBB—THE ANABASIS OF XENOPHON.—Books III. and IV., with the *Modern Greek Version* of Professor Michael Constantinides. Edited by Professor JEBB. Fcap. 8vo. 4s. 6d.

JONES—BROWNING AS A PHILOSOPHICAL AND RELIGIOUS TEACHER. By HENRY JONES, M.A., LL.D., Professor of Moral Philosophy in the University of Glasgow. Crown 8vo. Third Edition. 6s. nett.

"Mr. Jones is a diligent and appreciative student of Browning, and he handles the philosophical topics suggested by his subject with firm grasp and clear insight."—*Times.*

"A most absorbing volume. It is fresh, thorough, and judicious without dreariness."—*Christian Leader.*

JONES—A CRITICAL ACCOUNT OF THE PHILOSOPHY OF LOTZE—THE DOCTRINE OF THOUGHT. By Professor JONES. Crown 8vo. 6s. nett.

"This is a genuine contribution to philosophy. It amounts to a destructive criticism of the half-hearted attitude adopted by Lotze towards the problem of thought and reality."—Mr. BERNARD BOSANQUET in the *Pall Mall Gazette.*

KANT. *See* CAIRD'S KANT.

KANT. *See* WATSON'S KANT AND HIS ENGLISH CRITICS.

KANT—THE PHILOSOPHY OF KANT, as contained in Extracts from his own Writings. Selected and Translated by JOHN WATSON, LL.D., Professor of Moral Philosophy in the University of Queen's College, Kingston. Crown 8vo. Fourth Edition. 7s. 6d.

LEISHMAN—A SYSTEM OF MIDWIFERY. By WILLIAM LEISHMAN, M.D. Fourth Edition. 2 vols. Demy 8vo. 24s.

LOTZE. *See* JONES' LOTZE.

LOVE and ADDISON—DEAF-MUTISM. A Treatise on Diseases of the Ear as shown in Deaf-Mutes, with Chapters on the Education and Training of Deaf-Mutes. By JAMES KERR LOVE, M.D., and W. H. ADDISON. Demy 8vo. Illustrated. 9s. nett.

MACCUNN—ETHICS OF CITIZENSHIP. By JOHN MACCUNN, M.A., Professor of Philosophy in University College, Liverpool. Crown 8vo. Third Edition. 2s. 6d.

"A little book which, for general usefulness, far exceeds the massive tomes in which sociological philosophers are accustomed to impound the darkness of their cogitations. Its chief value is not for professional thinkers, but for the ordinary sensible man who wants to understand his duty to his country and his neighbours."—*Pall Mall Gazette.*

"There are ideas, and the courage of them, in 'Ethics of Citizenship'; indeed, the scholarly little treatise is mixed with brains."—*Speaker.*

MACDONALD—CATALOGUE OF GREEK COINS IN THE HUNTERIAN COLLECTION—University of Glasgow. Volume I. Italy, Sicily, Macedon, Thrace, and Thessaly. By GEORGE MACDONALD, M.A., Lecturer in Greek in the University of Glasgow. Demy 4to. 560 pages. With Plates of over 600 Coins. 63s. nett.

MACEWEN—Pyogenic Infective Diseases of the Brain and Spinal Cord. By William Macewen, M.D., LL.D., Regius Professor of Surgery in the University of Glasgow. Illustrated. Demy 8vo. 18s. nett.

MACEWEN—Atlas of Head Sections. 53 Engraved Copper Plates of Frozen Sections of the Head, with 53 Key Plates with Detailed Descriptions and Illustrative Text. By Professor Macewen, M.D. Demy 4to. 70s. nett.

"These volumes are of extreme value and importance; both as a record of successful work and as written and pictorial instruction to other workers they have rarely been surpassed."—*The Lancet.*

"It is hardly possible to imagine a more admirable text-book, from cover to cover, or a more difficult and important field of surgery."—*Edinburgh Medical Journal.*

M'KECHNIE—The State and the Individual : an Introduction to Political Science with Special Reference to Socialistic and Individualistic Theories. By William Sharp M'Kechnie, M.A., LL.B., D.Phil., Lecturer on Constitutional Law and History in the University of Glasgow. Demy 8vo. 10s. 6d. nett.

M'KENDRICK — Text-Book of Physiology. By John Gray M'Kendrick, M.D., LL.D., F.R.S., Professor of the Institutes of Medicine in the University of Glasgow; including Histology, by Philipp Stohr, M.D., of the University of Würtzburg. 2 vols. Demy 8vo. 40s.

(The volumes are sold separately, as follows)—

Vol. I.—General Physiology, including the Chemistry and Histology of the Tissues and the Physiology of Muscle 542 Pages, 400 Illustrations. 16s.

Vol. II.—Special Physiology, including Nutrition, Innervation, and Reproduction. 830 Pages, 500 Illustrations. 24s

MACKENZIE—An Introduction to Social Philosophy. By John S. Mackenzie, M.A., Professor of Logic and Philosophy in the University College of South Wales, Fellow of Trinity College, Cambridge. Second Edition. Crown 8vo. 7s. 6d.

"We can heartily recommend this book to all who are interested in the great social and vital questions of the day."—*Westminster Review.*

MACKINTOSH—The Natural History of the Christian Religion, being a Study of the Doctrine of Jesus as developed from Judaism and converted into Dogma. By the late William Mackintosh, M.A., D.D. Demy 8vo. 10s. 6d. nett.

MACLEHOSE — Tales from Spenser, chosen from The Faerie Queene. By Sophia H. Maclehose. Second Edition. Fcap. 8vo, ornamental cloth, gilt top, 3s. 6d. Also a Cheaper Edition in Paper Boards, 1s. 6d.

"The tales are charmingly and very dramatically told."—*Times.*

"This is a charming book of stories from the 'Faerie Queene.' It is just the sort of book for a good uncle to give to niece or nephew."—*Scots Observer.*

MITCHELL—Burns and His Times. As gathered from his Poems by John Oswald Mitchell, LL.D. Post 8vo. 3s. 6d.

MONRO—Raynaud's Disease (Local Syncope, Local Asphyxia, Symmetrical Gangrene) : its History, Causes, Symptoms, Morbid Relations, Pathology and Treatment. By T. K. Monro, M.A., M.D., Physician to the Glasgow Royal Infirmary. Crown 8vo. [*In the press.*

MOYES—Medicine and Kindred Arts in the Plays of Shakspeare by Dr. John Moyes, Largs, with Introduction by Dr. James Finlayson. Crown 8vo. 2s. 6d. nett.

MÜLLER—Outlines of Hebrew Syntax. By Dr. August Müller, Professor of Oriental Languages in the University of Königsberg. Translated and Edited by James Robertson, M.A., D.D., Professor of Oriental Languages in the University of Glasgow. Demy 8vo. Fourth Edition. 6s.

MURRAY—Attic Sentence Construction. By Gilbert . Murray, M.A., Professor of Greek in the University of Glasgow. 8vo. 1s. nett.

MURRAY—The Property of Married Persons, with an Appendix of Statutes. By David Murray, M.A., LL.D. Medium 8vo. 9s.

NEILSON—Annals of the Solway, until A.D. 1307. By George Neilson, author of "Trial by Combat," etc. Fcap. 4to. With 5 Maps. 3s. 6d. nett. [*This day.*

NEWTON—Sir Isaac Newton's Principia. Edited by Lord Kelvin, Professor of Natural Philosophy in the University of Glasgow, and Hugh Blackburn, M.A. Crown 4to. 31s. 6d.

NICHOL—Tables of European History, Literature, Science, and Art, A.D. 200 to 1888, and of American History, Literature and Art. By the late John Nichol, M.A., Professor of English Literature in the University of Glasgow. Fourth Edition. Royal 8vo, printed in Five Colours. 7s. 6d.
"About as convenient a book of reference as could be found."—*Spectator.*

OLRIG GRANGE. *See* Smith.

PATERSON—Nithsdale. A Series of Photogravures from Water-colour Drawings by James Paterson, R.S.W. With Letterpress. Folio, proofs on French and Japanese, £5 5s. nett; Ordinary impression, £2 2s. nett.

RAMSAY—ATLAS OF EXTERNAL DISEASES OF THE EYE. 48 full-page Plates in Colour and Photogravure, with full Descriptive Text. By A. MAITLAND RAMSAY, M.D., Ophthalmic Surgeon, Glasgow Royal Infirmary. Demy 4to. Buckram, gilt top. With 48 full-page Plates of the Eye in Colour and Photogravure and Descriptive Text. 63s. nett.

"A more beautiful and complete collection of coloured and uncoloured pictures of Eye Diseases does not exist."—Mr. G. A. BERRY in the *Edinburgh Medical Journal.*

RANKINE—SONGS AND FABLES. By W. J. MACQUORN RANKINE, late Professor of Engineering in the University of Glasgow. Illustrated by J. B. Second Edition. Extra fcap. 8vo. 6s.

RAWNSLEY—LITERARY ASSOCIATIONS OF THE ENGLISH LAKES. By the REV. H. D. RAWNSLEY, Vicar of Crosthwaite, Honorary Canon of Carlisle. With Map. 2 vols. Crown 8vo. 10s. nett.

Vol. I.—Cumberland, Keswick, and Southey's Country.

Vol. II.—Westmoreland, Windermere, and the Haunts of Wordsworth.

"A tramp of intelligence, however exacting, who carries the book in one pocket, and a good ordnance map in the other, will find himself amply provided for an exhaustive tour in the Lake Country."—*Illustrated London News.*

RAWNSLEY—LIFE AND NATURE AT THE ENGLISH LAKES. By the Rev. H. D. RAWNSLEY, Honorary Canon of Carlisle. Crown 8vo. 5s. nett. [*This day.*

"This pleasant volume is made up of about a score of papers, any one of which must interest anybody who has either been to the Lake Country or means to go there."—*The Scotsman.*

"Every lover of lake-land should secure these essays, for they afford unique casements opening on to a world of beauty."—*Manchester Courier.*

RAWNSLEY—HENRY WHITEHEAD, 1828-1896. A Memorial Sketch. By the REV. CANON RAWNSLEY. Demy 8vo. 6s.

RAWNSLEY—VALETE: TENNYSON AND OTHER MEMORIAL
POEMS. By REV. CANON RAWNSLEY. Crown 8vo. 5s.

ROBERTSON—LIFE AND LETTERS OF REV. WILLIAM B.
ROBERTSON, D.D., of Irvine. *See* BROWN.

ROBERTSON—HEBREW SYNTAX. *See* MÜLLER.

SCHLOMKA — A GERMAN GRAMMAR. With Copious
Exercises, Dialogues, and a Vocabulary. By CLEMENS
SCHLOMKA, M.A., Ph.D. Fourth Edition. Crown 8vo.
4s. 6d.

"Wonderfully clear, consecutive, and simple. We have no hesitation in
strongly recommending this grammar."—*School Board Chronicle.*

SCHLOMKA—GERMAN READER. Exercises for translating
German into English and English into German. With
Vocabularies for both. Third Edition. Crown 8vo. 3s.

SCOTTISH NATIONAL MEMORIALS. Extra pott folio,
with 30 full-page Plates, and 287 Illustrations in the Text.
£2 12s. 6d. nett.

"It will be enjoyed in equal measure by the Scotchman who is a student of
archæology and history, and by the Englishman who has time to saunter
through the sections into which it is divided, to sit down here and there,
and drink in the significance of the pictures of Scotch life in the past that
are presented to him in rich abundance and under the most fascinating
guise."—*Spectator.*

SMITH, J. Guthrie—STRATHENDRICK, AND ITS INHABITANTS
FROM EARLY TIMES : An account of the parishes of Fintry,
Balfron, Killearn, Drymen, Buchanan, and Kilmaronock.
By the late JOHN GUTHRIE SMITH, F.S.A.Scot., author
of 'The Parish of Strathblane.' With Memoir and Portrait.
Crown 4to. With numerous Engravings. 31s. 6d. nett.

𝔓𝔬𝔢𝔪𝔰 𝔟𝔶 𝔱𝔥𝔢 𝔄𝔲𝔱𝔥𝔬𝔯 𝔬𝔣 "𝔒𝔩𝔯𝔦𝔤 𝔊𝔯𝔞𝔫𝔤𝔢."

SMITH, WALTER C.

OLRIG GRANGE.   Fourth Edition.   Fcap. 8vo, cloth, gilt top.   5s.

KILDROSTAN.   Fcap. 8vo, cloth, gilt top.   5s.

A HERETIC, AND OTHER POEMS.   Extra fcap. 8vo. Blue cloth.   Edges uncut.   7s. 6d.

THOUGHTS AND FANCIES FOR SUNDAY EVENINGS. Second Edition.   Crown 8vo.   2s. 6d.

SELECTIONS FROM THE POEMS OF WALTER C. SMITH. Second Edition.   Crown 8vo.   Cloth.   3s. 6d.

"A graceful anthology, and sure of a welcome from his many admirers." —*The Times.*

SPENSER—TALES FROM SPENSER, CHOSEN FROM THE FAERIE QUEENE.   By SOPHIA H. MACLEHOSE.   Second Edition.   Fcap. 8vo, ornamental cloth, gilt top, 3s. 6d. Also a Cheaper Edition in Paper Boards.   1s. 6d.

"A delightful book for children.   It could not have been better executed had it been the work of the Lambs."—*Saturday Review.*

"A dainty volume.   It makes a charming introduction to a great poem."—*Guardian.*

STEVEN—OUTLINES OF PRACTICAL PATHOLOGY.   An Introduction to the Practical Study of Morbid Anatomy and Histology.   By J. LINDSAY STEVEN, M.D.   Cr. 8vo.   7s. 6d.

WADDELL—THE PARMENIDES OF PLATO.   After the Paging of the Clarke Manuscript.   Edited, with Introduction, Facsimiles, and Notes, by WILLIAM WARDLAW WADDELL, M.A., one of Her Majesty's Inspectors of Schools.   Medium 4to.   £1 11s. 6d. nett.

WADDELL—VERSES AND IMITATIONS IN GREEK AND LATIN.   By W. W. WADDELL.   Fcap. 8vo.   2s. 6d.

WATSON, Prof. John—SELECTIONS FROM KANT.   *See* KANT.

WATSON—CHRISTIANITY AND IDEALISM. The Christian
Ideal of Life in its relations to the Greek and Jewish Ideals
and to Modern Philosophy. By JOHN WATSON, M.A
LL.D., Professor of Moral Philosophy in Queen's University, Kingston, Canada. Crown 8vo. 5s. nett.

WATSON—AN OUTLINE OF PHILOSOPHY. By Professor
WATSON. Second Edition. Revised and greatly enlarged.
Crown 8vo. 7s. 6d nett.

" It is a book which attests on every page the ability of the author to
present his subject in a lucid and attractive way."—*International Journal
of Ethics.*

WATSON—HEDONISTIC THEORIES, FROM ARISTIPPUS TO
SPENCER. By Professor WATSON. Crown 8vo. 6s. nett.

WOTHERSPOON—THE DIVINE SERVICE. A Eucharistic
Office according to Forms of the Primitive Church. Arranged by the REV. H. J. WOTHERSPOON, M.A., Minister
of Burnbank. Fcap. 8vo, Paper Boards. 6d.

GLASGOW: PRINTED AT THE UNIVERSITY PRESS BY ROBERT MACLEHOSE AND CO.

Trieste

Trieste Publishing has a massive catalogue of classic book titles. Our aim is to provide readers with the highest quality reproductions of fiction and non-fiction literature that has stood the test of time. The many thousands of books in our collection have been sourced from libraries and private collections around the world.

The titles that Trieste Publishing has chosen to be part of the collection have been scanned to simulate the original. Our readers see the books the same way that their first readers did decades or a hundred or more years ago. Books from that period are often spoiled by imperfections that did not exist in the original. Imperfections could be in the form of blurred text, photographs, or missing pages. It is highly unlikely that this would occur with one of our books. Our extensive quality control ensures that the readers of Trieste Publishing's books will be delighted with their purchase. Our staff has thoroughly reviewed every page of all the books in the collection, repairing, or if necessary, rejecting titles that are not of the highest quality. This process ensures that the reader of one of Trieste Publishing's titles receives a volume that faithfully reproduces the original, and to the maximum degree possible, gives them the experience of owning the original work.

We pride ourselves on not only creating a pathway to an extensive reservoir of books of the finest quality, but also providing value to every one of our readers. Generally, Trieste books are purchased singly - on demand, however they may also be purchased in bulk. Readers interested in bulk purchases are invited to contact us directly to enquire about our tailored bulk rates. Email: customerservice@triestepublishing.com

You May Also Like

ISBN: 9780649692613
Paperback: 120 pages
Dimensions: 6.14 x 0.25 x 9.21 inches
Language: eng

Results of Astronomical Observations Made at the Sydney Observatory, New South Wales, in the Years 1877 and 1878

H. C. Russell

ISBN: 9780649669356
Paperback: 164 pages
Dimensions: 6.14 x 0.35 x 9.21 inches
Language: eng

Persecution and Tolerance: Being the Hulsean Lectures Preached Before the University of Cambridge in 1893-4

Mandell Creighton

www.triestepublishing.com

You May Also Like

ISBN: 9780649690602
Paperback: 114 pages
Dimensions: 6.14 x 0.24 x 9.21 inches
Language: eng

Reports of the Board of Directors and of the Superintendents of the State Hospitals for the Insane at Raleigh, Goldsboro and Morganton, North Carolina

State Hospital of North Carolina

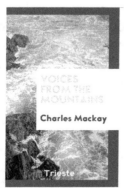

ISBN: 9780649730360
Paperback: 140 pages
Dimensions: 5.25 x 0.30 x 8.0 inches
Language: eng

Voices from the Mountains

Charles Mackay

www.triestepublishing.com

You May Also Like

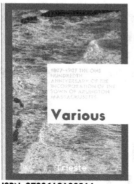

1807-1907 The One Hundredth Anniversary of the incorporation of the Town of Arlington Massachusetts

Various

ISBN: 9780649420544
Paperback: 108 pages
Dimensions: 6.14 x 0.22 x 9.21 inches
Language: eng

Biennial report of the Board of State Harbor Commissioners, for the two fiscal years commencing July 1, 1890, and ending June 30, 1892

Various

ISBN: 9780649194292
Paperback: 44 pages
Dimensions: 6.14 x 0.09 x 9.21 inches
Language: eng

www.triestepublishing.com

You May Also Like

ISBN: 9780649199693
Paperback: 48 pages
Dimensions: 6.14 x 0.10 x 9.21 inches
Language: eng

Biennial report of the Board of State Harbor Commissioners for the two fisca years. Commeneing July 1, 1884, and Ending June 30, 1886

Various

ISBN: 9780649196395
Paperback: 44 pages
Dimensions: 6.14 x 0.09 x 9.21 inches
Language: eng

Biennial report of the Board of state commissioners, for the two fiscal years, commencing July 1, 1890, and ending June 30, 1892

Various

Find more of our titles on our website. We have a selection of thousands of titles that will interest you. Please visit

www.triestepublishing.com

CPSIA information can be obtained
at www.ICGtesting.com
Printed in the USA
JSHW012343080922
30161JS00006B/324

9 780649 686759